ADAPTING AND WRITING LANGUAGE LESSONS

This work was compiled and pub_
lished with the support of the Office
of Education, Department of Health,
Education and Welfare, United States
of America.

EARL W. STEVICK

FOREIGN SERVICE INSTITUTE

WASHINGTON, D.C.

DEPARTMENT OF STATE

FOREIGN SERVICE INSTITUTE

BASIC COURSE SERIES

Edited by

AUGUSTUS A KOSKI

PREFACE

Each passing year sees more people exposed to more languages. The largest number are learning widely taught international languages such as English and French. Smaller, but growing even more rapidly, is the number of people who need competence in one or more of the seldom-taught languages of the world.

The seldom-taught languages are, for obvious reasons, the ones for which fewest textbooks are available. Yet any one course is necessarily of some one length, in some one pedagogical style, and with some fixed content. This fact, together with the paucity of materials, means that most prospective users of lessons will be dissatisfied with what they find. The decision is often to discard all that exists and start anew, or simply not to start at all.

The purpose of this book, which draws on twenty years of teaching 'neglected' languages in a wide variety of settings, is to do two things: first, to set forth guidelines for appreciating what does exist and adapting it to immediate needs; second, to suggest an approach to writing new materials that will be as adaptable as possible.

The Foreign Service Institute acknowledges its debt to the U.S. Office of Education for encouragement and support which made possible the writing and publishing of the report; and to the Peace Corps, which provided both facilities and financial support for much of the experimental work in which these guidelines were developed and refined.

James R. Frith, Dean
School of Language Studies
Foreign Service Institute
Department of State

TABLE OF CONTENTS

Preface   iii

Introduction   vii

1. What Seems to Be What in Language Teaching   1

2. Working Assumptions, and the Modular Approach to   28
    Materials Development

3. Evaluating and Adapting Language Materials   44

    Appendix A: Adapting a Dialog-Drill Format (Spanish) 66

    Appendix B: Adapting a 'Microwave' Format (Telugu)   74

    Appendix C: Adapting a Pattern-Practice Format   84
       (English)

    Appendix D: Adapting a Self-Instructional Format   96
       (Spanish)

    Appendix E: Adapting a Lesson Based on a Prose Text 115
       (Mauritian Creole)

    Appendix F: A Lesson for Discussion by Readers   123
       (Igbo)

4. Writing Adaptable Materials   131

    Appendix G: Mutually Derivable Materials in   154
       Technical Specialties (Thai)

TABLE OF CONTENTS

Appendix H: Mutual Complementation of English and   189
 Swahili Materials in Training for East Africa

Appendix I: Clusters as Supplements (Portuguese)   203

Appendix J: Relevance under Stress (Spanish)   215

Appendix K: Unsequenced Presentation of Structures 220
 (Swahili)

Appendix L: Materials for Discussion by Readers   225
 (French)

5. Learners Synopses   230

Appendix M: A Learners Synopsis of Thai   235

Appendix N: A Learners Synopsis of Swahili   258
 Structure

Appendix O: Part of a Learners Synopsis of Kirundi 284
 Structure

6. Cummings Devices   310

Appendix P: The Cummings Principle in Another   331
 Format (English)

Appendix Q: Cummings Devices in a Do-it-Yourself   337
 Kit (Kikuyu)

Appendix R: Cummings Devices in a Task-Centered   346
 Course (Ponapean)

TABLE OF CONTENTS

7. Microtexts   365

    Appendix S: Microtexts as Parts of a Basic Course   381
    (Luganda)

    Appendix T: Microtexts as Centers for Lessons   387
    (Swahili)

8. Routine Manipulations   391

    Appendix U: Manipulations Based on News Items   403
    (Swahili)

9. Perspective   431

References   433

Index   445

INTRODUCTION

The parts of this book may be read in any order, but its center is in Chapter 3.

Most chapters have appendices which show how their principal ideas have been applied to specific problems.

One theme of this book is that adaptation is inevitable; it ought therefore to receive more attention and more prestige than it usually does.

The other theme is that language study is inevitably a total human experience; writers and teachers ought therefore to act as though it is.

CHAPTER 1

WHAT SEEMS TO BE WHAT IN LANGUAGE TEACHING

> Language teaching has shared neither the
> honesty nor the self-knowledge of the fine
> arts. Whereas artists are willing to seek
> inspiration from the past, teachers, being
> cursed with the assumption that their
> discoveries are necessarily an improvement
> on what went on before, are reluctant to
> learn from history.

                                    Kelly, 1969

Of the making of many orthodoxies there is truly no end.
Harold Dunkel has reminded us that even in the 16th and 17th
centuries, language teachers faced much the same problems that
we face, and sought similar solutions.

> The student began study of the language at
> an early age with a large number of contact
> hours. He was required to speak the language
> at all times, he studied other subjects through
> it, and had opportunities for additional practice
> outside of class. He learned dialogues, and had
> visual aids.... How much the vernacular should
> be used in teaching was a matter of hot dispute,
> and to teach grammar inductively, yet systemat-
> ically, comprehensively, and efficiently was as
> difficult then as now.

                                    Dunkel, 1967

E. V. Gatenby in 1950 doubted whether any new principle had been
discovered since Gouin. Gudschinsky (1968, p. x) acknowledges
that most of the basic ideas in her book are found in Sweet (1900),
Cummings (1916), Palmer (1917) and Ward (1937). Yet in the pages
of our professional journals, applied linguists still cry back
and forth to one another in Viëtor's words of nearly a century

1

ago: 'Der Sprachunterricht muss umkehren!' As each linguistic
or psychological principle is (re)discovered, new materials must
be written to conform to it, and before us nothing was. Each
generation sees in its predecessors the dead hand of the past,
and each innovating coterie feels that in some sense it has finally devised a method that is 'as elastic and adaptable as life is
restless and variable.' (Jespersen, 1904, p.4). This was in one
way true of the Friesians, and in another way true of the same
audiolingualists who are lately being repudiated for having
espoused a 'sterile method based on parrotting and mechanical
habit formation.' So let it be with Caesar.

The second chapter of this book will outline certain
assumptions about materials for language learning. The present
chapter is an attempt to state some ideas that relate to language
learning as a whole. It begins with an interpretation of very
recent history, particularly the competition between 'behavioristic'
and 'cognitive' points of view. In this context, it then goes on
to discuss three fundamental problems: What is to be learned?
What is learning? What makes learning happen?

LANGUAGE TEACHING AS APPLIED LINGUISTICS

The next-most-recent orthodoxy stemmed from the work of linguistic scientists as language teachers during and after World
War II. Overlapping variants of this tradition have been labelled,
with some inevitable confusion, 'the oral approach,' 'the linguistic
method,' and 'audiolingualism.' Rivers (1964), in a well-known
and clear description of this school of thought, saw it as resting
on four assumptions. The first assumption was that foreign language learning is basically a mechanical process of habit formation.
This assumption had three corollaries: that habits are strengthen-
ed by reinforcement; that foreign language habits are formed most
efficiently by giving the right response rather than by making

mistakes; and that since language is behavior, then that behavior can be taught only if the student is induced to 'behave.' The remaining assumptions were that students learn more efficiently when speaking is presented before reading and writing; that 'analogy' is a better foundation for producing new sentences than is 'analysis'; and that meanings should/can be learned only in the matrix of allusions to the target culture.

The linguistic scientists who most influenced this approach to the task had come to language teaching out of a background of describing and analyzing hitherto unstudied languages. Their work had impressed them deeply with the fact that an adult outsider encounters such a language initially on its acoustic level, and that he can make sense of it only as he successively discovers its formal characteristics. He meets these characteristics first of all in terms of audible contrasts among sets of utterances that are partly like, and partially different from one another. American linguists of the postwar period were thus very much concerned with segmenting spoken utterances into parts, and making statements that would summarize the privileges and limitations of occurrence of these parts relative to one another.

It is therefore not surprising that the practitioners of what came to be called 'applied linguistics' resolutely concentrated their attention and that of their students on what we now think of as the surface structure of the language. So A. A. Hill, a leading descriptive linguist, in a paper (1959) on the relationship between language analysis and language teaching, urged the advantages of 'work[ing] through the formal characteristics [of the language] to arrive at functions and meanings.' Politzer (1965) and others have emphasized that a language is in some sense made up of sounds. Fries (1952) built his description of English structure on the assumption that 'all the signals of [grammatical] structure are formal matters that can be described in physical terms.'

CHAPTER 1   WHAT SEEMS TO BE WHAT

This view of linguistic description, when applied to language
teaching, led to two different sets of conclusions. One set
appears in the following series of statements which are reordered
but not reworded from Cornelius (1953, p. 12):

(a) The native language was memorized.

(b) Learning a new language is essentially
     memorizing the language in the same way
     that the native language was memorized:
     learning by heart innumerable forms from
     the language.

(c) The most important activities of classroom
     language study are continuous imitation
     and repetition of the model of the spoken
     language provided by the teacher.

(d) A knowledge of grammatical rules and
     terminology is independent of the ability
     to speak and understand a language.

Cornelius represented a strain of American applied linguistics
which placed heavy emphasis on the imitation and memorization
of authentic samples of speech. In fact, his instructions to
teachers stand among the most extreme statements of that point
of view. His references to the learning of structure as such
were both brief and vague: he mentions 'the word-sequence and
sentence-structure habits of the native speaker' (p. 7 f);
'explain[ing how] the language system functions, and drill[ing]
structural points through intensive repetition (22); 'the other
features of the language which accompany the sounds' (71).

Other applied linguists, most notably (within American practice) C. C. Fries, placed the heaviest emphasis not on memorization of texts, but on explicit, conscious practice of structural patterns. Politzer (1965, p. 8) sounded very different from Cornelius' statement when he told language students that 'even in your native language you have not learned by memory all of the sentences that you [need]. What you have learned is a system and how to use it.'

A number of textbooks have combined dialog memorization with pattern practice. Among the earliest and most conspicuous of these were the Audio-Lingual Materials. Brooks, who was a leading consultant in the preparation of these materials, provided what was in its day accepted as a fairly authoritative statement of American applied linguistics (1960). He said (p. 49) that 'a student learns grammar not by attempting to say everything that he will eventually want to say, but by familiarizing himself with structure patterns from which he can generalize, applying them to whatever linguistic needs he may have in the future.' 'The single paramount fact about language learning is that it concerns...the formation and performance of habits' (p. 47). The teacher should learn how to 'teach the use of structure through pattern practice' (p. 139), but 'structure is [also] learned in the form of dialogues based upon living situations' (p. 123). 'The principal method of avoiding error in language learning is to observe and practice the right model a sufficient number of times; the principal way of overcoming it is to shorten the time lapse between the incorrect response and the presentation once more of the correct model.' (p. 56).

The views of Cornelius, Brooks, and others in the twenty
years that followed World War II are examples of what Lane (1966,
p. 16) has termed the 'sunburn model of language learning,' according to which the teacher, as prime source of knowledge and
light, exposes the students to the material until the desired
effect is achieved. To say that linguistically oriented language
teaching in the 1950's was limited to promoting exposure in the
rather crude sense of some of the above quotations would be a
caricature and inaccurate; but to say that 'sunburn' (or at least
a good tan) was its immediate goal would not be unfair.

The beginning of the new decade brought with it what Lane
(ibid.) called the behavioral model of language learning. Its
distinctive emphasis, drawn from research on animal learning,
was on the shaping of behavior through positive or negative
reinforcement (i.e. rewarding) of the activities in which an
organism might engage. This period saw an upsurge of interest
in programmed instruction, teaching machines, and operant con-
ditioning. The cardinal principles of this approach, (adapted
from Valdman 1966, p. 136) are:

1. Rigorous specification of the desired changes
    in behavior.

2. Division of the subject matter to be taught into
    a gradual sequence of optimum minimum steps.

3. Active mode of response on the part of the student.

4. Immediate confirmation and (in the Skinnerian sense)
    reinforcement of student responses.

5. Revision and modification of the materials to
    accommodate individual student differences.

But although the behavioral model was in some respects undeniably more sophisticated and more effective than the sunburn model, its aim for many of its adherents remained 'to condition [the student's] verbal behavior to permit habitual autonomous manipulation of [the] second language' (Morton, 1968, p. 20).

In the last few pages, we have sketched some of the best known manifestations of what we may call A-L orthodoxy.[1] It is important to remember that A-L thinking consisted of at least two main strands, which were seldom separated from one another in the practice of that era, but which are nevertheless easy to separate in principle. These two strands were the linguistic and the psychological. Thus, attention to the surface structure of a language need not necessarily lead to spending most of class time in 'individual and choral repetition, of carefully guided conversations, of pattern practices, and the like' (Moulton, 1961).

BEYOND APPLIED LINGUISTICS

In the late 1960's, after two decades of controversy, conquest and prestige, A-L doctrine began to come under increasingly heavy criticism from a point of view which we may label T-C, for transformational-cognitive. Like A-L, this point of view has its linguistic component, drawn mainly from the work of transformational-generative grammarians, and its psychological component drawn from cognitivism. Again, the matching of the two was at least partially a matter of historical accident, rather than mutual deducibility.

––––––––––––––

[1]The letters stand for both 'applied linguistics' and for 'audio-lingual.' 'Applied linguistics' of course includes much besides language teaching.

It is instructive to look at some of the ways in which the
transformational-cognitive school (T-C) has been contrasted with
its immediate predecessor (A-L). An unusually clear comparison
is found in Kniesner (1969). According to Kniesner, A-L was characterized by a preoccupation with the differences between languages
rather than the similarities, and by the belief that any language
is a set of habits used in speaking (as opposed to writing). It
consists of the habits that its native speakers actually have, and
not either the habits that someone thinks they ought to have, or
linguistic statements about those habits. The goal of A-L language
teaching was 'fluent, error-free speech, without conscious attention to rules.' All the points in this summary, as well as
in Rivers' (p.2-3), may be easily and amply documented from the
writings of the leaders of A-L;[2] there is little use in denying
that they were characteristic emphases of the A-L tradition.

By contrast, Kniesner considers Chomsky's observations (1966)
to be typical of the T-C approach. Two of these draw principally
on the linguistic side of T-C thinking:

    1. The abstractness of linguistic representations.

    2. The universality of underlying linguistic structures.

Two more are primarily psychological:

    3. The creative aspect of language use.

    4. The role of intrinsic organization in creative processes.

In this view, the learner's task is _not_ 'to master a corpus'
(Kuno, 1969), but rather (Kniesner, op. cit.) 'to limit and test
hypotheses to find the generative rules which link surface manifestations with meaning-bearing underlying abstract structures

---

[2] For three key statements, see Fries (1948), Moulton (1961),
Brooks (1961).

and permit creation and understanding of an infinite number of novel utterances.' Some of the pedagogical implications of T-C, as seen by Kuno (1969) are:

1. emphasis on meaningful practice,

2. early use of reading and writing as well as speaking and listening,

3. instruction for conscious attention to the characteristics of language, especially its regularities,

4. emphasis on meanings of utterances,

5. the organization of course materials in terms of some deeper analysis of the language [than A-L either provided or used].

The positive thrust of T-C thought is clearer than the negative, for the bad, old, outmoded, behavioristic audiolinguists seldom gave full allegiance to the dogmas which the cognitivists attribute to them. (cf. Ney, 1968) Even when they proclaimed these doctrines, their common sense (with which they as well as their critics are endowed) usually prevented them in practice from reaping the consequences of excessive consistency which, as their successors point out, might logically have resulted from their theory. Most of Kuno's five points (above) were in fact found in stated precept as well as in actual practice within A-L.[3] One is tempted to agree with Rivers (1968, p. 78), that 'there is no reason to believe that [these] two positions are mutually exclusive.' There are differences, but they are differences of emphasis.

----

[3]To cite only a few examples from well before the T-C era, Fries (1948) was quite ready for structural patterns (cf. 'regularities' in Kuno's [3], above) to be pointed out and

CHAPTER 1   WHAT SEEMS TO BE WHAT

What are actually the issues at stake? Some writers give
the impression that a central disagreement is over the importance
of 'habit formation' (see for example Cooper, 1970). It would
be a mistake, however, to attach too much importance to what is
largely a terminological discrepancy between the two schools.

It is certainly true, and has been well documented by
quotations appearing earlier in this chapter, that many language
teachers of the past two decades have emphasized 'forming habits.'
It may also be true, as Chomsky (1966, p. 4) has charged, that
'there is no sense of "habit" known to psychology' in which
language use can be described as a matter of 'grammatical habit.'
Even though linguists have undeniably been influenced by what
has been going on in the field of psychology, their use of 'habit,'
if 'unknown to psychology,' is at least well known to the lexi-
cographers of everyday usage: 'a disposition or tendency, constantly shown, to act in a certain way' (ACD). To put the same
common notion in slightly different terms, when A-L language
teachers have spoken of 'forming language habits,' they have
meant something like 'obtaining unhesitating accuracy in the control of something in the target language.' That 'something'
might have been a sentence (<u>Habe ich Ihnen schon erzählt, wo ich
vorige Woche Donnerstag gewesen bin</u>?) or a structural problem

---

described to the student. The first two volumes of <u>Language
Learning</u> contained articles on an approach to reading
(Nida), the dictionary (one by Hill and another by Marckwardt),
and note-taking (Anthony, 1948). French (1949) counseled
that 'a student should be saying something that has meaning
for him personally, not only <u>after</u> he has learned the pattern
but also <u>while</u> he is learning it,' and this idea was found
also in Anthony (1949) and Reed (1948). Only the fifth point
cannot be matched from the proponents of the oral approach,
and this point depends on linguistic insights which were not
available before the late 1950's.

(English tag questions, Spanish _ser_ vs. _estar_, French partitive
constructions), or vocabulary. The trouble is that T-C writers
frequently seem to believe that their A-L colleagues thought only
of the first of these: 'great importance is placed upon mimicry,
memorization of prepared dialogs, and repetitive substitution and
transformation drills' (Cooper, 1970, p. 304; cf. also Valdman,
1966, p. 146). To this, T-C objects that in first-language learning
'we do not go around collecting sentences to hold in memory for
future use in speaking and understanding. Nor do we have to
search through our personal linguistic archives and carry out the
steps of solving a proportion whenever we want to say something'
(Langacker, 22).

But T-C is right in decrying habit formation only if the
phrase means nothing except 'memorizing sentences and solving proportions with them,' or if 'habits' are only behaviors which are
'acquired through the forging of stimulus-response bonds' (Cooper,
p. 309). If 'habit formation' means (or also means) 'attainment
of unhesitating accuracy,' then it is a goal at which adherents
of T-C themselves aim--or surely ought to.

T-C and A-L therefore have much in common. Both recognize
that languages are partly like and partly unlike each other,
although one school emphasizes the similarities and the other
the differences. Both schools agree that 'the behavior of the
speaker, listener, and learner of language constitutes...the
actual data for any study of language' (Chomsky, 1959, p. 56).
Both schools (and not just T-C) have always tried to produce
students who could understand all and produce only grammatical
utterances of the target language (Cooper, _op. cit._ p. 306),
regardless of whether the grammar of the language was described
structurally or transformationally. Both schools (and not just
A-L) aim at unhesitating accuracy in that behavior.

11

CHAPTER 1   WHAT SEEMS TO BE WHAT

The fundamental issues in language teaching, then, lie not here, but where they have always lain. We constantly seek--and occasionally obtain--new light on three different but related areas: What is to be learned? What is the nature of learning? What makes learning happen?

WHAT IS TO BE LEARNED?

Our understanding of the nature of what in a language has to be learned has been furthered in recent years by two developments within linguistic science. One is the interest in the ways in which all natural human languages are alike, which has followed (and been made possible by) several decades of emphasis on the ways in which they differ. The second is the increased attention to what Gleason (1965, p. 202) has called 'agnation:' the relation-ships among sentences with constant semantic relations among the same major vocabulary items, but with different (surface) structures:

> The cook used cornmeal.
> Cornmeal was used by the cook.
> ...use of cornmeal by the cook...
> ...the cook's use of cornmeal...
> ...the cook who used cornmeal...
>
> etc.

In all of these examples, it was the cook who used the cornmeal, and cornmeal was what he used, and what he did to the cornmeal was use it; but the configurations, or surface patterns in which these three concepts appear vary from complete simple sentence to relative clause to nominalizations of the whole idea.

12

The inclusion of such data as these in the study of language
has followed a long period in which linguists concentrated on
segmenting 'enate' sentences (sentences with identical surface
structures) and classifying the resulting parts:

The	cook	used	cornmeal.
The	people	ate	mush.
The	children	ate	mush.

To insist that the principal things to be learned in a language
are its 'patterns' is one thing, but this word may be interpreted
with the same latitude as 'habit' (see above). To define 'pattern' enately, as 'a sentence or phrase with all of the content
words removed'(Brown, 1967, p. xviii) is unnecessarily narrow.
In this sense, the sentences in the frame above would all represent the same pattern, which could be represented somewhat
as follows:

Article	Personal Noun	Transitive Verb	Noun

and the five phrases about the cook using cornmeal would be regarded as representing five different and presumably unrelated
patterns. To define 'pattern' in this way encourages the writer
of materials to ignore the extremely productive agnate relationships, such as connect the five sentences about cornmeal. But
this book is not the place for detailed discussion of either of
these matters.

CHAPTER 1   WHAT SEEMS TO BE WHAT

WHAT IS THE NATURE OF LEARNING?

Recent study of the learning process is leading to increased
appreciation of the importance of learning as opposed to teaching.
Newmark and Reibel (1968, p. 149) comment that

> the excessive preoccupation with the contribution of
> the teacher has...distracted the theorists from con-
> sidering the role of the learner as anything but a
> generator of interference; and preoccupation with
> linguistic structure has distracted them from con-
> sidering that learning a language means learning to
> use it.

and Valdman (in Mueller, 1968, p. 58) implies that 'programmers
and teachers [should] learn to observe rather than interfere with
the student's acquisition of the foreign language.' Carroll (in
Mueller, 1968, p. 64) suggests that 'we try to take more careful
account than we have, previously, of the learner's concept of
what it is that he is learning,' and (p. 66) that students 'using
basic language acquisition capacities,...<u>utilize the material</u>...
<u>to help themselves</u> develop towards language competence more or
less in the sense explicated by Chomsky' [emphasis mine]. In educational circles generally, there is a revival of interest in
student-centered and partially student-directed instructional
strategies. But we will not attempt to review here the development in organization of language instruction around the student.
For one point of view, see my 'Who's who in language transfer'
(<u>IRAL</u>, forthcoming).

But if the learner is indeed to be at the center of deliberate language transfer, we must no longer look at him only as 'linguistic man'--man regarded only as a potential internalizer and pro-
ducer of alien sounds, words and patterns. Any language student
is an entire social being, who inhabits (or consists of) an entire
physical organism. If he is a social being, then we cannot go
on 'perfecting the routine means...yet [remaining] oblivious to

14

its meaning and purposes' (Marx, 1970, p. 949). We cannot justify
dull practice (or even non-dull practice, or even a 'fun' language
course) solely on the basis of its contribution to learning, which
in turn contributes to the fulfillment of some future [economic
or] spiritual goal (Lado, 1964, p. 42). If the student is a
physical organism, we cannot remain content with our present
ignorance (Kandel, 1970, p. 70) of the neuronal mechanisms that
are the microphysiological counterparts of observed language
learning behavior.

Although Kandel very recently (op. cit.) and others (for
example, Chomsky, 1965, p. 57) have affirmed our inability to
explain in cellular terms what we know about behavior and learning in higher animals, writers and teachers continue to make assumptions about the neuro-mechanics of language acquisition.
Occasionally, they make these assumptions explicit, as in the
following quotations from Marvin Brown (op. cit.). According to
Brown, 'the student [must first] get the pattern ringing in his
ears.' Then, by repeating, 'he...acquires...muscular facility.'
Now a path may be 'built from ear to mouth' and 'from eye to
mouth.' Finally, the student 'burns the pattern into the brain
by going through the drill...many times at increasing speed'
(p. 4). Repeating and participating 'many times, constantly
pushing for slightly greater speed' is 'the payoff [and] the
step that builds the habit' (p. xviii). One may ask whether too
much of this kind of practice may not lead to habituation (learning to ignore stimuli that have lost novelty or meaning) rather
than to habit formation. But while some of the word pictures in
this description are obviously intended to convey methodological
rather than anatomical truths, the idea of strengthening selected
neural paths by sheer frequency of use is by no means new to
language teachers.

If, however, we recognize the uncertain and largely
metaphorical nature of what we can say in this realm, it is
still possible to sketch a view of language learning, somewhat
different from Brown's.

The National Library of Medicine in Bethesda, Md., once
had on display a model of part of a DNA molecule for one common
type of microorganism. The model is twelve feet long and two
feet in diameter, and contains hundreds of small colored balls
that represent individual atoms. We are told that a model of the
complete molecule on the same scale would be over 142 _miles_ long.
This particular molecule obviously has nothing to do with the
learning behavior of higher organisms, but it does suggest that
in the arrangements of atoms within biochemical molecules, and/or
in the arrangements of such molecules relative to one another,
lie immense possibilities for information storage. We may venture
the following postulates, stated in biochemical terms, but based
on other kinds of evidence:

1. The (sub?)molecular structure of a person's brain
plays a major role in determining how he will be able to respond
to what happens.

2. 'Learning' implies a change in how a person is disposed
to respond to what happens. (This is a commonplace.)

3. 'Learning' presumably involves rearranging something
in the molecules of the learner's brain.[4] Such a statement is

---

[4]Physiological evidence is not entirely lacking at this point.
Pribram, a neuropsychologist and neurosurgeon, in presenting his holographic hypothesis of memory storage argues
that 'the totality of [the memory] process has a more or
less lasting effect on protein molecules and perhaps other
macromolecules' (1969, p. 77).

not necessarily an assertion of materialistic behaviorism, since
it does not rule out the possibility of an acorporeal aspect of
the mind. It is surely compatible with any but the most extreme
of mentalistic views. In this sense, a new (sub)molecular arrangement may correspond to a new 'hypothesis,' or available basis
for action, whether or not the proprietor of the brain is consciously aware of the hypothesis.

4. Certain features of these (sub)molecular arrangements
are innate. Some of these innate features are shared by all
normal members of the species. They, for example, explain our
apparent inability to form the negative of a proposition by pro-
nouncing the phonemes of the affirmative in reverse order, even
though it is very easy for us to understand what such a process
would involve. This is in fact only one rather gross instance
of the language universals that enter into inferences about the
'base structure' that is common to all languages. It is in this
sense that linguists now talk about the innateness of language.

5. Certain things about these (sub)molecular arrangements
are not innate. With regard to the linguistic aspects of behavior, this is why nobody claims that anyone is born with the
ability to speak a language, but only with the propensity to
learn to speak one or more languages of an innately determined
kind.

6. Some of the non-innate arrangements become more permanent if actions that arise from them produce favorable results.
Otherwise, these arrangements are dissipated. These correspond
to what Skinner and others have called 'operants.' But note
that the changes that we are talking about are not limited to the
concatenation of 'behaviors:' learning to say _fool_ after _April_,
or _le_ before _monde_, or _a la esquina a tomar el autobus_. Nor are
they limited to 'solving proportions' using 'patterns' which are

17

'sentences with all the content words removed.' They may and do
include both of these, but they may also include the hypotheses
that correspond to the deepest, subtlest and most abstract units
or rules of the transformational-generative (or any other) style
of linguistic analysis.

But just as our view of the relevant 'operants' has sometimes been too simple, so it has also been too narrow in that
we have often failed to look beyond what we can describe in terms
of one or another brand of linguistics. To make the noises <u>What
sort of work do you do?</u> in a classroom or a lab because that is
the sentence that is supposed to follow <u>Yes, I'm an American</u> in
the dialog is a far different 'operant' from making the same
noises outside of class, in speaking to a new acquaintance,
because one wants to get certain information. The same is true
of saying <u>Mr. Grant is going to practice next Tuesday</u> as a response to the teacher's <u>Mr. Grant is going to practice next
Monday</u> followed by the cue word <u>Tuesday</u>, as contrasted with saying the same words in conversation with real people. We should
ask the student to 'do what we want him to learn' (Cooper, <u>op</u>. <u>cit</u>.,
p. 314), and what we want him to learn is not to produce and understand sentences, but to communicate through a number of channels,
one of which involves producing and understanding sentences.

There are, in addition, non-linguistic 'behaviors' which
are totally indispensable for linguistic success: willingness
to phonate, feeling that one has something worth phonating about,
expectation that the language can be useful--these and many others
deserve conscious and systematic encouragement from the teacher
at least as much as gender agreement or sequence of tenses do.

7. The arrangements to which we have referred in <u>5</u> and <u>6</u>
(above), at least insofar as they relate to speech, must consist
of a multidimensional network, much of it below the level of con-
sciousness. Disciplined exploration of some new dimensions has

been, at least from the language teacher's point of view, the
major contribution of post-Chomskian linguistics. Most evident
has been the study of relationships among surface structures,
with resultant postulation of deep structures. (cf. the discussion of enate and agnate relationships on p.12f, above.)

8. The job of a teacher consists of two parts:

   a. Somehow, he must induce his student to
      rearrange his own intracranial molecules
      in ways which will dispose him toward
      appropriate new kinds of behavior. The
      student may accomplish this rearrange-
      ment with the help of an explanation of
      the 'grammar point' that is involved.
      Or he may accomplish it as a result of
      consciously figuring out the system from
      examples which he encounters either
      systematically or non-systematically.
      Sometimes, perhaps, his rearranging of
      his molecules is done in sheer self-defense,
      as a way of rattling off dialogs or drills
      fast enough to escape being branded 'non-
      cooperative' (Brown, 1967, p.xvi) or inept.
      Adherents of one approach to this task are
      likely to scoff at the value, or even the
      practicability, of some or all of the others.
      Nevertheless, every 'method' ('an overall
      plan for the orderly presentation of language
      material' Anthony, 1963) must provide one way
      of achieving temporary rearrangement. This
      book is as neutral as possible concerning
      the choice of means to that end.

b.   Somehow, the teacher must see to it, before
the new arrangements have become dissipated,
that the student has some kind of experience
which will tend to make them permanent.

What do these changes of molecular arrangement correspond
to? Can one's brain be changed in such a way that an anecdote
memorized 25 years ago and not recalled once in the last fifteen
can still come back verbatim? Anyone who has ever memorized and
remembered anything in any language must answer this question in
the affirmative. Of course it happens. A-L makes much of it;
T-C makes considerably less. Can one summon up remembered sentences and use them to solve an immediate problem in sentence
construction? Again, this is a common experience of language
learners, and again the schools differ in the relative weight
that they give to this human ability. T-C errs only when it
claims that these phenomena should be totally excluded from the
methodology of language teaching.

Are there instances of speech that cannot be accounted for
in this way? Certainly there are, and T-C writers never tire of
furnishing examples. The assertion of T-C that 'a language is a
set of principles establishing correlations between meanings and
sound sequences' (Langacker, 1967, p. 35) is largely true. Indeed,
A-L writers have recognized its truth in many of their grammar
notes, and give lip service to it whenever they repeat after
Bloch and Trager that a language is a system (and not just a set)
of oral symbols. T-C, of course, is characterized by greater
emphasis on this undisputed fact, and A-L by less. What we mean
to emphasize here is that the neuronal molecules are inaccessible
to direct control from outsiders. Because they are inaccessible,
any method of teaching must come to terms with the learner. This
may take place in any of a number of ways, and these will be the
subject of the following section.

20

MOTIVATION

Motivation is whatever makes the learner ready and willing
to rearrange his own molecules, but what is that? Miller, a
social psychologist, and Wardhaugh, a linguist, express current
ideas on this topic in language that is strikingly harmonious and
at times almost identical. Motivation of course encompasses the
student's purposes (Wardhaugh, 1967, p. 23), and we should make
materials as relevant as possible to the live concerns of the
student, so as to increase the chances of individual involvement
(Miller, 1964, p. 40f.). But it also encompasses the social and
academic climate (Wardhaugh; cf. also the non-recent Wallace,
1949); we too often overlook or use unskillfully the forces within the learning group itself, and the quality of the interaction
of its members (Miller). Fear of inadequacy (Wardhaugh) and
failure (Miller), of change (Miller) and anomie (Wardhaugh) are
negative forces which teachers can identify and try to remove
(Miller).

We may picture these aspects of motivation in terms of two
intersecting axes of reality as it exists for the learner.[5]
The horizontal axis expresses the external aspect of his experiences: his relations with other people, his ability to talk
about past experiences, to interact with present waiters, taxi
drivers and friends, and to plan for the future. This outward-
looking kind of reality may in the long run be necessary for
motivation, but it is not by itself sufficient.

The vertical axis extends through reality that is internal
to the learner: his feelings, his anxieties, and his picture of
himself. Does he enjoy what he is doing, or not? Does he see

---

[5]This discussion of motivation in terms of two axes is taken
from Stevick (1971).

himself as succeeding, or as failing? Is he, in his own eyes, one
of the moving forces in the learning process, or is he only a pawn?

Emphasis on this vertical axis is one of the interesting
features of what Dr. Gattegno calls his Silent Way of teaching
languages. During the first part of the course, all talking is
about a set of small wooden blocks which differ from each other
only in length and color, and are little more than concrete
abstractions. At this stage, exploitation of the horizontal axis
has been reduced to what must surely be its very narrowest minimum. But it is this very annihilation of the horizontal axis,
coupled with the almost complete silence of the teacher, that
allows and indeed forces both student and teacher to focus their
attention on the introspective--on what resources are available
from within the student, on what is taking shape within his mind,
and what he is ready to do at any given moment. In the short run,
and with a teacher who can focus his attention on the inside of
the student's mind, the vertical axis may be sufficient for
motivation. In the long run, of course, it is not.[6] In fact,
motivation depends on connecting something on the horizontal
axis of external experience with something on the vertical axis
of the student's appreciation of himself. It is the vertical
axis, however, that language teachers talk and write about the
least.

Like our view of 'operants' (p.18), our view of favorable
results or rewards which will 'reinforce' those operants has been
too narrow. For long-term, extrinsic motivation we have placed
too much reliance on reference to 'spiritual goals,' or to 'an
experience which is essential to understanding the world [one]

---

[6]In Gattegno's system, the wooden blocks are followed by a
series of pictures which are still about as unrelated to
the horizontal kind of external, interesting reality as it
is possible for pictures of real objects to be, but which
provide the imaginative teacher with opportunities to begin
creative expansion of the student's vocabulary.

lives in' (Grittner, 1969, p. 36) or to 'the belief that what is learned in school will transfer to situations which the student will later face in life' (ibid.) For short-term, intrinsic motivation, we too often depend on some superficial reward: a 'feeling of accomplishment' (Stevick, 1959), grades, numbers on a counting device, candies, money, permission to go on to the next frame, and the like.

A more comprehensive view of motivation derives from what we may call Lambert's Principle.[6] This principle states that, other things being equal, a language course is effective in proportion to the breadth of its contact with the student's interests, and the depth of its penetration into his emotional life. The conditions that loosen up the atoms, or molecules, or electrons, of the brain so that they become available for rearranging lie outside the strictly linguistic realm. Both the teacher and the materials writer need to be aware of the full range of rewards and incentives that are available to the student:

(1) What needs, and what opportunities does the student have to gain satisfaction from having done something right? What he does may be very small, such as completing one line in a drill, or reciting a sentence out of a dialog, but the materials should

---

[6] Lambert and his colleagues have done much to elucidate the social psychology of second-language learning. They distinguish between 'instrumental' orientation, which looks toward the utilitarian values of linguistic achievement, and 'integrative' orientation of students who learn as if they desired to become potential members of the FL group (Lambert, 1963, section 4). Jakobovits (1970) cites Lambert frequently in his relatively full discussion of the complex psychological issues that may be involved in the study of foreign languages.

lay out very clearly--and more explicitly than most do--some of
the things that the student can do in order to gain approval.
Here is where programmed self-instruction is at its best. This
is also the aspect of 'intrinsic motivation' that has received
most attention.

(2) What needs, and what opportunities does the student
have to transmit and receive real messages? If the 'real messages' are to go much beyond the location of the chalk, and the
menu for the next meal, then there must be some area or areas of
shared genuine interest, whether these be planning the Spanish
club's annual picnic, or preparing for two years' residence in
Quito. This is one reason why integration of language study with
other components of a curriculum or training program makes so much
sense. Trainers have of course thought about this matter, but
usually with most of their attention on its 'extrinsic' or long-
term role, and very little exploitation of its potential for
'intrinsic,' day-to-day motivation.

(3) What needs, and what opportunities does the student
have to satisfy his drive to acquire knowledge that he can project
onto future events that he cares about? (Ritchie, 1967, p. 47).
Competence in generating and understanding new sentences is something that most learners require as a pay-off, not only in the
long run, but also immediately. (Reid, 1971)

(4) What needs, and what opportunities does the student
have to be aggressive in making sense out of nonsense--to acquire
skills and insights actively rather than having them 'skillfully
presented and sufficiently drilled' into him? Active inquiry,
even when it is not conscious, may result in active learning
(Kuno, 1969). Here is the value, for some students at least, of
the inductive presentation of grammar so dear to some A-L practitioners, and also of direct, monolingual teaching of meanings for
words and sentences.

24

(5) What needs and what opportunities does the student have
for developing personal relationships with people who interest
him? This question is related to the first two, for one 'does
things right' primarily in the eyes of other people, and it is
to other people that one 'transmits real messages.' But there
is no reason why a language course should confine itself to
helping the student 'get things right' and 'transmit real messages',
either through talking about books, tables, pens and blackboards
or through acting out imaginary episodes in the life of an
American who is living with a Sarkhanese family. Built into the
materials may be opportunities to become better acquainted with
instructors and classmates.

These opportunities may be of two different kinds. The
more obvious type is concerned with the content of the inter-
relationships: finding out about the other person's family his
likes and dislikes, his earlier experiences, and so forth. A
second type grows out of competition and cooperation in the common
tasks of studying and living together. The second kind of relationship may grow along with the first, or it may thrive without
it. This is another key feature of the first stage of Gattegno's
Silent Way of language teaching, in which very intense inter-
personal interplay is carried out in the context of discussing
abstract relationships among small colored wooden blocks.

CONCLUSION

When a student engages in activities that normally take place
only inside a language classroom, it is as though he were picking
up in his hands the stones from which he was to construct a wall.
These activities include memorization of word lists, dialogs or
rules, and performance of systematic drills; they also include

the gaining of insights about structure, and the generating of
sentences for the sake of generating them. To be sure, one can
hardly build a wall without picking up the stones, but if the
stones are not placed into the wall--if the activity does not
immediately produce rewards of several different kinds (points
1-5 on pp.23 -25 , above)--then the student simply sets one
stone down as fast as he picks another up. One cannot remember
what he has not in some sense understood, and he cannot put into
practice (i.e. use in a larger context) what he cannot remember.
This is the usual justification for many teaching practices today.
But we sometimes forget that the reverse is also true: what one
has not put into practice (used in a larger context) he will soon
forget, and what he has forgotten he no longer understands. Any
method is weak that emphasizes memory without understanding, <u>or</u>
<u>that is satisfied with memory and understanding in a narrowly</u>
<u>intraverbal context</u>.

To put the same matter in another way, a team of materials
developers must ask itself three questions:

1. What must the student <u>see</u>? The things he needs to see
include meanings of words and sentences, and also relationships
among them. The materials should make it easy for him to see
these things. It may very well be that the principal value of
the commoner types of drill is not, as we once thought, in sheer
repetition but in guiding the student as he explores the relationships between indicative and subjunctive, or affirmative and
negative.

2. What must the student <u>remember</u>? In contemporary practice,
these things are mostly words and examples of constructions. Some
materials try to make the student remember by requiring him to
memorize. Others emphasize multiple reintroduction of items to be
remembered. Some materials seem to ignore the matter altogether.

3. What can the student <u>do</u>? Where can he lay the stones
that he has just picked up, and what can he use for mortar?
What practical application can he make of his new ability to
choose between indicative and subjunctive French verbs, or how
many kinds of satisfaction can he gain from being able to form
the negatives of all the tenses of Swahili? <u>This is the point
at which materials writers most often abdicate to the teachers,
and where unskilled teachers are most often oblivious to their
opportunities.</u>

CHAPTER 2

WORKING ASSUMPTIONS, AND
THE MODULAR APPROACH
TO MATERIALS DEVELOPMENT

...one

One only, one thing that was firm, even no
Greater than a cricket's horn, no more than
A thought to be rehearsed all day, a speech
Of the self that must sustain itself on
Speech, one thing remaining, infallible,
Would be enough.

It can never be satisfied, the mind, never.

Wallace Stevens

The preceding chapter was concerned with the foundations of
language teaching and language learning in general. One of the
special problems within that area is the preparation of suitable
written or recorded materials, and that is the subject to which
we shall now turn. Continuous involvement in materials development for seldom-taught languages for 20 years in over a dozen
languages, and consultation with writers in dozens of others, has
frequently raised doubts whether those of us who sustain ourselves
on the speech of others can find even one thing infallible to
satisfy our minds. Instead, we shall present here five working
assumptions which have stood the test of time, and then outline
an approach which seems to be consistent with them. The assumptions concern respectively 'Usability,' 'Organization,' 'Responsiveness,' 'Responsibility,' and 'Pluralism.' The approach to
writing materials is 'modular.'

ASSUMPTION I   ('USABILITY').

> I know
> The power of words.
>
> It is nothing!
> A fallen
>
> Petal under
> A dancer's heel.
>
> But man
> In his soul, his lips, in his bones...

> Frederick Seidel

Man is by necessity a language-using animal, but as an adult he is only for convenience a language-learning one. The first assumption therefore is that people learn features of a language best if they use those features immediately for their own purposes, instead of just mimicking, memorizing and manipulating forms.[1,2] This assumption is inconsistent with the time-honored practice of delaying 'free conversation' until the student is 'ready' for it-- usually sometime near the end of the second semester or second year.

In this respect, it is worthwhile to distinguish between 'real' and 'realistic' use of language. I really use the question 'What time is it?' only if (a) I don't know what time it is and (b) I want to know what time it is. I can use the same question

---

[1] In Chapter 1, quoted material usually formed a part of the argument, and so was included in the body of the text. In this chapter most of the quotations are corroborative, in order to make the assumptions seem less idiosyncratic. Accordingly, they have been relegated to footnotes.

[2] Rivers (1964, p.128): 'If [the student's] work in a foreign

<u>realistically</u> if I can foresee the time when I might really use
it. Pictures, role plays, foreign coins and the like are stimu-
lants to sharpen the student's foresight in this sense, and in
this way to increase the available range of realistic practice.
Some completely grammatical sentences are susceptible of neither

---

language class has caused him to perceive the manipulation
of linguistic structures and the repetition of foreign
language phrases as "class exercises," unrelated to real-
life concerns, then these are not likely to spring to his
mind in a real-life situation.... [In order to bring about
good transfer of set and attitudes], the classroom must
simulate [real life] as closely as possible.' 'Important
as it is to make clear to the student what he is doing,
it is equally important to relate the drills to his own
interest.' (p.153)

Rivers (1968) '...students must be trained from the first
to apply what they have memorized, or practiced in drills,
in communication situations...' (p.46) '[After drilling],
the next, most important step is the opportunity for the
student to demonstrate that he can use the structure...
in...actual...communication.' (p.196)

Carroll (1966): Among the facts which have accumulated
in the study of verbal learning is: 'The more meaningful
the material to be learned, the greater the facility in
learning and retention.' (p.105)

Halliday et al. (1964): '[One of the propitious circumstances
that can favour language learning is] the amount of experience
of the language received by the learner, provided that this
experience is meaningful.' (p.181) 'Human beings learn more
rapidly and effectively if they have a reason for doing so.'
(p.182)

Prator (1964) puts the matter more bluntly:
    1. Communication is always accompanied by understanding.
    2. Communication requires that the student himself sup-
        ply the sounds, words, and structures needed to ex-
        press his thought.

30

real nor realistic use: 'The child sees vegetables in the after-
noon.' Others might possibly find real use, but in such restricted
circumstances that realistic practice is impossible to arrange:
'I live in the eighth city.'

Even 'real' communication in a foreign language may or may
not be 'authentic.' If it is in the language that for the two
interlocutors would be the natural one to use at that time, on
that topic, then it is authentic; otherwise it is not. One of
the peculiar skills, and a mark of dedication of a good language
teacher (provided of course that he could be communicating with
the student more easily in some other language) is his ability
and willingness to carry on communication that is at the same
time real and non-authentic. One of the mistakes of the unskilled
teacher is to assume that because communication is not authentic,
it can at best be realistic.[3]

---

3. This concept of communication may prove more
    important to the language teacher than either
    programed learning or transformational analysis.

Compare also 'Lambert's Principle,' Chapter 1, p. 23.

[3]This emphasis on real communication, although it receives
strong support from many authorities (footnote 2), is of
course by no means universally accepted. So Benton
(1970, p.   ), introducing a textbook which makes almost
no provision for exploitation of the present realities of
a training site, urges the student to 'be willing to
cooperate in that "suspension of disbelief" which will
enable him to become a real participant in an imaginary
event.'

The degree of tolerance for pretense (i.e. non-real and/or
non-authentic use of words) may in fact be a major component of
what looks like a difference in language aptitude between academ-
ically-oriented trainees (e.g. Peace Corps 'A.B. generalists')
and other kinds of trainees (e.g. older Volunteers, skilled craftsmen). One recent training program not only used materials (see
Appendix L) which were drawn from the trainees' trade (diesel
mechanics), but also brought in monolingual French-speaking ap-
prentices for the trainees to teach their trade to. Results were
encouraging, though a single experiment is necessarily inconclusive.

Corollary 1 to the assumption on usability. Each new word and
each new grammatical feature should be used (not just practiced),
either really or realistically, as early as possible. It should
be used as often as necessary to integrate it into the student's
repertoire and to improve his chances of retaining it.

Corollary 2 to the assumption on usability. Other things being
equal, spontaneous material is better than pre-existing printed
material. This is because language is really used only as a part
of life. Printed materials are at best a record of past life (or
of a past guess as to what the present would be like); at worst,
they bear very little relation to life past, present or future.

ASSUMPTION II ('ORGANIZATION')

On the elementary level, there must be order in the introduction of new phonological, grammatical and lexical problems,
and systematic drill on alien mechanical features, and some way
of organizing classroom procedures.[4]

----

[4]The professional consensus on the need for organization
hardly needs documentation. As stated by Hutchinson (in

ASSUMPTION III ('RESPONSIVENESS').

> Hawthorne and Emerson met on the wood paths of
> Concord, and passed on, Emerson with his head
> full of bright futurities and relevances,
> Hawthorne with his head full of the irrelevant
> past.... We revere Emerson, the prophet whose
> prophecies came true..., but we find in [Hawthorne's]
> work a complex, tangled and revolutionary vision
> of the soul, which we recognize as our own.
>
> Emerson spoke nobly about relevance.
> Hawthorne <u>was</u> relevant.
>
> The moral is that it is hard to tell at any
> given moment what is relevant.
>
>   Robert Penn Warren

Our third assumption is that individuals, but also groups,
vary widely not only in general language aptitude, in their
emotional involvement with the new language, and in the degree
of pre-existing motivation, but also in the lexical content that
they can make immediate use of, in the approaches that they will
put up with, and in the methods that are appropriate for them.

Valdman, 1966, p. 225) 'Language is complex; language learning is complex. It takes a variety of organized activities
to teach language successfully, for the art and science of
teaching include the judicious selection, timing, measuring
and blending of the many ingredients involved.' The level
of agreement on this point is exceeded only by the level of
disagreement on just what principles, procedures and formats
should provide that organization. A good general treatment
in terms of 'limitation,' 'grading,' 'presentation' and
'testing' is found in Halliday <u>et al</u>. (1964) chapter 7;
Mackey (1965), especially in Part 2 (<u>Method Analysis</u>), is
encyclopedic on this subject. Kelly (1969) provides a
readable diachronic view of the same matter.

Some students, but only some, can profit from spending the first
15 hours of class on phonological drills; some students, but only
some, want to start out with 'What's your name and where are you
from?'; some but only some thrive on the memorization of dialogs;
one group plans to drill wells for two years, another group plans
to teach English, and still another expects to monitor radio
broadcasts. Tolerance for one or another approach depends partly
on the coordinator or supervisor of the program, partly on the
past experience of the students themselves.[5]

The assumption about 'responsiveness' is close to the issue
of 'relevance' that looms so large in the entire world of education today. We must not be too facile either in accepting a
language text as 'relevant' merely because it is job-related, or
in rejecting it as 'irrelevant' just because it spends most of
the first lessons in talking about colored blocks of wood. As
we have pointed out in chapter 1 (p.23f), the needs and interests
that any student has, and to which a course may relate, are many
and complex. Nevertheless, there are irrelevant courses, and
almost any textbook may be made either more or less relevant to a
given class.

-----

[5]To cite one of a number of possible sources, Carroll (in
Valdman 1966, p.96) asserts that 'one of the best-establish-
ed findings of educational research is that a major source
of variation in pupil learning is the teacher's ability to
promote that learning. Exactly what this ability consists
of is not certain, but we have strong evidence that along
with knowledge of subject matter there is involved the
teacher's ability to organize this content and present it
with due regard for the pupil's ability and readiness to
acquire it.'

ASSUMPTION IV ('RESPONSIBILITY')

> ...the students [of history] read what they
> pleased and compared their results. As
> pedagogy, nothing could have been more tri-
> umphant.... No difficulty stopped them;
> unknown languages yielded before their at-
> tack, and customary law became as familiar
> as the police court.
>
>   Henry Adams

We assume that, other things being equal, the program will
be more effective if the students and instructors feel that they
have some control over both content and method. Materials ought
therefore to provide for transferring to the users as much responsibility as they are prepared to handle. There are undoubt-
edly certain functions which will remain with the teacher and
supervisor throughout the training period, but in general, growth
in the skills and attitudes of increasing self-sufficiency in
language study are an important part of the aims of any
well-run language program.[6] Note that this assumption is inconsistent with exclusive or nearly exclusive reliance on programmed
self-instruction or other highly authoritarian systems of teaching.

---

[6]Thus Ruopp (1969, p.6) 'Techniques [for any kind of train-
ing] should involve the trainee in the learning process as
actively as possible, and the process should itself equip
him for adapting and improving his field performance. That
is, the activities he engages in during training should be
consistent with the problem-solving behavior expected of
him [on the job].'

ASSUMPTION V   ('PLURALISM')

> I do not think that we should assume that
> there is always one point of vantage from
> which we can equally see the front and the
> back, the inside and the outside, the left
> and the right.
>
>   Fred Householder

Householder's words about phonological theory apply also to
language teaching. Our final assumption is that no one format,
and no one system however ingenious, can be sufficient for even
one student or group of students. What has been seen only once
will not be perceived, and what has been perceived from only one
point of view will not be assimilated.[7] If a student uses the
Swahili verb stem -kaza 'set, emphasize' with genuine understanding, or as a native speaker would, then he must have met it more

---

[7]Valdman (in Mueller, 1968): '...a foreign language course
[should not] be based on too narrow a model of language
learning.'

G. Miller (quoted in Rivers 1964, p. 123): 'The process of
organizing and reorganizing is a pervasive human trait,...
motivated at least in part by an attempt to make the best
possible use of our mnemonic capacity.'

Rivers (1964, p.94): 'If [the teacher] wishes to induce
each [student] to behave, he must see to it that the methods
he employs are sufficiently varied....'

In my discussion (Stevick, 1963) of techniques, I have
sometimes forgotten that what may be 'blind alleys' under
some circumstances may be useful 'technemes' (Stevick,
1959) under others.

than once. If he has met it five times, he has met it in five
different contexts. He has not only met the word in varied contexts, he has also seen that -kaza is related to -kaa 'stay, sit,
reside' as -jaza 'fill' is related to -jaa 'become full.' Or
again, the student who can really handle tag questions (isn't he,
didn't they, etc.) in English has probably memorized them (intentionally or not) as parts of fixed phrases or whole dialogs,
he has explored them systematically either through drills or in
some more overtly 'cognitive' way, and he has used them in un-
structured conversations. Procedures and systems and approaches
supplement one another more than they supersede one another.

Anisfeld (in Valdman 1966, p.114) quotes William James:
'The secret of a good memory is...the secret of forming
diverse and multiple associations with every fact we
care to retain.' Anisfeld then goes to show how the
experience that was behind James' statement can be
interpreted better when seen from the point of view
of information processing.

CHAPTER 2   WORKING ASSUMPTIONS

A MODULAR APPROACH TO MATERIALS DEVELOPMENT

Most language courses violate some or all of these five
assumptions. One reason is that they attempt to be too massive
and too permanent. Great quantities of curricular concrete and
steel are assembled and formed into a mighty bridge across the
chasm, in anticipation that the oncoming traffic (the students)
will want to cross at just the point where the bridge is.

This anticipation is often disappointed. When it is, the
Golden Gate-style course fails on responsiveness (Assumption III),
it almost always fails to provide for user responsibility (Assumption IV), and often it is not directly usable (in the sense
of Assumption I). Its one strength (unless it is poorly constructed even by its own standards) is in organization, and
superior organization alone will not produce superior results.

Most of the textbooks that this writer has used or helped to
produce have tried to be more or less massive bridges. The needs
and the mood of the students have never been exactly those that
the course was written for, but the discrepancies have often been
small enough so that some kind of useful result could be achieved.
In this, as in many other respects, experience with Peace Corps
language training has provided stimulating, if discomforting,
ventilation of old complacencies. Students' specialized interests
are at the same time more specialized; trainees are more conscious
of their own dissatisfaction with both content and method;
instructors are mostly willing but inexperienced, brought up in an
educational system that knows nothing of audio-lingual materials.
Peace Corps programs have also demonstrated the value of giving to
the users--both the students and the instructors--a certain amount
of leeway for their own creativity. These observations point
toward a new approach to materials development, one which has seemed
more appropriate for Peace Corps needs, but which also seems promis-
ing for programs of a more conventional sort.

The label that has been applied to this approach is
'modular.'[8] The modular principle may be applied on at least
two different scales. On a large scale, it means that instead
of a single volume, with drills, notes, dialogs and what-not all
printed and bound in fixed order relative to one another, there
are separate fascicles, or 'modules,' which can be used (or
discarded!) individually, or in various combinations with one
another. Instead of building a bridge, we supply a set of
pontoons. Each major component of the course takes the form of
one or more modules. One fascicle may consist of phonological
drills; another may be a very brief reference grammar that covers
only those matters that are of high text frequency; another may
consist of dialogs, with cross references to the short grammar in
lieu of separate grammatical notes. Some of the less common types
of module are described in Appendices G,H,J,K,L,M,N,O,P,R,S,T,U.

Within a single 'lesson,' or 'unit,' the modular principle
suggests that the several components (dialogs, drills, etc.) be
designed so that they may be rearranged to suit the convictions
of various kinds of user, and so that the individual components
may be replaced with minimum disturbance to the rest of the lesson.
For examples, see Chapter 4 and Appendices G,I,J,K.

One advantage of modular construction is that it allows for
more user responsibility (Assumption IV): a class that wants to
spend the first 15 hours on phonology can do so, but a class that
finds that kind of activity unmotivating can wait until what is

---

[8]One of the first to apply this term was William F. Mackey.

for them a more appropriate time. Dialog memorization, newspaper
reading and study of grammar may proceed in any order, or simul-
taneously. A second advantage is that, for example, a set of
readings or dialogs appropriate for well-diggers may be replaced
by a set appropriate for TB control workers without tearing the
whole course apart. (For examples, see Chapter 4 and Appendix G.)

In any case, modular construction may lead to greater responsiveness (Assumption III) and hence to greater usability
(Assumption I). An incidental advantage for the overworked
writer who is producing materials on marginal time is that one
fascicle can be completed and put into use in a small fraction
of the time it takes to write a complete course.

It may be objected that drawing on an array of modules and
combining them into a successful course places heavy demands on
the teacher's ingenuity and judgment. That is certainly true.
But exactly the same is true if one is to teach successfully
from a printed course, bound between covers, conceived and written
by strangers who were removed by many months and many hundreds of
miles from one's present students.

Modularity is a principle or an approach, and not
a method. Specifically, as Allen Weinstein has pointed out
(private communication)

> If a student needs a certain amount of material,
> and the material exists in a corpus, then break-
> ing that corpus up into a series of 'modules'
> which may be presented in any order at his choice
> does not represent a modular approach, since all
> paths eventually lead to the same spot.... If a
> student has to use all the available modules to
> reach his goal, his instruction has not been
> modular.

The modular principle is of course not new. It is implied by the existence of alternate, parallel versions of some courses, and by series of optional readers that have been prepared for some of the more widely taught languages. Beyond that, however, it has seldom been followed either consciously or very far. To my knowledge, the earliest deliberate attempt to produce an array of modules was in Swift (1963), for Kituba.   This was a set of one central and five optional fascicles which for reasons of economy were bound in a single volume. According to Swift's introduction:

> This course consists of a 'primer' in the language and five subject-oriented groups of lessons. The primer is intended to introduce the major grammatical structures of the language, to develop in the student an adequate pronunciation, and to present a certain amount of useful vocabulary for a variety of situations. The primer is prerequisite to the rest of the course, and the student is expected to go through it in order, as each unit presupposes the vocabulary and the grammar of the earlier ones.

> The subject-oriented lesson groups all presuppose the vocabulary and grammar of the entire primer, and each group is intended to be studied from the beginning--the vocabulary within a given group being cumulative. However, no subject-oriented lesson group depends in any way on any other group so that the student is free to pursue his study of these lesson groups in any order after he has finished the primer.

> This arrangement is intended to provide maximum flexibility. The class with only a few hours of time to devote to classroom drill with an instructor may find it possible to cover the primer only. Students with more time will wish to select such of the subject fields covered in the later lessons as are of most interest to them. Students in intensive courses with at least 300 hours of class and laboratory will be able to cover the entire content of the course. An additional element of flexibility is provided in that the primer may be used as an introduction to be followed by more specialized subject-oriented lessons which are not included in this course but which may be constructed by an instructor or a linguist to meet the specialized needs of particular students.

Similarly, in the introduction to Adams, Modular Vietnamese (1970, unpublished) we read:

> This elementary course in Vietnamese is composed of several different 'modules.' Each module is a series of related lessons which will guide the student toward accurate conversation on a particular topic. It does not matter whether the student begins his study of Vietnamese conversing, say, about geography, street directions, or personal matters; each module begins at the beginning.

In 1968, MacDougall produced for the Peace Corps her deliberately modular Active Introduction to Sinhala. In this set of materials, one module introduces the writing system. A second is a grammatical sketch of Sinhala. The third consists mainly of a series of Cummings devices (p. 310 -314). This series is broken into a subseries on classroom expressions, a subseries on matters of general conversation, and further subseries on specialized topics such as rice growing and the preparation of food.

A set of fourteen modules has been developed by Goodison and the staff of the Foreign Service Institute's Russian language section. These materials are designed especially to fit the scope and nature of Russian training at the Institute, and are therefore unpublished. They include an introduction to pronunciation and to printed and handwritten letters; a series of lessons based on using a simplified table-top model of Moscow; narratives and conversations suitable for use with the table-top model; introductory, intermediate and advanced readings taken from newspaper advertisements and announcements; general or specialized newspaper stories, charts and maps on the economic geography of the Soviet Union; selections from a sixth-grade geography book used in the Soviet Union.

This book is itself written on the modular principle.
Chapter 3, which explains much of the distinctive terminology,
should not be omitted, but the chapters may otherwise be read
in any order. Most chapters are followed by one or more appendices, many of which are also largely self-contained.

CHAPTER 3

EVALUATING AND ADAPTING LANGUAGE MATERIALS

INTRODUCTION

With the growing shortage of time and money for writing
new textbooks, particularly in the seldom-taught languages,
there is a premium on making effective use of what already
exists. We have sometimes acted as though, for any given set of
materials the choice was only between using them and rejecting
them. Adaptation, as a third alternative, has received very
little either of time or of money or of prestige. Rewriting, a
fourth possibility, is often viewed both as unjustifiably
troublesome for the rewriter, and as an affront to the original
author.

Yet among the many dozens of language teachers who have
been consulted in the preparation of this book, there has been
scarcely one who does not claim that he or she makes some
changes or additions to the printed textbook, even if it is
supposedly of the programmed self-instructional variety. Many
of those interviewed described major changes. A few operate
with a minimum outline and a few props, and recreate the course
every time they teach it. Under these circumstances, two
points need emphasis: First, the various degrees of adaptation,
augmentation and rewriting form a continuum, at the far end of
which stands the preparation of original materials. Second,
before one can begin to adapt or augment or write or rewrite,
and before one can even decide which of these four to undertake,
it is necessary to evaluate what is available. This chapter
offers guidelines for evaluation, and outlines a general procedure for adaptation. The guidelines and the procedure

receive detailed illustration in the appendices, and particularly
in Appendices A-F.

EVALUATION

More than courses in French, Spanish, German or English,
a course in a seldom-taught language is likely to be the brain
child of one author, conceived in desperation, brought forth in
obscurity, and destined to be despised and rejected of all other
men. Sometimes rejection is inevitable, but often it is the
result of hasty, or unperceptive, or unappreciative examination
of the existing book. The following guidelines for evaluation
may be applied to the efforts of others, but also to one's own
handiwork both before and after it is completed. The guidelines
are stated in terms of three qualities, three dimensions, and
four components.

EVALUATION: THREE QUALITIES

Every lesson, every part of every lesson, and even every
line may be judged on three qualities, which we shall call
'strength,' 'lightness' and 'transparency.' As we shall use
these terms, their opposites, weakness, heaviness and opacity
are usually undesirable. There are however situations in which
a certain amount of heaviness and opacity can be useful, and the
same may even be true for weakness (see, for example, Appendix D).
It would be a mistake, therefore, to assume that strength,
lightness and transparency are absolute virtues, or that an
increase in one of these values necessarily means an improvement
in the lesson. Nevertheless, weakness, heaviness and opacity
are in general warning signs, and their presence calls for
special justification in terms of the lesson or the textbook
as a whole.

CHAPTER 3   EVALUATING

Strength

'Does it carry its own weight by means of the rewards
that it makes available?' As we pointed out in Chapter 1
(p. 23f), rewards may be of at least five different kinds;
they _must_ be valid in terms of the values of the learner, and
not of the materials writer only.

In the evaluation of an entire course, concern about
strength will lead to such questions as:

> Is the content relevant to the present and
> likely future needs of the trainees?

> Does the textbook provide for the tools,
> both in vocabulary and in structure, that
> students will need in order to reach what-
> ever goal has been set?

> Are the materials authentic both linguistically
> and culturally?

Looking at a single lesson from the same point of view, one may
ask:

> Will the students derive from this lesson
> satisfactions that go beyond the mere
> feeling of having mastered one more lesson,
> and being ready for the next? (see below,
> p. 54f, and Chapter 1, pp. 23f.)

> In particular, to what extent will the students
> be able to use the content of this lesson imme-
> diately, in a lifelike way?

On the smallest scale, a sentence like 'your horse had been old'
(cited by Jespersen, 1904) is weak to the point of being feeble,
because there is no situation in which anyone can use it. The
cliché 'The book is on the table' is stronger, because the situations in which it _can_ be used are fairly frequent. But we must
distinguish between the ease with which a situation can be created
in the classroom, and the frequency with which it actually gets

commented on in real life. In this latter respect, 'The book is
on the table' is still relatively weak. A sentence like 'I need
a taxi' (Taylor, p. 50) is potentially stronger because most
people are more concerned about being able to verbalize this need
than they are about being able to describe the most obvious
location of a book. In the same way, 'I need a taxi' is stronger
for most students than 'I need a hinge.' But other things being
equal, strength is always relative to the needs and interests of
the students: some people talk about hinges every day and never
see a taxi. For this reason, we cannot build strength as a permanent and absolute quality into any fixed set of materials.

It is impossible to give simple directions for determining
what would make materials strong for any given class. Questionnaires may help, and being psychically 'with' one's students may
help. Certainly it is necessary to be more than a purveyor of
words and a master of drill techniques. This problem is discussed
under 'specification' in Chapter 4 (p.135ff); pp. 21-25 in
Chapter 1 and pp.54 - 57 in this chapter also relate to it.

Lightness

'Is a single "unit" so long that the student wearies of it
before it is finished, and loses any sense of its unity?' 'Does
an individual line weight heavily on the student's tongue, either
because of the number of difficult sounds or because of its sheer
length?' Insofar as new words or structures, by virtue of their
newness alone, make a line or a lesson tiring, they may also be
said to contribute to its weight, but lightness is intended here
to refer primarily to sheer physical characteristics. With respect to lightness, 'Your horse had been old' and 'I need a taxi'
are approximately equal. Heaviness in this sense may vary with
the language background of the learner: many would find 'I need

a hinge' to be noticeably heavier than 'I need a label,' depend-
ing on whether the native language has initial /h/ (German has,
French and Spanish have not), or final voiced stops (French has,
German and Spanish have not).

In general, of course, we try to make early lessons rather
light. But Alex Lipson is one authority who advocates putting
some heavy items into the very first sessions of a new class,
while the students are in their freshest and most open state.
This is one example of how none of the three qualities has
absolute positive value, and temporary lack of one of these
qualities is not necessarily bad.

Transparency

Transparency is primarily a cognitive problem: how readily
can the user of the materials see the units and their relationships? Looking at a textbook as a whole, we may ask:

>   Do these materials make clear at least one way
>   in which the teacher may use them in class?
>
>   Is it easy to find where a given point of grammar
>   has been covered?

With regard to single lessons, we may ask:

>   To what extent does the student know what he is
>   doing and why?
>
>   How easily can a teacher or adapter find places
>   where he can make changes or additions without
>   destroying the lesson?

With regard to single lines, we may ask:

>   Can the meaning be put across without translation?
>
>   Can the student see the structure of this sentence
>   clearly enough so that he will be able to use it as
>   a help in composing or comprehending new ones?

Once again, transparency is not an absolute value. One good aspect of inductive teaching of grammar, for example, is the fun of working one's way out of a temporary structural fog.

Needless to say, opacity is to be calculated from the point of view of the learner. If the writer or adapter knows the language too well, he may forget that what seems obvious to him may be perplexing for students from a very different language background. On the other hand, writers sometimes spend much effort in elaborate explanation of a point that really causes the students no trouble.

Summary comments on the three qualities

The differences among the three qualities may perhaps be clarified by looking at the following sentences:

Weak, light, transparent: The book is on the table.

Weak, heavy, transparent: The big red book is on the little table by the open window.

Weak, heavy, opaque: The seldom commented-upon but frequently observed location for a book is that in which we now find this one.

(Potentially) strong, heavy, opaque: The repast which the cook, for our enjoyment and his own self-satisfaction has (in a manner of speaking) prepared for our lunch today is pizza.

(Potentially) strong, light, opaque: I paid half the then going rate.

(Potentially) strong, heavy, transparent: We're going to have pizza with mushrooms, anchovies and pepperoni.

(Potentially) strong, light, transparent: We're going to have pizza for lunch!

Obviously, in even the best of lessons some lines will be stronger than others, every line has some heaviness, and many

will be partly opaque. Furthermore, the three criteria will often
conflict with one another: a line may be very strong but also
heavy, or transparent but also weak. Even so, they may be worth
the attention of anyone who is writing or evaluating language
lessons. Lightness and transparency can conceivably be made
permanent attributes of permanent lessons, but only constant
adaptation will keep strength from deteriorating.

EVALUATION: THREE DIMENSIONS

The content of a textbook, or a lesson, or a drill, or a
single line may be plotted in each of three dimensions: linguistic,
social and topical.

The linguistic dimension. ('How well must they speak?)

In a course as a whole, the linguistic content that is needed
is relatively independent of the age, occupation or special interests
of the prospective students. This content consists mainly of phonological patterns and structural devices. Because this aspect of
content is so dependable, text writers have too often accorded the
linguistic dimension absolute primacy: Social and topical content
need not be absorbing, but only plausible and appropriate for
illustrating a series of linguistic points. This is particularly
likely to happen when the materials developer is also a trained
linguist, intent on sharing with the readers his enjoyment of the
intricacies and symmetries of linguistic structure. Even before
the ascendancy of linguistic science, of course, one type of textbook subordinated everything else to the purpose of conveying
patterns. (That must surely have been the purpose behind 'Your
horse had been old.') But in the absence of resolute and
meticulous planning for other sources of reward, strength is drawn

primarily from the social and topical dimensions. This is one
reason why some linguistically brilliant textbooks have been
pedagogical flops.

The social dimension ('Who is talking with whom?')

It is therefore a good idea, before starting to adapt existing lessons, to draw up a simple two-dimensional matrix. The
social dimension lists the kinds of people with whom the student
most urgently needs to interact, by occupation of course, but
also according to their social status with reference to the communication event. The choice of interlocutors determines not
only the content of what one says, but also the style in which
one says it. If the training site is a junior high school in an
entirely English-speaking town, the original list might include
only the teacher and the other students. The reality to which
the matrix refers may be prospective as well as immediate, however.
Many teachers prefer to operate on the principle of 'now now and
later later:' stick to present realities while the students are
coping with the rudiments of the language, and begin to use more
distant ones in the intermediate stage. Policemen, taxi drivers,
landlords and many others may thus be added to the matrix. But
they may only be added if the prospect of encountering them is
psychologically real to the students themselves. To add them at
the whim of the teacher or for the convenience of the materials
writer would result in a spurious matrix, invalid from the point
of view of the student, and a source of weakness rather than
strength.

The same principle applies to the training of adults who
expect to go immediately to jobs where they will use the language.
The roles that make up the social dimension will be more numerous,
and the prospects will be more clearly defined, but care in
selecting and defining the roles can still make the difference
between strength and weakness. 51

CHAPTER 3   EVALUATING

    Most writers give some attention to the social dimension
when they are writing dialog material, although there have been
some exceptions. Drill materials, on the other hand, are usually
treated as socially neutral. They are not always completely so,
of course. Any German, French, Russian or Spanish sentence in
the second person must necessarily imply choice as to level of
respect, and the same is even more true for many other languages.
Some drills may in fact concentrate on the contrast between tu-
forms and vous-forms. This is fine as far as it goes, but it is
not enough. Even the lowliest substitution drill can be checked
for its social implications ('Who might say these things to
whom?'). Thus, 'Have you received an invitation?' and 'Have you
met the ambassador?' are compatible with each other, but not with
'Have you brushed your teeth?' Any internal inconsistencies
should have some clear justification.

The topical dimension ('What are they talking about?')

    At right angles to the social dimension, the topical dimension
lists the things that the trainee is most likely to want to talk
about: greetings and general phrases for getting a conversation
started, expressions needed in conducting a class, street directions, diagnosis of poultry diseases, and so forth. Some topics
are of interest to trainees of almost all kinds, while others are
highly specialized. The problem, for the writer who wants to produce strong materials, is that the trainees' most specialized
interests are often the very ones that are most vivid for them.
Even for a generally useful topic like street and road directions,
the actual locales that excite most interest will vary from one
class to another.

The socio-topical matrix

The intersection of the social and topical dimensions produces a set of boxes. For some situations, the boxes might be labeled as follows:

	Greetings, etc.	Street directions	Food	Work schedule	etc.
Adult Stranger					
Small Child					
Policeman					
Colleague					
Host					
etc.					

Note that not all the boxes will be equally plausible: one will not expect to praise the policeman's cooking or ask directions of a four-year-old child.

This kind of matrix[1] is useful both for making an inventory of what is in an existing book, and also for plotting the needs of a particular group of students. With the addition of a linguistic dimension, as in Chapter 4, p. 142, such a matrix may

---

[1]A matrix with a social dimension was suggested to me by Dr. Albert R. Wight (private communication).

serve in planning entire courses. For the adapter's needs,
however, this two-dimensional grid is easier to manage, and
almost as effective.

Ted Plaister (private communication) has suggested how
selected boxes from such a matrix might be placed on individual
cards or sheets of paper and made into starting points for
adaptations or for complete lessons.

EVALUATION: FOUR COMPONENTS

Earlier drafts of this chapter ventured the guess that a
successful lesson needs components of four--and only four--kinds.
Subsequent experiments, and discussions with many dozens of language teachers, have turned this hunch into a belief. The four
essential components,whether for speech or for writing or for
both, are: occasions for use, a sample of the language in use,
exploration of vocabulary, and exploration of (phonetic,
orthographic or grammatical) form. To make this assertion is
not, however, to prescribe a method or a format. Each of the four
components may take any of countless shapes, and the student may
meet them in any of several orders. It should also be pointed
out that the order in which the components are written need not
be that in which they are placed before the student.

Component 1: occasions for use

Every lesson should contain a number of clear suggestions for
using the language. Each of these suggestions should embody a
purpose outside of the language itself, which is valid in terms
of the student's needs and interests. Insofar as these purposes
relate to the external world (see Chapter 1, p.21f), most of them
will fall under one or more of the following rubrics:

1. Establishing or further developing real social relation-
    ships with real people, including classmates. Simple
    examples are greetings, introductions, autobiographical
    matters including personal anecdotes, participation in
    games, exploration of likes and dislikes.

2. Eliciting or imparting desired information. What is
    the climate like at various times of year in Sarkhan?
    How does the currency system work? How is a certain
    dish prepared? How does the electrical system of an
    automobile work?

3. Learning or imparting useful skills: sewing, dancing,
    playing soccer, thatching a roof.

4. Learning to make culturally relevant judgments: distin-
    guishing ripe from unripe fruit, candling eggs, predict-
    ing the weather, estimating water depth.

5. Doing things for fun: humor, games, singing, relaxation.

Some of the 'occasions for use' should involve muscular activity:
playing, pointing, handling, writing, etc.

As many occasions for use as possible should be written in
the form of 'behavioral objectives:' what students are to do
should be described so clearly that there can be no question as
to whether any one student's performance meets the requirements.
There should be some overt way in which each student can know
(a) that he has performed, and (b) how well he has performed.
For example:

> '<u>Tell your instructor</u> the names of the people in the
> family with whom you are living, and how they are
> related to one another.'

is better than:

> '<u>Find out</u> the names of the people in the family with
> whom you are living, and how they are related to one
> another.'

Even the latter is better than:

> 'Try to use this vocabulary (i.e. kinship terminology)
> outside of class.'

Occasions for use, then, should be both <u>useful</u> and <u>specific</u>.
But they should also be <u>stimulating</u> and <u>open-ended</u>. Excellent
examples of such suggestions are to be found in the sections on
<u>Using the Materials</u>, in Appendix R, pp.346- 364. Rehg (private
correspondence) comments on some of these examples as follows:

> An important aspect of Ponapean culture is the title
> system. Each adult, unless he is something of an
> outcast, is assigned a title, and is subsequently
> known by that title in all formal and many informal
> situations. However, most foreigners do not know these
> alternate 'names.' A student who has learned the
> relevant structures and vocabulary can be assigned
> a task of the following kind:
>
> (a) Elicit the titles of the adult members of the
> family you are staying with. Record this information,
> and bring it back to your instructor.
>
> (b) What are the literal meanings of these titles?
>
> (c) Within the Ponapean title system, how important
> are these titles?
>
> Completion of these tasks accomplishes a number of
> objectives. Part (a) gives the trainee an opportunity
> to use the language that he has learned in a manner
> that is <u>useful</u> following an assignment that is <u>specific</u>.
> Part (b) provides him with the basis for countless hours
> of interesting discussion on a topic that fascinates
> most Ponapeans; therefore, the task is <u>open-ended</u>. Part
> (c) brings the student to grips with the power structure
> of the community. Foreigners seem to be very curious

about the matter of titles, and so the task is also
<u>stimulating</u>. Students very quickly recognize busy
work, so a useful, specific, open-ended but non-
stimulating task will probably be non-productive.

We have discussed 'occasions for use' before the other three
components because writers and teachers so often slight them, or
ignore them altogether. It is true that the student normally
performs them at the end of a lesson, if at all, but a writer or
adapter would be wise to begin thinking about them as soon as he
has chosen a lesson. Even in the student's book, the planned
occasions for use might be listed at the head of the lesson, so
that the student can form a clearer idea of the potential strength
of the rest of the lesson. Occasions for use should certainly
affect the writing or revision of every other component.

Component 2: a sample of language use

Every lesson should contain a sample of how the language is
used. The sample should be:

1. long enough to be viable. (Two-line dialogs, no
    matter how timely or realistic, have proved <u>not</u> to
    meet this requirement.)

2. short enough to be covered, with the rest of the lesson,
    in 1-4 hours of class time.

3. related to a socio-topical matrix that the students accept
    as expressing their needs and interests.

The sample may take any of several forms. Many courses in the
past 25 years have used the 'basic dialog' to fulfill this role,
but other kinds of sample are more useful for some purposes. The
most concrete is probably the 'action chain' (or 'action script'),
which lists a series of activities that normally occur together.

The most familiar example is 'I get up. I bathe. I get dressed
...,' but the same format may accommodate discussion of technical
processes, negotiation with a landlord, public ceremonies, and
many other topics. Another kind of sample, particularly suitable
after the first 50-100 hours of instruction, is a <u>short</u> passage
of expository or narrative prose (see Chapter 7).

Whatever form the sample takes, it should contain at least
one or two lines that lend themselves to lexical and/or structural
exploration of the kinds that will be discussed in the next two
sections of this chapter. If the sample does not contain such
lines, then it will become an isolated compartment within the
lesson, rather than a productive part of it. Appendix C illustrates this danger. Appendix G, among others, shows what we would
consider to be a more desirable relationship between the sample
and the rest of the lesson.

'Language in use' of course implies 'language as one part
of a communication event,' and spoken language is always accompanied by other bodily activity, including gestures, facial
expressions, posture, nearness to other people, and so forth.
These aspects of communication ought to receive attention also.
See Appendix B for examples.

Component 3: lexical exploration

In this and the following section, we have made frequent use
of the word 'exploration.' This word is perhaps confusing, and
hence ill-chosen. We have used it in order to emphasize the
active, creative, partially unprescribed role of the learner,
and to avoid an image of the learner as one whose every footstep
is to be guided by a pedagogue. 'Exploration' in this sense stands
in contrast to 'inculcation.'

'Lexical exploration,' then, refers to those aspects of a
lesson through which the student expands his ability to come up
with, or to recognize, the right word at the right time. The
simplest kind of lexical exploration uses lists of words, sometimes with a sentence or two illustrating the use of each. In
a well-constructed lesson, there may be a number of sub-lists,
each related to some part of the basic sample. Thus, the basic
dialog for Unit 2 of French Basic Course (Desberg et al., 1960)
contains the line:

> C'est ça, et reveillez-moi   Fine, and wake me to-
> demain à sept heures.   morrow at seven.

and the section devoted to Useful Words provides the expressions
for 'one o'clock' through 'eleven o'clock,' plus 'noon' and
'midnight.' The dialog for Unit 5 includes the words for
'autumn' and 'winter,' and the Useful Words add 'spring' and
'summer.'

For a more coherent lesson, it would be desirable to relate
lexical exploration not only to the basic sample, but also to
the projected occasions for use. One way of approaching this
goal is through use of 'Cummings devices' (Chapter 6). In a
Cummings device, a question or some other line from the sample
may be presented along with a number of sentences which are
alternative answers or other rejoinders to it. The device may
also include other questions that are very similar to the first.
Both questions and answers should be chosen with careful attention
to how the student can use them for more than mere linguistic
drill. For example, in one set of lessons in Mauritian Creole
(cf. Appendix E), a narrative sample of the language describes
a woman going to market. It contains the sentence:

Zaklin aste rasyŏ komã too le semen.	Jacqueline buys groceries as [she does] every week.

A Cummings device that focusses on the lexical exploration of
this sentence is:

Questions:

Lil Moris, eski zot aste dipẽ too le zoor?	In Mauritius, do they buy bread every day?
Lil Moris, eski zot aste doori too le zoor?	In Mauritius, do they buy rice every day?
etc.	etc.

Rejoinders:

Zot aste dipẽ too le zoor.	They buy bread every day.
Zot aste doori too le semen.	They buy rice every week.
etc.	etc.

Students first learn to pronounce, understand and manipulate
these sentences, and then go on immediately to use them in the
form of two-line conversations. Note that these conversations
remain in touch with reality, for this Cummings device contains
accurate information about the frequency with which various items
are bought. Because of differences in marketing practices and
refrigeration facilities, the student will find certain differences
between Mauritius and his home. A factually inaccurate answer to
one of these questions is just as wrong as a linguistically incorrect one. Thus, as the student practices a new construction ('too
le zoor/semen'), he is also learning some down-to-earth facts
about the place where he expects to live.

Component 4: exploration of structural relationships

The final essential component of a language lesson guides
the student in exploring such matters as the relationship in both
form and meaning between the third person singular present subjunctive of a verb and the corresponding third person singular
present indicative; or between two different ways of embedding
one sentence in another; or between the definite and the indefinite
article. These relationships are the subject matter of what is
usually called 'the study of grammar.' Bosco (1970, p. 79)
distinguishes among three 'modes of representation.' Following
his analysis, the exploration of structural relationships may take
the form of drills ('enactive' mode), charts and diagrams ('iconic
mode'), or grammar notes ('symbolic' mode). Much past and present
controversy among language teachers turns on the relative prominence to be assigned to each of these modes, and the order in
which they should occupy the student's attention. Learners
synopses (Chapter 5) are principally symbolic presentations of
major structural relationships.

Lado (1958) may have been right in speculating that 'it is
possible to learn a language without ever repeating the same
sentence twice.' To do so, however, would require extraordinary
materials, extraordinary teachers, and probably extraordinary
students as well. For some structural relationships, adequate
exploration may require a certain amount of retracing one's steps,
both within and between lessons. This may involve one, two, or
all three of the 'modes.' What we usually call drills may in this
sense be regarded as 'reiterated enactive exploration,' to use a
phrase which is as monstrous as it is descriptive. Looking at
them in this way is probably better than inflicting them as
'necessary neuromuscular inculcation.' This matter is discussed
in Chapter 8.

61

CHAPTER 3   ADAPTING

Because the sentences in any one Cummings device are often
grammatically similar to one another, the device has advantages
in structural, as well as lexical, exploration.

A FINAL WORD ON EVALUATION

Instructional materials do not consist of qualities, dimensions and components. Nor do the descriptions of the qualities,
dimensions and components provide a blueprint for writing or adapting. Rather, the three terms stand for ways of looking at materials, and these ways are not merely restatements of one another. We
have said that strength is often derived from appropriate socio-
topical resources in a lesson, but a socio-topically relevant
lesson that is poorly organized may still be weak, and some teachers know how to make lessons amply rewarding and strong with
almost no relation to external reality. Similarly, occasions
for use contribute to but do not guarantee strength.

ADAPTATION

Throughout recorded history, and probably longer than that,
language teachers have been reminding one another of the necessity
for 'bridging the gap' between manipulation and communication,
or between the classroom and life. One of the ways in which they
quite properly attempt to do so is through adapting old textbooks
to fit new needs. Most, however, tend to place the center of
gravity of their bridges on one side of the gap or another. To
put the same thing in another way, they focus their attention
either on the original textbook or on the rewards and relevancies
of the project at hand, and slight the other. In the original
sense of the word 'focus,' the first kind of adapter seems to be
working his way out from the warmth and comfort of a hearth (the

printed lesson) toward a perimeter (the end of the lesson)
beyond which lies darkness. He sees his task as providing additional activities (dialogs, drills, games, or whatever) that lie
not too far beyond the perimeter, and which may help to extend
it. If this adapter were a plant, he would be a morning glory
vine in the springtime, putting out its tendrils in search of
anything at all to which it can attach itself. The second kind
of adapter warms himself by a portable hearth wherever the interests
of the students seem to lie, and may forget where home was;.botani-
cally he would be a dandelion whose seeds are scattered by the wind.

In this book, we suggest that a prospective adapter begin
by making a careful survey of both sides of the gap he is trying
to bridge. Once he has done so, he can connect the two sides by
using whatever devices he is most comfortable with. The point
is that he is working with two basic documents and not just one.
Certainly he must take account of the lessons that he has set
out to adapt, but just as certainly he must exploit the socio-
topical matrix that summarizes his students' interests. He must
satisfy the demands of the textbook, but in ways that will be
satisfying to those who learn from it. He works around two foci,
and not just one. Depending on the nature of the original
materials, he may find himself preparing Cummings devices to go
with dialogs, or dialogs to go with Cummings devices, or drills
to go with either or both, or all of these to flesh out an existing set of grammar notes. In all cases, his most creative contribution will probably lie in suggesting how the learners can
make early and convincing use of what they have just learned to
manipulate.

CHAPTER 3   ADAPTING

Obviously, in view of the great variety both of original
textbooks and of student objectives, adaptation is and will remain
an art. We cannot here offer a mechanical procedure for accom-
plishing it. Nevertheless, on the basis of the principles outlined earlier in this chapter, we may venture to suggest an
overall strategy:

1. Predict what the students will need and respond to in
    each of the three dimensions: linguistic, social and
    topical.

2. Make an inventory of the material at hand, in the same
    three dimensions.

3. Compare the results of the first two steps, in order
    to form a clear picture of what you need to add or
    subtract.

4. Draw up a list of ways in which the students may use
    the material. This is the most delicate step in adapta-
    tion because the list should be as heterogeneous as
    possible, yet stated in terms of actual behavior that
    the students are to engage in. It is also the most
    important step, however, because it opens up such
    valuable sources of motive power.

5. Supply whatever is necessary (dialogs, drills, Cummings
    devices, etc.) in order to bring the students from
    mastery of the existing materials to the uses which
    you have listed in Step 4. Politzer (1971) has pointed
    out that changes may be in rate of progress, or in the
    means employed, or in the goals themselves. Adaptation
    of rate may take the form of added materials to make
    more gradual the transition from one part of the existing

materials and another. It may also take the *form of*
more complete instructions for the teacher, or detailed
checklists to show the student what he should get out
of each part of the lesson. Changes in the means employed
will depend on what the adapter and the prospective users
find mutually congenial. Changes in goals should take
account of one fact that some teachers seem not to be
aware of: <u>any topic may be treated at any degree of
linguistic difficulty</u>, from the simplicity of 'What is
this? It is a (papilla, colony, Petri dish, centrifuge,
etc.)' to the complexity of 'The never before published
volume lying at an angle of approximately 37° to the
edge of the table is wholly supported by it.'

This chapter is incomplete without one or more of its appendices.

CHAPTER 3   A DIALOG-DRILL FORMAT (SPANISH)

APPENDIX A

TO CHAPTER 3

ADAPTING A DIALOG-DRILL FORMAT (SPANISH)

The courses produced for use at the Experiment in International Living, in Putney, Vermont, are variations on a basically audiolingual schema. One of the most widely used of that series is EIL Latin-American Spanish. The first lesson of this book provides an excellent opportunity to show how the principles of textbook evaluation in Chapter 3 may guide the adaptation of that type of course.

From a socio-topical point of view, Lesson I is based on the situation in which a Latin-American and a young speaker of English discuss the latter's forthcoming trip to Chile. The lesson contains two 'samples of language use' (p. 57): a dialog and a short expository paragraph. The dialog consists of 12 lines, with a total of 20 sentences which range in length from 2 to 14 syllables. The Spanish dialog is followed by an English translation, but the paragraph is not.

ANTES DEL VIAJE

Julio: ¡Hola Mario! ¿Cómo estás?

Mario: Bien, gracias. ¿Y tú?

Julio: Muy bien. ¿Sabes que mañana viajo a Sudamérica?

Mario: ¡Verdad! ¿Estás contento?

Julio: ¡Por supuesto! Tengo muchas ganas de ir a Sudamérica.

Mario: ¿Dónde vas a vivir?

Julio: En Santa Ana. Voy a vivir con una familia.

Mario: ¿Dónde está Santa Ana?

Julio: En el norte de Chile. Es una ciudad bastante grande.

Mario: ¿<u>Tú hablas español</u>?

Julio: <u>Si, un poco</u>. <u>Estudio español en la escuela</u>.

Mario: Entonces, buena suerte y buen viaje.

BEFORE THE TRIP

Julio: Hi Mario! How are you?

Mario: Fine, thanks. And you?

Julio: Fine! Do you know that I leave for South America
tomorrow?

Mario: Really? Are you excited?

Julio: Of course! I really want to go to South America.

Mario: Where are you going to live?

Julio: In Santa Ana. I'm going to live with a family.

Mario: Where is Santa Ana?

Julio: In the north of Chile. It's a fairly large city.

Lexical exploration (Chapter 3, p.58) beyond the basic
dialog is provided principally through a number of short lists
of 'related vocabulary,' including both single words and some
short, useful expressions.

Structural exploration (Chapter 3, p.61) is both phonetic
and grammatical. Phonetic exploration is in terms of lists of
words that contain respectively /j, d, gr, b/. In the grammar
drills, the student chooses correct forms for person-number
agreement in the present tense of <u>-ar</u> verbs, and repeats
sentences that exemplify singular and plural articles, the
periphrastic future, and the negative <u>no</u>. The same matters,
except for the future, are explained succinctly in a 'grammatical synopsis' at the end of the lesson.

CHAPTER 3   A DIALOG-DRILL FORMAT (SPANISH)

The lesson also contains one occasion to do something
with Spanish. The expository paragraph and the questions that
follow it allow the student to demonstrate that he can comprehend a text that consists of novel utterances, and go on
to talk about it with novel utterances of his own. Other
opportunities for use of the Spanish of Lesson I can be found,
but they are not made explicit in the lesson as it now stands,
and may be overlooked by some instructors.

The lesson ends with a 'cultural supplement' which consists
of an exposition of El Alfabeto Español, with the suggestion
that it 'may provide ideas for cultural inputs into the
classroom.'

In its present form, then, Lesson 1 contains all of the
four components (p. 54ff) that we have claimed are necessary for
a complete unit, and its general socio-topical content is
suitable for almost anyone who would enroll for a Spanish
course in the first place. As language lessons go, then, it
is excellent.

There are, however, reasons why a prospective user might
want to reject this lesson, or at least tinker with it. The
students may be more interested in Puerto Rico or Spain than
in Chile. They may not be planning on a homestay with a
family. They may not expect to leave for Latin America on
the following day. More seriously, they may feel strong
antipathy toward a lesson that depends on memorizing a dialog,
or may find that the dialog is too long for them. Their
teacher may dislike some stylistic detail of the wording.
There may be objection to some of the superficial inconsistencies in a set of materials which were, after all, produced
primarily for in-house use. Accordingly, revision of each

of the four components may take the form of replacing what
is inappropriate and supplementing what is inadequate for
a particular group of students.

The authors of the text have themselves made a first step
toward greater flexibility in the 'sample' component by underlining approximately half of the lines of the dialog. They
suggest that only the underlined sentences be used if an
abbreviated version is preferred.

It will be instructive to take a closer look at this
dialog. The underlined portion (we shall call it Part A)
contains 13 of the 20 sentences, including most of the short,
very frequent, and relatively invariable phrases such as
greetings, 'really?' and 'of course.' It also contains the
two longest and 'heaviest' sentences. All of the second-
person verbs, all of the exclamation points, and all expressions of emotion are in the underlined sentences.

The sentences that are not underlined (Part B) are more
nearly uniform in 'weight.' Except for the last, they consist
of factual questions and answers. Part B will therefore be
relatively more susceptible to 'lexical exploration,' through
Cummings devices (Chapter 3, p.59, and Chapter 6) or in other
ways.

Adaptation of the dialog itself is likely to be slight
and superficial. Some teachers will feel that if only one
form of the second person is to be taught in the opening
lesson, it should be the formal rather than the informal one.
Most students will have destinations other than Santa Ana,
Chile. Some will expect to live in hotels or dormitories
rather than with a family. All of these changes can be made
without disturbing the basic structure of the dialog.

CHAPTER 3   A DIALOG-DRILL FORMAT (SPANISH)

For purposes of lexical exploration, the entire dialog
lend itself to the writing of Cummings devices:

From Part A:

¿Adónde viajas? Viajo a (Sudamérica, Chile, etc.)
¿Cuándo viajas a (Sudamérica)? Viajo a Sudamérica
    (en julio, mañana, etc.)

From Part B:

¿Dónde vas a vivir? Voy a vivir en (Santa Ana, etc.).
¿Dónde vas a vivir? Voy a vivir (en un apartamento, etc.).
¿Qué vas a hacer (en Chile)? Voy a (estudiar, vivir con
    una familia, etc.).
¿Dónde está (Argentina, Santa Ana, etc.)?
    Está en el (norte, etc.) de (Sudamérica, Chile, etc.).
¿Cómo es (Santa Ana, etc.)? La ciudad es (grande, etc.).

In exploration of structure, many of the existing drills
require the student either simply to repeat families of
sentences, or to substitute a word without making related
changes elsewhere in the sentence. An example of the first
kind is:

        Voy a comer en casa.   'I'm going to eat at home.'
        Vas a comer en casa.
        Va a comer en casa.
                etc.

An example of the latter is:

        Voy a estudiar con unos hermanos.
        _____ tíos.

70

_____ padres.

_____ profesores.

_____ primos.

The rest of the drills require the student to supply appropriate person-number forms of certain verbs, as he changes the subject pronouns:

Yo viajo a Bogotá.   'I'm travelling to Bogotá.

Tú _____.

Nosotros _____.

     etc.

A teacher who is concerned about courtesy levels may want to add a constant-change drill in which the student subtitutes formal for informal second-person forms, and vice versa:

Tú estás en la clase.   Usted está en la clase.

Tú viajas a Bogotá.   Usted viaja a Bogotá.

Tú hablas español.   Usted habla español.

    etc.   etc.

Such a drill might involve the use of non-verbal cues (e.g., pictures, gestures) to dramatize the difference, since it does not exist in English on the level of verb inflection. Looking ahead to occasions for use which involve questions, one might also explore briefly the changes in word order that are found in the formation of questions like those that appear from place to place in this lesson:

question:	cf. statement:
¿Es pequeña la ciudad?	La ciudad es pequeña.
¿Viajan ustedes hoy?	Ustedes viajan hoy.
but:	
¿La tía habla español?	La tía habla español.

With changes and additions like these, this lesson may lead to the fulfillment of a number of rewarding occasions for use:

1. Talk fluently for 15 seconds (or less fluently for 30 seconds) about your travel plans.

2. Converse with a Spanish speaker other than your own instructor about your travel plans. Try to make a good impression.

3. Tell where each person in the class is going, and say something factual about the city where he expects to stay.

4. Using a map, give a lecture on the geography of the country that you expect to visit.

Once the lesson has been adapted in these ways, its center of gravity in the linguistic dimension has moved outside of the basic dialog. To put the same point into a different metaphor, the dialog remains but is no longer basic. Those users who prefer to start with drills or with Cummings devices are free to do so. The dialog may then become, to the student, a culmination rather than a commencement—a happy concentration of elements that he had met earlier, one or two lines at a time. Or the dialog may remain as the starting point. In any case, the social and topical dimensions of the lesson have been 'customized' in an orderly way, and all three dimensions converge on a set of demonstrable non-linguistic objectives.

CHAPTER 3   A 'MICROWAVE' FORMAT (TELUGU)

APPENDIX B

TO

CHAPTER 3

ADAPTING A 'MICROWAVE' FORMAT. (TELUGU)

In recent years, particularly under the auspices of the
Peace Corps, a number of language courses have been written which
have consisted entirely, or almost entirely, of Cummings devices.
Some of these courses have been surprisingly successful in spite
of their lack of variety in pedagogical format. A relatively
good example is <u>Conversational Telugu</u>, written in 1965 by Judith
Beinstein. At the time of this writer's visit to Brattleboro in
August 1970, staff members of the Experiment in International
Living under the direction of Ray Clark were adapting this course
for a Peace Corps training program. Their work illustrates some
of the principles of Chapter 3.

The first lesson in the original course consisted of a single
Cummings device (Chapter 3, p. 59, and Chapter 6): 'What is (this,
that)?' '(This, that) is a (banana).' The individual lines are
short and the things that they name are concrete, portable, and
demonstrable; accordingly, they are relatively light and transparent. Because the things named are edible and everybody gets
hungry, the lesson is also fairly strong.

But 'strength' in this sense is always relative to the needs
and interests of a particular class. In this instance, the materials were being used to train Peace Corps Volunteers who were to
help in conducting workshops for science teachers in Andhra
Pradesh, India. The adapter's first step was to replace the nouns
of the lesson, substituting instead the names of eight tools
which the students would be using early in the technical part of

A. idi ēmi?   What is this?

                                    1.1

idi sutti	This is a hammer.
idi rampamu	" saw.
idi paṭṭakaru	" pliers.
idi screwdriveru	" screwdriver.
idi skēlu	" ruler.
idi mēku (cīla)	" nail.
idi barama	" drill.
idi cadaramu	" square.

adi ēmi?   What is that?

adi sutti	That is a hammer.
adi rampamu	" saw.
adi paṭṭakaru	" pliers.
adi screwdriveru	" screw-driver.
adi skēlu	" scale.
adi mēku (cīla)	" nail.
adi barama	" drill.
adi cadaramu	" square.

B. idi ēmiti?   What is this?

idi sutti	This is a hammer.
idi nā sutti	This is my hammer.

adi ēmiti?   What is that?

adi rampamu	That is a saw.
adi mī rampamu	That is your saw.

Notes

1. There is no difference in meaning or usage between /ēmi/ and /ēmiti/.
2. Telugu does not use the verb is in this situation.

75

CHAPTER 3   A 'MICROWAVE' FORMAT (TELUGU)

their training. He added the words for 'my' and 'your', together
with two very brief grammar notes (see p. 75).

At this point, the lesson still consisted of a single
Cummings device, which explored one small section of the vocabulary
of Telugu, and at the same time exemplified one very simple and
very useful structure. Its two lines actually make up what might
be considered to be an embryonic conversation. The question
'What is (this)?' can furthermore be used to elicit the names of
other objects in which the student is interested. The adaption
is therefore highly appropriate and was presumably successful.

Experience with Cummings devices in many languages has however raised the question of whether a two-line conversation is
really viable as a 'sample of language use.' Certainly it can
simulate communication within the confines of a classroom, but it
is seldom adequate for genuine interaction in the outside world.
Would it be possible to provide a closer approximation to genuine
interaction without a prohibitive increase in the length and difficulty of the lesson?

Such a 'sample of language use,' might take the form of a
Telugu counterpart of the following English dialog:

          Please hand me the _____.

          Here you are.

          Thank you.

          Do you want the _____?

          No, thanks.

This dialog adds five new sentences, but except for the list of
tools, each sentence is to be treated as an indivisible unit.
Each of these sentences is extremely useful. The longest consists of 9 syllables. At least three of them provide opportunities

for learning courteous non-verbal concomitants such as facial
expressions, gestures, and body postures.

The grammatical structures that are of interest in this lesson are: (a) equational (is, are') sentences with no verb, (b) 'this'
vs. 'that', (c) 'my' vs. 'your.' Since the first of these is exemplified in every line, there is no occasion for practicing it in relationship to something with which it contrasts. The second and
third points, with respect to their 'symbolic' and 'iconic' re-
presentations,[1] are perfectly clear to a speaker of English, since
the Telugu demonstratives apparently correspond closely to English
'this' and 'that,' and the possessive pronouns precede the nouns
they modify. From the 'enactive' point of view, however, there
is still exploration to be done. This might, for example, be
accomplished through the use of substitution drills in which the
student is given nouns, possessives and demonstratives as cues,
and has to decide which slot of the model sentence he should put
each cue word into. Such drills could either be done as pure
linguistic manipulation, or accompanied by appropriate pointing
actions.

If the lesson is adapted in this way it can lead to such
occasions for use as the following:

1. Hand to an Indian colleague each of a set of tools, as
    he asks you for them. Observe and use any gestures or
    other expressions of courtesy that are appropriate in
    this situation.

2. Outside of class, learn the names of two objects that
    you want to be able to talk about. Teach these to your
    classmates tomorrow.

_____

[1]For explanation of this terminology, see reference to
F. Bosco, in Chapter 3, p. 61.

3. Make (or draw on the blackboard) a tool rack, with outlines of the various tools. One person points to a
   space, and another asks him whether he wants a particular
   tool.

4. Speak Telugu for 30 seconds so as to impress a stranger
   with your fluency.

Note that each of these 'occasions' has a social side as well as
a linguistic side.

The second lesson of the original course introduced the
negative of the pattern that was covered in the first lesson. The
instructors working in this training program, however, felt that
the negative would cause too much confusion at this point, so it
was postponed. The second lesson in the new series therefore was
structurally identical with the first, and differed only in socio-
topical content: 'What is (this, that)? (This, that) is a tree,
etc.)' The vocabulary consisted of some gross physical features
of the training site (see p. 79).

Although the format and grammatical content of the second
lesson as it stands are identical with the first lesson, the socio-
topical difference leads to some interesting differences in further
development. Instead of two colleagues in a workshop, we have
students with their Telugu teacher, improving the time as they
walk across the campus. The 'sample' might therefore take the
form of another dialog:

What's that, _please_?

It's a (tree).

('Tree')_?_

That's right.

78

APPENDIX B

A. idi ēmi?   What is this?   1.2

        idi ceṭṭu   This is a tree.

        idi kāru   This is a car.

        ịdi konḍa   This is a hillock.

        idi gaḍḍi   This is grass.

        idi pandu   This is fruit.

        idi hostel   This is a dorm.

        idi āsupatri   This is the infirmary.

        idi kukka   This is a dog.

B. adi ēmi?   What is that?

        adi ceṭṭu   That is a tree.

79

<u>And</u> that?

That's a (car).

That's a (dorm). <u>Right?</u>

No, it's (the infirmary).

<u>Thanks</u>.

The parts of this dialog that go beyond the Cummings device have been underlined. As in the dialog for Lesson 1, what is done through words in English may be done in some other way in Telugu, and in any event the non-verbal aspects of communication should receive attention along with each spoken sentence.

This lesson also differs from Lesson 1 with respect to the occasions which it can provide for using Telugu. Some possibili- ties are:

1. At your own initiative outside of class, ask one of the Telugu speakers (preferably not your own instructor) the name of something you see, or check with him/her to be sure that you have the word right. Report how many times you actually did this within a 24-hour period.

2. With reference to a rough map of the campus, ask and answer questions about what things are.

3. Look at a series of 4-8 color slides of India, and talk with your instructor about them within the Telugu that you have learned in these lessons.

4. Have the same slides shown in the same sequence, each for no more than 5-10 seconds. Students take turns narrating the entire sequence. Then do the same thing but with the slides in random order. (For a humorous final touch, put slides in backward, upside down, and sideways.)

Note that Lesson 2 provides more opportunities than Lesson 1 for transferring initiative to the trainees (in Occasion 1) and for transferring from present reality to prospective reality (in Occasions 3, 4).

Where Lessons 1 and 2 in the new series had to do with identifying objects, Lesson 3 (p. 82) is concerned with identifying people. It is based on Lessons 3, 4 and 5 of the original course: 'Who are you? Who is he? Who is John?' The answers are in terms of general classifications (girl, man, etc.), occupations (teacher, student), or personal names. An obvious way to tailor the vocabulary to the training project is to include the names of all instructors, as well as the names of any other Telugu speakers known to the trainees. As for structural exploration, the difference between abbāyi and abbāyini requires some sort of explanatory comment or diagram, as well as practice in making sentences that contain those words. So do the differences between formal and informal reference, a contrast that was introduced into the revised lessons at the insistence of the instructors. If there is a significant contrast between mīru evaru? and evaru mīru?, then this also deserves attention. The relationship between īyana, 'he here' and āyana 'he there' may be related to the difference in Lessons 1 and 2 between idi 'this' and adi 'that.'

Some objectives for use will be reminiscent of Lessons 1 and 2: learn to identify all instructors by name, in formal or informal style as appropriate; learn the names and occupations of service and administrative personnel with whom you have dealings; identify photographs of people who will be important to you during your time in India. But the introduction of personal names also provides an unexcelled opportunity for working on pronunciation. One of the hard facts about teaching pronunciation is that human beings cannot be equally strict at all times. A teacher may insist

81

1.3

A. mĩru evaru?   Who are you?

    nẽnu Subhanu.   I am Subha.

    nẽnu vidyārthini.   I am a student

    nẽnu ammāyini.   I am a girl.

    nẽnu abbāyini.   I am a boy.

    āyana evaru?   Who is he? (there)

    āyana mastarugāru.   He is the master.

    āme evaru?   Who is she?

    āme maithili.   She is Mythili. (informal)

    āme rajammagaru   She is (Mrs.) Rajamma (formal)

B. John evaru?   Who is John?

    John abbāyi.   John is a boy.

    evaru mĩru?   Who are you?

    nenu tĩcarini.   I am a teacher.

    evaru iyana?   Who is he? (here)

    iyana mastargāru.   He is the master.

    atanu evaru?   Who is he (there) (familiar)

    atanu vidhyārthi.   He is a student.

82

on maximum phonetic accuracy for short periods, but most of the
time he has to be satisfied if he is getting back a reasonably
high percentage of correct phonemes. In the area of people's
names, however, phonetic accuracy coincides with personal courtesy.
The teacher's standards are likely to be higher and the student's
efforts greater, particularly if the owners of the names are
fellow-residents of the same school or training site.

It may be objected that the original Telugu lessons are
hardly recognizable after so much adaptation and supplementation,
and that the adapter might as well have started from scratch. If
the course were no longer than these three sample lessons, that
might be true. But the existing course has picked out a large
number of points to be learned, has placed them in one practicable
order, and has provided as examples materials which are themselves
usable. It thus provides a framework on which the adapter and his
staff may hang their own ideas and their own efforts, and a fabric
of lessons that they can press into service if their own adaptations fall behind schedule.

CHAPTER 3   A PATTERN PRACTICE FORMAT (ENGLISH)

APPENDIX C

TO

CHAPTER 3

ADAPTING A PATTERN-PRACTICE COURSE (ENGLISH)

One of the most pregnant sentences in history of language
teaching was Fries' dictum that 'a person has "learned" a
foreign language when he has...mastered the sound system...and
...made the structural devices...matters of automatic habit.'
(1947, p. 3). Even though the person who has done these
things may not be a fluent speaker, 'he can have laid a good
accurate foundation upon which to build' through the acquisition of 'content vocabulary' (ibid.). Since its publication,
the last half of this formulation has determined the strategy
of much 'scientific' language teaching, just as the first
half has determined the tactics. The priority, both logical
and chronological, of the basic structural habits goes unchallenged in many circles, and we sometimes act as though
we think the best way to 'internalize' the 'structures' is to
concentrate on them to the virtual exclusion of everything else.

A relatively recent and sophisticated representative of
this tradition is the series Contemporary Spoken English, by
John Kane and Mary Kirkland (Thomas Y. Crowell, 1967). The
first lesson of Volume 1 contains two short dialogs (total
approximately 2 pages), pronunciation, rhythm and intonation
drills (7 pages) and grammar drills (10 pages). The dialogs,
which consist of simple introductions and greetings, have no
integral relation to the drills, which concentrate on present
affirmative statements with be. Most of the substitution drills
may be summarized in three tables:

I	'm	in class
you	're	at church
he	's	in bed
she		etc.
Sue		
John		
we		
they		

I	'm	a farmer
Dick	's	a lawyer
		etc.

I	'm	hungry
we	're	married
		tired
		etc.

In addition, the rhythm and intonation drills include:

this		a pen
that	's	a coat
it		etc.

In keeping with one interpretation of the Friesian emphasis on
structure, there is nowhere in the book any indication as to
when or how the teacher is to put across the meanings. (Many
would be easy to picture or dramatize, but 'lawyer,' and the

CHAPTER 3   A PATTERN PRACTICE FORMAT (ENGLISH)

difference between 'in school' and 'in class' might pose
problems.) The nearest reference to meaning is a statement
(p. viii) that the vocabulary has been drawn from 'basic
semantic fields.' Echoing Fries, the authors state that their
goal is to teach 'with a limited vocabulary of high-frequency
words, those features of English phonology and syntax which
students should be able to comprehend and manipulate before
proceeding beyond the intermediate level' (p. vii).

Teachers who are philosophically in communion with the
authors will welcome their work and will probably adopt it.
Those who reject the philosophy will also reject the book.
In the field of English as a Second Language it makes little
difference, for if one book is cast aside, there are still
dozens of others waiting to be examined.

The same is not true for seldom-taught languages, where
the available courses usually number between 1 and 5. All
too easily, a new teacher or language coordinator despairs of
all that is in print and decides to set out on his own.
But such a decision is expensive in money and time, and dubious
in result. A Swahili proverb tells us that 'there is no bad
beginning,' and so the newcomer, encouraged by the ease with
which he has pleased himself with his first few lessons,
launches yet another material-writing project.

This appendix, then, is <u>not</u> a review of Kane and Kirkland's
<u>Contemporary Spoken English</u>. It is primarily addressed, not
to practitioners of TESOL, but to prospective teachers and
lesson writers in the so-called 'neglected languages.' Its
purpose is to demonstrate how, by following a particular set
of principles, one may adapt and supplement existing materials
instead of rejecting them. English has been chosen for this
illustration only because examples are easier to follow in a

widely known language. To this end, we shall pretend that
<u>Contemporary Spoken English</u> is one of only two or three ESOL
courses in print.

The first step toward adaptation is to form a clear
picture of the students, their needs and interests. This
picture may take the form of a simple socio-topical matrix.
Let us assume that we are adapting for an evening class of
adults who live in one major part of a metropolitan area,
and who speak a number of different languages but little or
no English. In general, the matrix can be more specific and
more accurate in smaller groups, but even the largest and most
diverse class has in common its classroom or training site,
and current events both local and worldwide. The matrix will
also be more effective if the students feel that they have
had a hand in designing it or at least adding to it. For
the purposes of this illustration, however, we shall have to
be content with guessing that a partial matrix might look
something like this:

	getting from place to place	greetings and courtesy formulas	meetings and appointments	shopping	role as guest or host
neighbors	2	1			
clerks in stores					
English teacher		1			
fellow students		1			
people on street	2				

CHAPTER 3   A PATTERN PRACTICE FORMAT (ENGLISH)

The next step is to analyze the existing lesson for its
content in all three dimensions: linguistic, social, and
topical.

Linguistic content:

Dialogs: Eleven sentences, invariable except for substitution
of personal names, suitable for use in introducing oneself and
in exchanging morning greetings. Intonation contours are
marked.

Pronunciation sections: Lists of monosyllabic words containing the diphthongs which the Trager-Smith transcription writes
/iy, ey, oy, ay, aw, ow, uw/, and short phrases or sentences
that include these words. (The authors do not assume that
these words and phrases will be intelligible to beginning
students.) Lists of phrases and sentences with the common
231↓ statement intonation pattern, realized in short utterances that have various stress patterns. Stress and intonation are portrayed 'iconically,' with an effective system
of lines and geometrical figures.

Grammar sections: The sentence patterns represented on p. 85
(above), requiring the student to produce person-number agreement between a subject and the present tense of 'be,' followed
by four kinds of complements. Nouns standing for locations
follow prepositions, with no intervening article; all other
nouns have the indefinite article.

Social content:

Dialogs: Generally suitable for adults who don't know each
other, or who are not close friends. May be used 'for real'
among members of the class.

Pronunciation sections: Strictly speaking, no social content
at all, since they are intended only for practice in repetition.

Grammatical sections: Quite non-specific. Even the teacher
and the student can hardly be said to be playing genuine social
roles in a substitution drill of the type:

	Dick's in school.
in class	Dick's in class.
at home	Dick's at home.
at church	Dick's at church.
	etc.

Topical content:

Dialogs: As stated above, introductions and morning greeting.

Pronunciation sections: None. (see above)

Grammatical sections: Statements about locations, occupations,
states, classification (see substitution frames on p. 85). The
content words in the grammatical sections are either common
nouns, personal names, or adjectives. Except for the personal
names, none of the content words that appear in one type of
statement ever appears in another. Each list of nouns refers
to several different real-life contexts, e.g. class, church,
bed.

In summary, the linguistic content of this lesson is
delineated with unusual clarity; the topical content is clear
enough, but is unified only in terms of a grammatical criterion;
the social content is almost entirely concentrated in the
dialogs, which have no close relationship to the rest of the
lesson.

CHAPTER 3   A PATTERN PRACTICE FORMAT (ENGLISH)

The third step in preparing to adapt a lesson is to check its components: Does it include (1) a convincing sample of language use? Does it provide for both (2) lexical and (3) grammatical exploration beyond the sample? Does it suggest (4) ways in which the students can put their new linguistic skills to work for non-linguistic purposes that they can accept as their own?

The lesson under consideration does contain two short samples of genuine use, in the form of the dialogs. The lists of words in the drills provide for lexical exploration, and the grammar drills themselves lead the student to explore a bit of English structure. The fourth component is not overtly represented in the lesson itself, and is only hinted at in the introduction.

Finally, one may look at the individual lines of the various components and judge them according to their lightness, transparency, and strength. (Chapter 3, pp. 45 - 49)

The sentences of this lesson, with an average of three syllables apiece, show up very favorably with respect to the first of these three qualities. Most of the meanings could be put across easily without translation, and the structures are lucidly presented; accordingly, the lesson also rates well on average transparency of sentences.

Where this lesson leaves most to be desired is in what we have called 'strength.' Here is a striking demonstration that high-frequency vocabulary may still produce sentences that are relatively weak. As the lesson now stands, the students can do very little at the end of Lesson 1 except introduce themselves, greet one another, and go on to Lesson 2.

90

As we have seen, the dominant dimension in this course and the one according to which the lessons are sequenced, is the linguistic. The goal of an adaptation will therefore be to enable the students, in relation to the existing linguistic framework as much as possible, to use the language in a connected and communicative way in one or more contexts that are meaningful to them. We shall aim at non-linguistic occasions for use that have the students getting acquainted with each other and with the immediate area in which they live.

The most obvious and also the simplest first step is to change 'good morning' in the second dialog to 'good evening,' since our students go to night school. A much larger step, also in the lexical realm, is to introduce the names of local destinations: 'grade school, high school, gas station, restaurant, parking lot' etc., alongside or instead of the non-specific 'work, class, bed' etc. There are four advantages in doing so: (1) The destinations may be readily and cheaply brought into the classroom by means of locally produced color slides. (p. 92) At the same time, the slides themselves are 'stronger' in our sense because they portray places that the students have actually seen and will be seeing in real life. (2) The same list of nouns can now appear in two different substitution frames: This is a ____ and We're at a ____. (p.85). This helps to unify the lesson in the topical dimension. (3) These words and slides will be useful in later lessons, and thus strengthen the continuity of the whole book. (4) They will help clarify the grammatical facts in Lesson 1. We have noted that as the lesson now stands, nouns that follow a preposition do not have an indefinite article, while all the other nouns do. In talking about local destinations, nouns have the article both without a preposition (This is a____.) and with it (We're at a____.)

The suggestion that an adaptation should introduce pictures and new vocabulary should not be taken as a criticism of the

original lesson for lacking them. What will be most live and real in the night schools of Arlington County, Virginia, will necessarily fall flat everywhere else. On the other hand, expertly chosen vocabulary and technically excellent pictures would have been specific for nowhere, and would only have added to the cost of publication.

Having (as we hope) livened the lesson up topically by bringing in new words and color slides to illustrate them, we would like to do the same in the social dimension. The simplest way to do so is to convert at least three of the substitution frames (p. 85) to Cummings devices. (Chapter 3, p.59 and Chapter 6) We can do so by teaching the questions 'What is this? Where are (we)? What are (you)?' Where formerly we had only repetition and substitution drills, we now have some two-line embryonic conversations.

There is of course a price to be paid for the Cummings devices, because they introduce wh-questions. The authors of the original, who introduced yes-no questions only in Lesson 4 and wh-questions in Lesson 6, might object that this price is in fact prohibitive, since it disrupts their carefully planned sequence of structures. But each of the new question patterns is closely related to one of the statement patterns that are already in the lesson, and the mechanical aspect of changing from an interrogative sentence to its corresponding statement is the same throughout. This is then a much less serious change in the structural sequence than, say, the introduction of present tense of content verbs. The question is whether the extra weight of the new engine is more than compensated for by the gain in power. My guess is that it is.

Another slight addition in the linguistic dimension would open up further opportunities for interesting conversation. The construction with 'this' plus a noun would enable the students to handle a Cummings device like:

93

CHAPTER 3   A PATTERN PRACTICE FORMAT (ENGLISH)

> Where is this (gas station)?
> It's (near here, on Fairfax Drive,
>   at Parkington, etc.).

Going still further, if one is willing to introduce yes-no
questions at this stage, then the students could use questions
like 'Is this a parking lot? Are we at the library?' and also
learn each other's marital status and inquire about such states
as fatigue and hunger. But this too is a question of balancing
new communicative potential against increased length and complexity of the lesson. Would such an extension be justifiable?
The most important fact about this kind of question is not whether
the answer is yes or no, but rather who is qualified to answer it.
We sometimes forget that a worthwhile answer can only come from a
classroom teacher who understands its implications, and that even
he or she can answer it for only one class at a time. Someone
writing a case study like this one can only guess at the answer,
but the same is true for the textbook writer himself. This is one
reason why published textbooks are so often rejected by prospective users. It is also one reason why we must give to adaptation
much more thought, time, and prestige than we have been accustomed
to doing.

The final proof of the lessons, as we have said, is in what
the students can now do that they recognize as immediately useful
or enjoyable in its own right, or potentially so in the immediate
future. Greetings and introductions, marked (1) in the matrix on
p.87, are certainly socio-topical 'behavioral objectives' in this
sense, and these were in the lesson from the beginning. New
'objectives' relate to the boxes marked (2) in the matrix. Although
the student is still unable to carry out sustained conversation
with neighbors on the subject of getting around in Arlington, he
at least has some of the most crucial sentence patterns and vocab-

94

ulary items.   In the meantime, he can demonstrate his new ability
to ask and answer questions about (pictures of) places in his
immediate vicinity.   This activity may be varied by reducing the
time each picture is on the screen, or by putting slides in back-
wards, upside down or sideways.

Referring once more to Fries' famous definition, we may
question whether, in fact 'to have learned a foreign language'
is it itself a serious goal for any adults except a few professional linguists and other language nuts.   Certainly in addition
to extrinsic motivations like fulfilling a requirement or preparing for residence abroad, one needs the intrinsic rewards of
esthetically agreeable activities with frequent rewards of various
kinds.   But the work of Lambert and others[1] indicates that even
the extrinsic motivations vary dramatically in their driving power,
according to the breadth and depth of their integration with the
total personality of the learner.   That principle must be both
the adapter's raison d'être and his guiding star.

---

[1]See Chapter 1, p. 23.

CHAPTER 3   A SELF-INSTRUCTIONAL FORMAT (SPANISH)

APPENDIX D

TO

CHAPTER 3

ADAPTING A SELF-INSTRUCTIONAL PROGRAM (SPANISH)

The Foreign Service Institute's Spanish Programmatic Course (SPC) was chosen for this illustration of the principles of adaptation for three reasons: (1) It is a successful example of programmed self-instruction (PSI). (2) Among PSI courses, it employs a minimum of technology: only a book and an ordinary tape recorder. It is thus relatively inexpensive and easily accessible. (3) Contact with its author and with some of its most experienced users was available on an in-house basis, within the Foreign Service Institute and the Peace Corps.

The format of a typical early lesson may be seen in the excerpt from Unit 2, which is reproduced on pp. 97-99. The lesson opens with a programmed introduction, of which the last six frames appear on the top half of p. 97. The introduction shapes behavior, either phonetic or grammatical or both. In Unit 2, there follows a short dialog, which the student first comprehends, then pronounces under guidance from the tape, and then becomes fluent on. Finally, he goes to his instructor for a 'checkout' session. In later lessons (e.g. Unit 15), the dialog is longer, and is followed by guided observation, practice, and variation, leading to the applications reproduced on pp. 100-103.

Spanish Programmatic Course differs from some PSI in that it provides for regular 'check-out' sessions of conversation with a live instructor at the end of each unit. This arrangement has at least three points in its favor: (1) The student knows that a live human being is following his progress and appreciating it. (2) He enjoys the feeling that he can converse with a Spanish-

96

y- of <u>you</u> change to something resembling the sound '-ch-', and <u>we</u> normally say something like 'donchou'. In the dialog of this Unit, you will find a change of the kind called a reduction, or 'shortening'. Here are the two words.

(a) (a)   (b) (b)

69.   In normal speech, there is this reduction.

(a)   (b)   (a+b)   (a+b)

70.   Here is another example from the dialog of a change. First, listen to the two words said separately.

(a) (b)   (a) (b)

71. Listen to the combination.

(a)   (b)   (a+b)   (a+b)

72.   In order to 'pin-point' it more clearly, let's illustrate this by using word (a) but followed only by the first sound of word (b).

(a)   (-)   (a+-)   (a+-)

73.   Finally, here it is again, in its natural form.

(a)   (b)   (a+b)   (a+b)

74.   (You are now ready to begin learning the dialog.)

<u>DIALOG</u>

(Recorded)

Every Unit will have a conversation in Spanish which must be memorized. To help you achieve this memorization, the conversation has been recorded in four different manners, each of which is a progression toward <u>complete</u> <u>memorization</u>:

<u>Step 1</u>.   Comprehension.

<u>Step 2</u>.   Pronunciation.

<u>Step 3</u>.   Fluency.

<u>Step 4</u>.   Participation.

Before working each Step, <u>read the instructions for that particular</u> <u>Step</u>.

Person A: Hi! How are you?   (1)

Person B: Fine. And you?   (2)

                    Person A: So-so.   (3)

                              Where is S_____   (4)

                    Person B: In his office.   (5)

Recordings.

Step 1: Comprehension.

Listen to the tape, and don't repeat. The purpose of Step 1 is to learn the meanings of each line. So, just listen, and then take these small Identification 'tests' as they are announced on the tape.

Identification test 1. (Lines 1 & 2)

You will hear lines 1 and 2 read to you in Spanish several times, in a mixed order. You are to 'keep score' and identify how many times you hear line 1 or line 2, by making a little mark in the appropriate 'box' in the chart that follows.

Identification test 2.

Same procedure as in No. 1, but using lines 1, 2, and 3.

Identification test 3.

Same procedure, using lines 1, 2, 3, and 4.

Identification test 4.

Same procedure, using lines 3, 4, and 5.

Identification test 5.

Same procedure, using lines 1 through 5.

CHART   (Answers on last page of Unit 2.)

	Test 1	Test 2	Test 3	Test 4	Test 5
No. 1: Hi! How are you!					
No. 2: Fine! And you?					
No. 3: So-so.					
No. 4: Where is S_____					
No. 5: In his office.					

Step 2: Pronunciation.

Imitate everything you hear to the best of your ability. Replay Step 2 two or three times, or more to assure yourself of a good pronunciation.

Step 3: Fluency.

This time, each full line will be said twice. Repeat each time, paying close attention to the rhythm and the intonation.

Replay this part several times, four or five times or more, until you feel completely relaxed with the entire group of sentences.

Step 4: Participation.

Your instructor will engage you in the conversation which you have been memorizing. As a preparation for this exercise with your instructor, Step 4 has been prepared.

Part A: Your instructor's voice on the tape will take the role of 'Person A', and he will leave a blank space for you to insert the role of 'Person B'.

Practice Part A three or four times before going to Part B.

Part B: Your instructor's voice will now take the role of 'Person B', and you are to fill the blank spaces with 'Person A'. Since 'Person A' begins the conversation, the voice on the tape will announce when you are to begin.

As in Part A, repeat this part three or four times.

If you are not able to perform Step 4 smoothly and without any effort, you need to work Steps 2 and 3 a little more.

Answers to Identification Tests:

	No. 1	No. 2	No. 3	No. 4	No. 5
Test 1:	5	6			
Test 2:	3	4	5		
Test 3:	4	6	3	6	
Test 4:			5	5	6
Test 5:	4	4	3	3	5

END OF UNIT 2

Practice 10. (Recorded)

  Substitution-transformation drill. Based on the model shown below, make the substitution and the necessary changes as each number is announced. This time, the substitutions may occur in any part of the sentence.

  Model: 'José quiere estudiarlo.'

    1. tiene ... ('José tiene que-estudiarlo.')

    2. José y yo ... ('José y yo tenemos que-estudiarlo.')

    3. Acabamos ... ('José y yo acabamos de-estudiarlo.')

    4. Venderlo ... ('José y yo acabamos de-venderlo.')

    5. (Etc.)

Application

Part 1.

  How would you say the following thoughts in Spanish?

  1. I sold /it/ yesterday. 2. I sold (him) my car. 3. I know /him/. 4. I know /her/. 5. I sold her my car. 6. I brought the car to her. 7. I didn't bring her the car. 8. I didn't bring her to the party. 9. José sold me his car. 10. Gómez sold us his car. 11. Gómez sold them his car. 12. I defended them (boys). 13. I defended them (girls). 14. I prepared the exercise for her. 15. I offered him my book. 16. A modern exercise. 17. A modern saying. 18. We want to use the famous one (book). 19. We want to study in a modern one (class). 20. That book is necessary. 21. That lesson is necessary. 22. That class is exclusive. 23. That teacher (man) is famous. 24. Sometimes you can say that. 25. We have to use it without Jones. 26. María and I want to use the car tomorrow. 27. José and I have to decide that tomorrow. 28. Say, Jones! I have to ask ('preguntar') (you) something. 29. How's that? You have to ask me something? 30. Yes, I have to ask you: where were you born. 31. I have to ask you also: in what year were you born. 32. You have to ask me: when I was born? 33. Ah, now I understand! You asked me: where was I born. 34. In which what? 35. I was born in 1930. 36. I wasn't born yesterday! 37. José was born in 1930 also. 38. That doesn't exist in Spanish. 39. Yes, you're right; I want to go, but I can't go without José. 40. No, I don't want to, but I have to go. 41. We don't have to finish it

today without Nora. 42. We don't have to prepare it today.   43. I don't want to write her today.   44. José doesn't want to write him today.   45. He doesn't have to go until 4:00.   46. They have to go tomorrow; they can't go today. 47. I had to go yesterday, but I don't have to go today.   48. Yes, sir, we can decide that today.   49. I'm very sorry, but I can't study with 'you-all' until 10:00.   50. José is planning to stay in his office until 4:00. 51. I don't know what it means.   52. He asked me: what does año mean.   53. I asked him: what does nació mean.   54. He asked us:when is the party.   55. He asked me: where does that exist.   56. He asked them:why can't they go tomorrow. 57. He asked them:where were they born.   58. He asked us:where were we born. 59. He asked us:where did we use it.   60. I asked them:where did they use it.

Part 2.

Prepare an oral answer to the following questions:

1. ¿Qué le-preguntó el profesor a Clark?
2. ¿Clark le-entendió al profesor?
3. ¿De veras no le-entendió?
4. ¿Y dónde nació el señor Clark?
5. ¿En qué año nació?
6. ¿Clark entendió la frase 'en qué año'?
7. ¿Qué quiere decir 'en qué año'?
8. ¿Usted entiende todas las frases?
9. ¿Dónde nació usted?
10. ¿Ustedes tienen hijos?
11. ¿En qué año nació su hija mayor?
12. Usted tiene 30 años, ¿verdad?
13. ¿Cuándo nació su-esposa(-o), en 1930?
14. ¿Su-esposa(-o) no es americana(-o)?
15. ¿Qué es su-esposa(-o), colombiana(-o)?
16. ¿Usted tiene que-preparar la lección siempre o a veces?
17. ¿Usted no preparó la lección?
18. ¿Clark tampoco preparó la lección?

Part 3.

Be prepared to be engaged by your instructor in the following conversation.

Note: In some conversations you will find English and Spanish phrases. This can be confusing to you as to what you are supposed to do with them. Do not translate those English portions which appear in parentheses.

A:

Sir, how does one say (He told me)?

--- One says 'me-ɖijo'.

Me ɖijo.   And how does one say (was going)?

--- But, who (was going)?

José.

--- Fine. One says 'iɓa'.

Can I say 'Me-ɖijo iɓa'?

--- No. You have to use 'que'.

Where?

--- Me-ɖijo que iɓa.

Thank you. And how does one say (I was going)?

--- 'Iba'.

Really? Don't tell me!

--- Yes, really.

And how does one say (I told him)?

--- One says le-ɖije.

Well, now I can say 'Le ɖije que iɓa.

---I'm glad.

Dije-traje. Dije-traje. Dijo-......?

Can I say trajo?

--- Of course! Dije-traje. Dijo-trajo

Very well! I can now say (José brought me the car yesterday.)

--- How does one say that?

One says José me-trajo el carro ayer.

--- Very well.

B.

Sir, what does i∅a mean?

--- It means (I was going) or (He was going.)

Well, if i∅a means (I was going), I can now say (He asked me if
I was (were) going.)

--- Fine. How does one say that?

One says Me-preguntó si i∅a.

Is it necessary to use que?

--- No, it isn't necessary; sometimes one uses que, but
    with si it isn't necessary.

Very well: Me-preguntó si i∅a.

I can now say (I asked him when he was going.) One says:

(Note: Include here what you could say.)

--- Very well.

C.

Mr. Clark, ¿en qué mes nació usted?

--- How's that?

I asked you en qué mes you were born.

--- You asked me in which what I was born?

¡Mes! ¡Mes!

--- Oh, now I understand.

--- I was born in May (mayo).

In what month was Mr. Jones born?

--- I don't know. I think that he was born in April (a∅ril).

--- Were you born in April or May? ... How's that? ... He
    said that he was born in May.

You're right. Mr. Jones was born in April and you were born
in May.

END OF UNIT 15

103

speaker, if only simply, almost from the very first day. (3) His strengths and weaknesses can be catered to as they become evident, on a day-to-day basis.

This course shares with most other PSI a concern to lead the student one step at a time, with relatively few errors, to a command of phonological and grammatical structures which will be superior to what he would get in a conventional class. It assumes (probably correctly) that premature attempts at fluency and lexical range are sure to reward and hence reinforce defective approximations to both pronunciation and grammar. It therefore adopts the strategy of building into the student the best set of structural habits it can, before tempting him with much vocabulary or with completely free conversation.

One conspicuous feature of SPC is in fact the smallness of its vocabulary. The first 100 hours contain only about 4.2 new words per hour, even if different forms of the same verb are counted as separate words. It is therefore necessarily almost devoid of cultural or topical content. This may from one point of view seem to be a shortcoming, but it probably makes the work of augmentation easier. In terms of the three checklists (Chapter 3), SPC concentrates almost entirely on the linguistic dimension. Its individual lines are generally light and transparent. The principal problem is lack of strength. (These terms are explained in Chapter 3, pp. 45-49 .)

In the other case studies, we have spoken of 'adapting' an original textbook. The care with which a good PSI course has to be worked out, however, and the delicate balance of one part with another, make tampering by outsiders unadvisable or at least prohibitively expensive. In this appendix, therefore, we shall speak not of 'adaptation,' but of 'augmentation:' assuming that the student will complete a unit of the program exactly as it stands, what can be <u>added</u> to provide additional strength without too much increase in the weight and opacity of the total unit?

Augmentation in this sense may be more cautious in adding to the original, or less so. The suggestions in this appendix lie in three different 'orbits'[1] around each of the first five units of SPC:

> Inner orbit: Student pronounces few
> or no words that the program has
> not taught him to pronounce.

> Middle orbit: Student uses some new
> words, but within structures that
> he has learned from the program.

> Outer orbit: May contain new structures
> as well as new words.

<u>Unit 1</u>.

This unit is devoted entirely to matters of pronunciation, but the student himself says nothing at all in English during the whole unit. There is not even any treatment of the vowels and consonants of the language. The student is required only to show by means of his English or non-linguistic responses that he can (1) differentiate stressed from unstressed syllables, and (2) identify three different intonation contours. The lesson may therefore be analyzed as follows:

> <u>Linguistic content</u>: Word stress and sentence
> intonation contours.

---

[1]The word 'orbit' is intended for use only in this appendix.

CHAPTER 3   A SELF-INSTRUCTIONAL FORMAT (SPANISH)

Social content: Difference between familiar
and polite intonation for questions.

Topical content: None.

The lesson as it stands contains no non-linguistic 'occasions for
use,' no 'connected sample of language use,' no 'lexical exploration,' and only the slightest 'exploration of structure.' It is
socio-topically about as neutral as it could possibly be. On the
other hand, it at least contains nothing that would be socio-
topically in conflict with the needs of any group of students.

For purposes of this appendix, let us assume a class that
consists of Peace Corps trainees who are studying at some central
location but living with Spanish-speaking families. Their job
assignments will be in the fishing industry, in three different
Latin American countries. A number of possible 'augments,' grouped
into 'orbits,' are the following.

Inner orbit (no new structural matters brought to student's
attention, no production of Spanish by student beyond what
is in the original lesson).

1. Tape recording of a Spanish-speaking teacher taking the
roll in class. Students identify stress patterns on surnames,
and incidentally hear what a Spanish roll-call sounds like.

2. Tape-recorded or live, list of nouns related to fisheries.
Students are not told meanings, but are only assured that they are
names of things connected with fishing. As above, identify stress
patterns.

3. Live or recorded, list of names of persons (teachers,
co-workers, neighbors, government officials) who are or will soon
be important in the students' lives. It seems likely that such a
list would be significantly stronger than a mere list of 'typical
Spanish names.' Again, identify stress patterns. Meanings might
be supplied in the form of pictures, or in the form of identifying

106

phrases in English: 'President of Chile,' 'teacher from Mayagüez,' etc. If meanings are supplied, the students may work toward the objective of being able to point to the appropriate picture or other identifier when they hear the name.

Middle orbit (some production by the student beyond what the program has taught him to say).

4. Students learn to pronounce some of the items in (2) and (3), above, with special attention to stress and intonation. Teacher should select items so as to avoid sounds such as /r/ that the student is most likely to mispronounce. In any case, there is no need to show the students how the words are written, and to do so would only increase the chance of a spelling-pronunciation using English sounds.

5. Using the items from (4), point to the appropriate pictures or other items. If the items are objects used in fishing, handle them (cf. (3), above.)

Outer orbit (new structures).

6. Cummings devices (Chapter 3, p. 59, and Chapter 6) based on the items in (2) and (3), with multiple answers to the questions 'Who is that?' and 'What is that?'

7. Classroom instructions for students to respond to. In this augment, instructions that are actually needed in the conduct of the class (e.g. Open, close your books.) are preferable to instructions that are not normally given to adult students (e.g. Stand up.).

Unit 2.

Linguistic content:

(1) Identification of pure, unreduced vowels in contrast to some common English substitutes for them. Repetition of isolated syllables with special attention to these matters. 107

(2) A dialog of five sentences, with meanings in English (see pp. 97 - 98).

<u>Social content</u>: Polite (<u>usted</u>) forms between adults who already know one another.

<u>Topical content</u>:

(1) A perfunctory greeting formula.

(2) 'Where is (a person)?'

This unit, unlike Unit 1, does have a brief sample of language use, in the form of a dialog. Its exploration of structure is confined to phonology, and there is no provision for exploring new vocabulary. Exchanging the greeting formula outside class constitutes a possible occasion for use, but this is not made explicit in the book. Some possible augments are the following.

Inner orbit.

1. Using the lists of names and technical objects from augments (2) and (3) of Unit 1, relearn pronunciation with special attention to the vowels.

2. Students use English to elicit the names of the people in the families with whom they are living. Bring the names to class and practice them as in (1), above.

3. Questions of the type 'Is (Sr. Martinez) in (Las Cruces)?' 'Is (Sra. Gomez) in (the kitchen)?' Students answer with <u>sí</u> or <u>no</u>. Names are of people who mean something to the students, and places are ones where these people may characteristically be found. Otherwise, this augment will add more weight than strength.

Middle orbit.

4. Cummings device consisting of the question '¿Dónde está (Sanchez)?' and answers, using the same information as in (3),

above. The difference between (3) and (4) is that the student must pronounce the names of the new locations.

5. Cummings device, again with the question '¿Dónde está _____?' involving the locations of pieces of fishing gear named in the augments of Unit 1.

Outer orbit.

6. Dialog and/or Cummings devices to enable students to introduce themselves, and ask in Spanish for the information in (2), above.

7. Simple greetings beyond ¡Hola! ¿Cómo está? which are in the original lesson.

Notice that the use of the same names and objects from one unit to the next provides a longitudinal continuity which should add to the strength of the entire course.

Unit 3.

Linguistic content: Identification and production of un-aspirated /p, t, k/ in contrast to the aspirated stops of English.

Social content: Adult acquaintances or co-workers who address one another by surnames, without titles.

Topical content: (1) Greeting. (2) Inquiry about the time of a coming event.

Inner orbit.

1. Using the technical nouns and personal names from Units 1 and 2, relearn pronunciation with special attention to /p, t, k/.

CHAPTER 3   A SELF-INSTRUCTIONAL FORMAT (SPANISH)

Middle orbit.

2.   Cummings device based on the dialog sentence   ¿Cuándo es
la fiesta?, substituting other events in place of la fiesta, and
answering with hours of the day and/or days of the week, as appropriate. If this augment is to be worth its weight, it must
deal only with events that the students are likely to want to talk
about. Note that this does not allow for questions which require
content verbs, such as 'When does the class end?' Note also that
this augment can be shifted into the inner orbit by casting it in
the form of yes-no questions.

Outer orbit.

3.   Cummings device for learning the occupations of people,
beginning with those in the lists from Units 1 and 2: Presidente
de Bolívia, pescador, maestro, etc.

Occasions for use based on outer orbits of Units 1-3: (1) Say
as much as you can about various individuals; (2) take a true-false
test concerning at least ten Spanish-speaking people who will have
a role in your life; (3) have two small panels of students compete
in answering questions.

Unit 4.

Linguistic content: voiced fricatives.

Social content: two adult male friends at a party.

Topical content: asking who a third person is.

Inner orbit.

1.   Relearn pronunciation of items from earlier units, with
special attention to the voiced fricatives.

2. Using English as the contact language, make a kinship diagram of the family with whom you are living. There may be cross-cultural problems here of a non-verbal nature: Under what circumstances is this kind of inquiry acceptable? What must one avoid asking about? Whom should one ask?

Middle orbit.

3. Based on the original dialog:

¿Usted conoce (a) (Juan Martínez)?
 (Lo/La) conozco.

or

No (la/lo) conozco. ¿Quién es?
Es (el padre, la hija, etc.) de (Miguel).

¿Quién es (Raúl Quintana)?

Outer orbit.

4. Cummings device: ¿Dónde vive (usted)?
(Vivo/Vive) en (la calle Cristina).

5. The Spanish dialogs and/or Cummings devices to enable students to perform augment 2, above, in Spanish instead of English.

Unit 5.

Linguistic content:

(1) Review of segmental pronunciation points covered in units 2-4.

(2) First steps in teaching pronunciation of /r/.

(3) Meanings of verb endings without meanings of verb stems: (a) 1 sg. present vs. 1 pl. present, (b) 1 sg. present vs. 2/3 sg. preterite, (c) 1 sg. preterite vs. 2/3 sg. preterite.

111

CHAPTER 3   A SELF-INSTRUCTIONAL FORMAT (SPANISH)

Social content: continued from dialog of Unit 4.

Topical content: describing and identifying people.

Inner orbit.

1. At the end of the unit, the student is shown four simple
conversations made up of material that he has already mastered.
He is told to 'be prepared to carry out these conversations...
with your instructor.' Instructors should of course be sure that
the students take 'Role A' as well as 'Role B' in these conversations. It might be well, in addition, to change the directions so
that they read 'be prepared to initiate and maintain conversations
like these with your instructor.'

Middle orbit.

2. Cummings device(s) for describing and identifying people
(height, complexion, age, sex, etc.). Note the possible areas
for cross-cultural sensitivity here. Apply this to local people.

3. By adding first person soy, estoy, use the above vocabulary in self-description.

4. In Unit 3, augment 2, the students began to talk about
their daily routine, but without verbs. Now, add 1 pl. and 1 sg.
present content verbs to form an action chain based on the remaining parts of the routine: 'We get up at (6:00), we eat breakfast at (7:00), etc.' To maintain strength, much should be made
of each student also answering factually for himself where
individual schedules vary.

Outer orbit.

5. 'What is your address?' 'Where is your house?' Cummings
devices and/or dialogs, with a map of the area.

SUMMARY

The augments that we have listed here are just a beginning.
C. Ray Graham, director of language instruction at the Peace Corps'
Escondido Training Center, points out several other directions in
which to look for more: use of blackboard cartoons as a simple,
enjoyable and flexible source of present reality; reference to
the trainee's past, his parents, etc., in addition to his present
and his future; directed dialogs ('A., ask B. where Sanchez is.')

But all these suggestions are suggestions, and only that.
They apply to one actual situation, but by that very fact they
will be inapplicable in others. Their purpose is to demonstrate
how the principles of Chapter 3 might work themselves out in one
setting, and to stimulate the creative imagination of any reader
who may need to augment SPC or another programmed course in some
other setting.

What we are calling 'augmentation' does not just add something; it adds something for a purpose. The purpose is to move
from the secure base provided by the Units, and toward doing in
Spanish things that the student needs or wants to do anyway.
Every 'augment' should give the student something to do; it should
also give him at least two reasons for doing it. One reason will
be linguistic: he is gaining practice with a particular sound or
sentence pattern. At least one reason, however, must be non-
linguistic: he is doing something that he wants to do at the
moment, or he is preparing for some clearly defined effect that
he wants to have on Spanish speakers in the foreseeable future.
He may, for example, be learning to pronounce their names in a
non-irritating manner, or making himself able to produce the names
of people, places and things that may soon be part of his world.
It is this constant, close tie-in with the student's non-linguistic

113

purposes that keeps a good 'augment' from being just more 'additional material.' It is this same tie-in that keeps the writer
of the original materials from putting augments into the textbook
itself.

APPENDIX E TO CHAPTER 3

ADAPTING A LESSON BASED ON A PROSE TEXT

(MAURITIAN CREOLE)

In the spring of 1970, a group of Mauritians working at the request of the Peace Corps Representative in Mauritius produced a set of lessons in Mauritian Creole. These lessons were then sent to the Peace Corps training site on St. Thomas, V. I., for use in training the first group of Volunteers for Mauritius. The lessons varied somewhat in format, but in general were a valuable contribution to both the linguistic and the cultural sides of the training program.

This appendix illustrates briefly how one part of Lesson 5 was adapted for use. The lesson as a whole consisted of the following:

a. A narration (about 180 running words) with
    English translation.   (2 pages)

b. Numerals to enable the trainee to handle
    numbers up to 1,000,000.   (4 pages)

c. Nine adjectives and their opposites. (½ page)

d. Eleven names of colors.   (½ page)

e. Twenty words which indicate quantities. (1 page)

f. Six ways of showing degree with adjectives.
                             (1/3 page)

g. Four sentences illustrating passive voice.

h. Lexical drills. A series of sentences in which
    some consecutive members differ only by substi-
    tution of a single word, but others are much

less closely related. The sentences illustrate
the use of the words listed in c-f, above.

(2 pages)

i. Question and response drills. Like the lexical
   drills, except that each item in the series
   consists of a question and one answer. (1 pages)

j. Substitution drills. Like usual substitution
   drills, except that in going from one sentence to
   the next, substitution was sometimes required in
   more than one slot.   (2 pages)

k. Questions involving 'how much/many?', with one
   answer for each question.   (1 page)

As the lesson stood, then, it seemed to raise four
problems with regard to teachability:

a. There was no indication of how the narrative
   passage was to be used: how the trainees were
   to acquire and demonstrate short-term mastery
   of the material in the passage.

b. It was often not possible to predict one line of
   a drill by referring to the preceding line plus
   a cue. For this reason, the drills seemed to
   depend on reference to the English translations
   of the individual sentences.

c. There was no clear indication of how the material
   in the lesson might be employed in uses (Chapter 3,
   p. 57f) of the kind we have mentioned, which would lead
   to longer-term mastery, and integration with the
   trainee's previous knowledge of the language.

d. There was no provision either in this lesson or
   in the rest of the series, for any reference to

the realities of the training site. This problem
was of particular importance in the mind of the
person who was to serve as language coordinator
for the project.

In general, then, the pedagogical devices of this lesson
were rather indistinctly articulated.

At the same time, Lesson 5 (and the entire series) had
certain very important strengths. The Creole-speaking
members of the materials development team were quick to point
out that it was in general very authentic, both linguistically
and culturally. The content had been chosen under the supervision of the Director under whom the Volunteers were to serve,
and hence carried prima facie credibility with respect to
'coarse-grained specification'(Chapter 4, p.135). All vocabulary
items were potentially very useful.

The strategy of the adapters was therefore to present
the material of Lesson 5, using clearer pedagogical devices,
but rewriting as little as possible. Most of their work went
into presentation of the narrative. For this purpose, they
followed four steps:

a. Break the narration into sections of 2-4
   consecutive sentences.

b. After each section, write numerous comprehension
   questions.

c. Write Cummings devices (p. 59) based on a few of
   these questions, and use them as occasions to
   review vocabulary relating both to the training
   site and to Mauritius. Where possible, write
   them in a way that will promote the trainee's
   knowledge of Mauritian life.

117

d. Write drills only for new points of grammar that
the trainees might want to explore.

The narration is preceded by an English sentence which
sets the stage for the reader, by telling him that Jacqueline
goes first to the shop, and then to the market.

Section 1

Original text: Samji fin vini. Zaklin aste rasyõ komã
too le semen. Li sarye en zoli tãt vakwa dã so lamẽ.
(Saturday has come. Jacqueline buys groceries as
(she does) every week. She carries a beautiful 'vakwa'
basket in her hand.)

Comprehension questions:

Eski Zacqueline pou alle asseté ration zourdi?
Qui zour Zacqueline asseté ration?
Eski Zacqueline asseté ration tous les sémaines?
Eski Zacqueline asseté ration tous les zours?
Eski Zacqueline pou asseté ration?
Eski Zacqueline pou asseté linze?
Eski Zacqueline apé sarrié ene tente?
Qui qualité tente li apé sarrié?
Qui li apé sarrié?
Eski tente vacoas lá zoli?
Eski li sarrié tente lá lors so latête?
Eski li sarrié tente lá lors so lédos?
Eski li sarrié tente la dans so lamain?

These questions cover the section rather thoroughly.
Some groups of questions elicit very much the same answer,

118

but place an increasing load on the student:

> Is J. Carrying a <u>tãt</u>?
> What kind of <u>tãt</u> is she carrying?
> What is she carrying?

In the first of these questions, the student has only to understand it and choose between 'yes' and 'no.' In the second, he must remember <u>vakwa</u>, and in the third he must supply the entire phrase <u>tãt</u> <u>vakwa</u>.

<u>Cummings devices</u>.

The questions that were chosen to figure in Cummings devices were those that contained 'every/day/week' (because this was a new construction) and 'carry' (because this was a new verb). The team also found opportunities to interject some superficial but useful information about how the people of Mauritius live: which groceries they have to buy daily, and which on a weekly basis, and how various objects are customarily carried.

<u>C. d. 1</u>

M1

Zot asseté dipain tous les zours.	They buy bread every day.
Zot asseté dilait tous les zours.	They buy milk every day.
Zot asseté douriz tous les sémaines.	They buy rice every week.
Zot asseté dil'huile toutes les sémaines.	They buy oil every week.

CHAPTER 3   A PROSE TEXT (MAURITIAN CREOLE)

M2

L'Ile Maurice, eski zot
asseté dipain tous les
zours?

In Mauritius, do they buy
bread every day?

L'Ile Maurice, eski zot
asseté douriz tous les
zours?

etc.

En plis dé ça, qui zot
asseté tous les zours?

C1

L'Ile Maurice, eski zot
asseté (douriz) tous les
zours?

Non, zot asseté (dipain)
tous les zours

En plis de ça, qui zot
asseté tous les sémaines?

Zot asseté (lentilles)
tous les sémaines.

C. d. 2

M1

Zacqueline sarrié tente
dans so lamain.

Zacqueline carries a basket
in her hand.

Marsand bazaar sarrié
panier bazaar lors so
latête.

The bazaar merchant carries
his/her panier on his/her
head.

Marsand bazaar sarrié
panier bazaar lors so
bicyclette.

The bazaar merchant carries
his/her panier on his/her
bicycle.

M2

Comment Zacqueline sarrié so tente?	How does Zacqueline carry her basket?
Comment marsand bazaar sarrié so panier bazaar?	How does the merchant carry his/her panier?
En plis dé ça, qui zaffaire zot sarrié dans zot la main?	In addition to that, what things do they carry in their hands?

C1

Comment (Zacqueline) sarrié
(so tente)?

(Zacqueline) sarrié (so tente)
(dans) (so la main).

Eski li sarrié ene (panier)
(lors so latête)?

Non, li sarrié ene (tente)
(dans) (so lamain).

Drill. The expression corresponding to 'like every day/week'
is new enough and useful enough to be made the subject of a
drill. The cue sentence is always of the form 'Did you_____
today?' and the response is always 'Yes, I_____today,
like every day.' Instead of providing information about
Mauritius, this drill allows the instructor and trainees to
review vocabulary relating to life at the training site:

CHAPTER 3   A PROSE TEXT (MAURITIAN CREOLE)

Drill 1

Eski to fin lévé six ere grand matin
                              zourdi?

Oui, mo fin lévé six eres comment
                tous les zours.

Eski to fin boire café zourdi?

Oui, mo fin boire café comment
                tous les zours.

Ask some more questions about everyday activities and make
sure the students use "comment tous les zours" in their answers.

    Note that the 'occasions for use,' which in Chapter 3
we listed as one of the four essential components of a lesson,
are built into the Cummings devices and the drills.

APPENDIX F TO CHAPTER 3

MATERIALS FOR DISCUSSION (IGBO)

Blass, Johnson and Gage (1970) list no fewer than five sets
of teaching materials produced for the Igbo language within the
1960's. The most recent is Welmers and Welmers (1968). The
subject of this appendix is 5 of the 10 pages of Lesson 1 in
that book. Later lessons are a little longer, but are generally
similar in format. In the introduction to their book, the authors
say:

> Since these lessons are intended to be intensely practi-
> cal, it may seem strange that they do not start right out
> with some lively, useful daily conversations. There is
> good reason, however, for the procedure used. For one not
> used to a second language, and particularly a tone language,
> accurate pronunciation is difficult to achieve; but it is
> also crucially important. The drills that may seem monotonous
> at first are actually a golden opportunity to learn to con-
> trol pronunciation at the outset, so that habits of sloppy
> pronunciation will never have a good chance to develop. At
> the same time, every utterance in every drill is a perfectly
> good and natural utterance that will be found useful in
> daily life.
>
> The details of Igbo pronunciation will be outlined step
> by step in the early lessons. Try to imitate every detail
> accurately, but don't expect everything to be explained at
> once; concentrate on the points emphasized in each drill
> as you go along. The same is true of grammar: don't try
> to anticipate new forms and constructions, or you will only
> confuse yourself and everyone else. Don't worry about what
> you haven't learned to say; concentrate on saying what you
> have learned, and saying it accurately. The goal is to
> speak not so that you <u>can</u> be <u>under</u>stood, but so that you
> can<u>not</u> be <u>mis</u>understood.

1. With reference to the distinction between audiolingual
   habit formation and cognitive-code learning (Chapter 1,
   p. 7 ff.), does this textbook seem to be predominately
   A-L, or T-C?

123

CHAPTER 3   MATERIALS FOR DISCUSSION (IGBO)

2. Comment on the strength, lightness and transparency of
   the individual lines in this lesson, and of the lesson
   as a whole.

3. To what extent does this lesson include what we have
   listed as the four basic components?

4. What kinds of reward (Chapter 1, p.23f) are available
   to the student from this lesson as it stands?

5. What special obstacles does the Igbo language present
   to the would-be adapter?

6. Suggest ways of adapting or augmenting a lesson in this
   format so that new strength would probably justify added
   weight or opacity.

Lesson 1.

In a fairly long Igbo sentence, there may be a large number of different levels of pitch; but every pitch can be described in terms of one of three alternative possibilities at any particular point in the sentence.

First, the mark ´ represents a phenomenon which we will call "step". The pitch of a vowel or m or n or ŋ so marked is never low. In any Igbo utterance, each "step" is a little lower than the preceding one. You can only step down, and once you have done so you cannot climb up again until you come to a pause at the end of a phrase or sentence. Thus the sequence "step - step" is something like a child's call, "Daddy!", or like the melody at the beginning of the song "Chlo-e".

Second, the mark ` indicates "low". A "low" is distinctly lower in pitch than a "step" either before or after it. The sequence "step - low - step" is something like the melody at the beginning of the World War I song "Over There".

Third, any vowel (or m, n, ŋ as will be explained later) which is unmarked has the same pitch as that indicated by the last mark before it. Such unmarked syllables after a "step" will be called "same". After "low", following unmarked syllables will also be labelled "low". The sequence "step - same" is thus two syllables on a monotone; the second syllable must be on exactly the same pitch as the first. The sequence "low - low" (in which only the first low is marked) is also level within a sentence, but on a lower pitch than "step - same". At the end of a sentence, "low - low" may go a bit downhill in pitch, but it sounds nothing like two successive "steps", nor like "step - low". In an isolated two-syllable word, the first "low" in "low - low" may be noticably higher than the second; but the interval is not nearly as great as for "step - low". A final "low" is relaxed, much like the ending of a simple declarative sentence in English.

Igbo has eight vowel sounds. Not one of them is exactly the same as any English vowel, but you will not find all of them difficult to recognize or reproduce. The vowels are written: i, į, e, a, ọ, o, ụ, u; the marks under some of the letters (usually a dot or a short vertical stroke rather than the cedilla used here) are part of the vowel symbols themselves; to a speaker of Igbo, the vowel written ụ is as different from u as it is from o. For the time being, imitate these vowel sounds as carefully as you can, though the major point emphasized in the first several drills is tone. There are also some consonant sounds that will be strange to you; you will be helped with them as difficulties arise.

Drill 1. Each of the following sentences begins with the sequence "step - low", and continues with syllables that are "low" to the end. Thus each sentence has a melody somewhat like the English sentence "THEY were coming." Remember that in Igbo, however, the higher pitch at the beginning has absolutely nothing to do with emphasis. After the English is read aloud, each student should repeat each sentence in direct imitation of the model until his pronunciation is acceptable.

It's a bed.	ọ́ bụ̀ akwa.
It's a pot.	ọ́ bụ̀ ite.
It's a rope.	ọ́ bụ̀ ụdọ.
It's a bag.	ọ́ bụ̀ akpa.
It's a drum.	ọ́ bụ̀ ịgba.
He saw a bed.	ọ́ hụ̀rụ akwa.
He saw a pot.	ọ́ hụ̀rụ ite.
He saw a rope.	ọ́ hụ̀rụ ụdọ.
He saw a bag.	ọ́ hụ̀rụ akpa.
He saw a drum.	ọ́ hụ̀rụ ịgba.

Drill 2. Each of the·sentences in this drill differs in tone from those in Drill 1 only in that the very last syllable is a "step"; that is, the pitch goes up again with the last syllable, but not quite as high as the initial "step".

It's a cup.	ọ́ bụ̀ ikó.
It's an egg.	ọ́ bụ̀ akwá.
It's a dress.	ọ́ bụ̀ uwé.
It's a box.	ọ́ bụ̀ igbé.
It's a compound.	ọ́ bụ̀ ezí.
He saw a cup.	ọ́ hụ̀rụ ikó.
They saw an egg.	há hụ̀rụ akwá.
They saw a dress.	há hụ̀rụ uwé.
They saw a box.	há hụ̀rụ igbé.
They saw a compound.	há hụ̀rụ ezí.

(Note: ùwé may also refer to a blouse, shirt, or other sewn garment. èzí 'compound' is the area on which a house and subsidiary buildings are located.)

126

Notes.

The five groups of nouns used in the above drills are typical of the majority of Igbo nouns: two syllables, the first being a vowel or a syllabic m or n or ŋ, the second beginning with a consonant and ending with a vowel, all accompanied by one of the five tone sequences illustrated above. There are some three-syllable and longer nouns in Igbo, and some nouns beginning with consonants, but they will give little trouble once these five basic types are mastered. In isolation, the five types of nouns are labelled and written as follows:

1.	Low – low:	àkwa	'a bed'
2.	Low – step:	àkwá	'an egg'
3.	Step – same:	óce	'a chair'
4.	Step – step:	égó	'money'
5.	Step – low:	ákwà	'cloth'

In the sentences on which you have drilled, the initial low tone of the first two of the above types has, of course, not been marked, because the last preceding marked tone was low. If you want to keep a vocabulary card file, be sure to mark the tones as above, not as they appear in full sentences.

As you begin to learn Igbo vocabulary, remember that the tone is an integral part of the word, and must be learned along with the consonants and vowels. It is true that tones sometimes undergo alternations that will surprise you, somewhat as the f in English wife changes to v in the plural wives. But the existence of this alternation in English does not permit us to interchange f and v whenever we feel like it; neither does the existence of variant tonal forms in Igbo permit us to ignore tone. First learn the words as they have been introduced, including their tones; the alternations follow statable rules, and will be systematically presented as the lessons progress.

A few words about consonants, consonant clusters, and syllabic nasals. The writings kp and gb represent single consonants, not sequences of k and p or g and b. The closure at the back of the mouth for k or g, and at the lips for p or b, is simultaneous; the releases are also simultaneous. These may not be easy consonants at first, but with practice you can learn them. You have probably used a consonant similar to the Igbo kp in imitating a hen cackling; in Igbo orthography, a common American imitation would be written "kpó kpọ kpọ kpọ kpọ". After a vowel or syllabic nasal, the syllable division always precedes the consonants kp and gb; it does not come between them.

127

The writings kw and gw (and ŋw, which you will meet later) also represent single consonants as far as Igbo structure is concerned. kw and gw are not particularly hard to recognize or reproduce, but again remember that the syllable division precedes them, never splits them.

The letter c represents a consonant much like that which is written ch in English (and in most written Igbo); c always represents this sound in our writing of Igbo, so that there is no need to add another letter to show what the sound is.

The letters m and n (and ŋ, which you will meet later) sometimes appear before vowels; in such cases, they are consonants just like k or b. However, they may also appear before consonants; in such cases, they are syllables by themselves, with their own tone. Be sure you don't use a vowel either before or after such a syllabic nasal; just hum-m-m it and then go on-n-n to the next consonant. As you will soon learn, m is also frequently written as a word by itself; in such cases also, it is syllabic and has its own tone. Syllabic m also appears occasionally at the end of an Igbo word; apart from a few cases of this type, all Igbo words end with vowels.

Review of Lesson 1:

Twenty-five nouns have been introduced in this lesson, and at first it won't be easy to remember which is which. For further practice on pronunciation, and to help learn the vocabulary, use the following procedures:

1. Have the model pick a sentence at random from this lesson, say it clearly, and call on a student first to repeat the Igbo sentence and then, if he can, to give the meaning. If the student gives the wrong translation, or cannot remember the meaning, the correct English should be given immediately. Continue with Igbo sentences selected at random, calling on students in random order.

2. Call on students at random to say any Igbo sentence in this lesson that they happen to remember hearing, and to give the meaning if they can. Correction of pronunciation, especially tone, should be strict. If the English equivalent is not given immediately, call on another student to give it, or supply it without permitting long intervals of silence.

3. Call on students at random, supply any of the English equivalents from this lesson, and ask for the Igbo sentence. If the reply is not reasonably prompt, supply the correct Igbo. After some drilling of this sort, much of the vocabulary will be learned.

Recognition Test: 1

Students: DO NOT TURN TO THE NEXT PAGE.

A. Below are ten Igbo words without tone marks. Each one has either the sequence step-same (like ánu̠) or the sequence step-low (like ázù̠). You will hear each word pronounced at least twice. Mark the tone in either of the above ways, as you hear it. (The words should be read to the students from the following page.)

1.	a t u̠	6.	i k w e
2.	e l e	7.	u̠ g b o̠
3.	o̠ b a	8.	e g b e
4.	a k p u̠	9.	e z i
5.	i g w e	10.	a k a

The correct markings will now be given to you. Indicate each error by a check mark, and then make the appropriate correction.

B. Below are another ten Igbo words without tone marks. This time, each word has either the sequence low-low (like ìte) or low-step (like ìkó). Mark each word in one of these two ways as you hear it.

1.	o k e	6.	o k p u
2.	ŋ k e	7.	ŋ g b e
3.	o̠ k w a	8.	o̠ s a
4.	a t o̠	9.	i s e
5.	u d u	10.	a l a

Again you will be given the correct markings. Indicate each error by a check mark, and then make the appropriate correction.

On the following page, the correct forms of the above are given, with their English meanings. Most of these words will become part of your vocabulary within the next few lessons.

The results of this test may indicate a need for further drill or explanation.

Recognition Test: 1 -- Instructor's Key

Each of the following is to be read twice, with a few seconds between, in a clear voice, but not too slowly.

A. 1. átụ   'chewing stick'   6. íkwè   'mortar'

    2. éle   'antelope'   7. ụ́gbọ   'vehicle'

    3. ọ́bà   'calabash'   8. égbè   'gun'

    4. ákpụ   'cassava'   9. ézì   'pig'

    5. ígwè   'iron; bicycle'   10. áka   'hand'

(The correct markings should be given as "Number one: step-same; Number two: step-same; Number three: step-low", etc.)

B. 1. òké   'rat'   6. òkpú   'cap'

    2. ị̀ke   'thing'   7. ị̀gbe   'time'

    3. òkwa   'partridge'   8. ọ̀sá   'squirrel'

    4. àtọ́   'three'   9. ìsé   'five'

    5. ùdu   'water jug'   10. àla   'ground, land'

(The correct markings should be given as "Number one: low-step; Number two: low-low", etc.)

(The nouns from this test can be used for supplementary drill by asking students to construct sentences such as "He saw an antelope", "It's a rat", etc.. Do not attempt to use the numerals at this stage.)

CHAPTER 4

WRITING ADAPTABLE MATERIALS

THE PROBLEM

> If the blind lead the blind, shall
> not both fall into the pit?
>
>   Luke 6:39

The preceding chapter suggested ways of adapting and using language materials that are already at hand. Whoever rejects what is at hand and writes his own lessons assumes a double responsibility: to produce something that really is better for his purposes than what existed before, and to reduce the likelihood that those who come after him will feel that they in turn have to write their own courses. Chapter 4 applies to the writing of new materials many of the same principles that guided adaptation in Chapter 3 and its appendices.

Writing lessons for seldom-taught languages and writing them for commonly-taught ones differ in much more than the names of the languages. Students in seldom-taught languages are likely to be more mature, and many have already in mind some imminent and very definite use to which they hope to put the language. Yet in the development of language study materials, writers are only rarely qualified to speak for the public among whom the prospective students are to live and work. Sometimes, the materials-writing 'team' consists of one person, who is biologically coextensive with the only student. It is for this situation that we have Gudschinsky's How to Learn an Unwritten Language (1967; cf. also Ward [1937] and Bloomfield [1942]). Most frequently, however, the materials writers directly represent neither the student nor his future audience. All too often, they have begun and completed

131

their work without even seeing either the students (because they have not yet been enrolled) or the audience (because they are remote either geographically or socially or both). The plight of such writers is implicit in the following quotation from the introduction to one textbook:

> This grammar is designed for a highly heterogeneous audience, composed primarily of the following groups: (1) area specialists interested in language- or culture-studies of all parts of tropical Africa; (2) ethnographers focussing on the social structure of the Edo-speaking peoples; (3) historians working directly or indirectly on the Benin Project sponsored by Ibadan University; (4) linguists more concerned with analytical procedures than with specific languages or language-groups; (5) missionaries in the Benin area who wish to reach their parishioners more immediately than they can in English; and (6) Bini-speaking teachers and writers who seek a more exact understanding of their own language than conventional training in English grammar offers them. As though this assemblage were not already diverse enough, the grammar is intended secondarily for any and all foreign visitors to Benin Province who may find a description of one of the Edo languages useful or interesting. The author's hope is that this volume may have something to offer to each of the above-mentioned audiences, though he fully appreciates the very real possibility that it may fall between scholarly stools in such a way as to leave all of its prospective audiences unsatisfied.
>
> Wescott, A Bini Grammar, page 1

Except where materials are being prepared in the midst of an ongoing training course, consultation with students is obviously impossible. (Consultation with students must take place during adaptation, and it is largely to enhance the status of adaptation that we have placed that chapter ahead of this one.) Getting preliminary information from spokesmen for anticipated audiences is not impossible, however, and writers should be willing to spend some time and considerable effort in assembling it. At the same

132

time, they must remember that the potential audience for a student going to Greece is not just undifferentiated 'Greeks.' Potential audiences for different trainees interested in the same country will be partly alike and partly different, even within a series of programs sponsored by a single sending agency.

All this uncertainity, instead of filling writers with diffidence and godly fear, seems to send them forth to sin all the more bravely. The result has been publication of much that is idiosyncratic, some of which is good, some of which is useful to others, and some of which is neither. In the 1960's, when money for such enterprises was more freely available, this profusion was either inspiring, amusing or annoying, depending on one's point of view. In the 1970's, however, we can no longer afford to invest many thousands of dollars in a course which embodies the theories, needs or prejudices of its own writers, but which may then be rejected by most other prospective users. This is particularly true for the less-frequently taught languages.

The problem, then, is how to minimize the likelihood that a set of materials will be rejected by new programs operating with different aims, different kinds of students, different theoretical convictions, and different prejudices. The solution that is proposed here depends on building into the materials a number of clearly-defined options relating to the choice of material, its possible replacement, and the ways in which it may be used. On the other hand, too much flexibility may be just as disastrous as too little. For those who want to follow, materials must give firm guidance; for those who want to tamper, there must be clear indications of how to select, rearrange, and complement without destroying.

CHAPTER 4   WRITING ADAPTABLE MATERIALS

The goal which we have set for this chapter is more delicate
than for any of the other chapters. We are attempting to tell
others how they can do something (write adaptable materials)
without telling them how they must do it. To put the same
dilemma in another way, if suggestions are to be helpful they
must be fairly concrete, yet the whole purpose of these suggestions will be defeated if they are taken as prescriptions for yet
one more ultimate format. This chapter therefore presents a somewhat idealized scheme for materials development, which will be
partly exemplified and partly contradicted in the appendices which
follow it. Like Jabberwocky, it is supposed to fill the reader's
head with indefinite ideas; unlike Jabberwocky, it is supposed to
help the reader to produce very definite ideas when he applies it
to any specific problem in materials development.

A WAY

One of the most noteworthy (and least noted) attempts to
view the writing of materials for seldom-taught languages is
John Francis' Projection (1969). Using Francis' analysis as a
point of departure, we may say that the writing team must provide
for three 'functions' (specification, presentation, articulation)
on each of two 'scales' (coarse-grained, fine-grained). The flow
chart (Fig. 1) shows how these are related to one another:

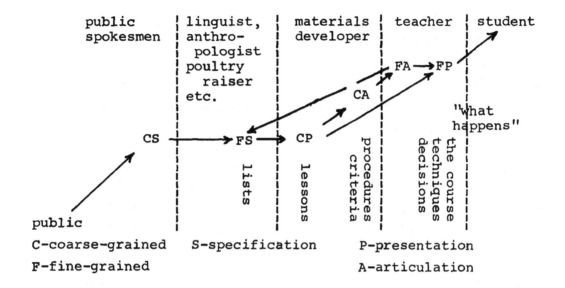

Fig. 1

Coarse-grained Specification. This is the responsibility of
a qualified spokesman for the potential audience. Just who is
qualified for this role depends on who is being trained for what.
The spokesman may be a group of community representatives, or a
ministry of agriculture, or a Peace Corps country director. For
the Thai materials described in Appendix G, the principal spokesmen were two returned Peace Corps Volunteers, one of whom had spent
two years in malaria control and one of whom had spent the same
amount of time in leprosy work. In Appendix H, coarse-grained
specification was provided by a director of area studies in a
stateside training program. In Appendix I, it was provided by
teachers, but by teachers who had had observed at first hand
the way their students might need to use the language.

Coarse-grained specification answers questions in each of the
three 'dimensions' of Chapter 3:

135

1. _Socio-cultural_. ('What will be the trainee's _position_ relative to speakers of the language -- and bearers of the culture -- in which he is interested?') This information may be given in the form of a careful prose description. The source of the information itself may be discussion, questionnaires, surveys, or some combination of these.

2. _Topical_. ('What kinds of _messages_ will the trainee need to handle?') This information is best given in the form of a list of problems or tasks. Some of these may involve social situations of interest to a broad spectrum of trainees, while others will be within special fields of interest or technical specialization.

3. _Linguistic proficiency_. ('_How well_ will the student need to understand, speak, read and write the language?') This information as it comes from spokesmen for the future audience will not be in technical linguistic terms, but will be stated functionally, perhaps somewhat as follows:

> The trainee must learn to participate effectively in all general conversation; he must be able to discuss leprosy control and health education with reasonable ease; comprehension must be quite complete for a normal rate of speech; his vocabulary must be broad enough so that he rarely has to grope for a word; his accent may still be foreign, but his control of the grammar must be good enough so that his errors never interfere with understanding, and rarely disturb a native speaker.

The above statement, which is based on an official description of the Foreign Service Institute's widely-circulated S-3 rating, represents a rather high goal. Much less demanding would be:

> The trainee must learn to ask and answer questions on topics that are very familiar to him; he may not understand even simple sentences unless they are repeated at a slower rate than normal speech; he may

> make frequent errors of pronunciation and grammar,
> and his speaking vocabulary may be inadequate to
> express anything but the most elementary needs, but
> he must be able to make himself understood to a
> native speaker who is used to dealing with foreigners;
> he must be able to take care of his need for food,
> street and road directions, matters of personal
> hygiene and cleanliness, including laundry, tell
> time, and handle basic courtesy requirements.

This, of course, describes only a very rudimentary (actually,
pre-rudimentary) control, labelled S-1 on the Foreign Service
Institute's scale. In between these two is S-2:

> The trainee must learn to handle with confidence,
> though perhaps not with facility, most social
> situations including introductions and casual con-
> versations about his work, family and autobiographi-
> cal information; the same applies to limited business
> requirements, in that he must be able to handle routine
> matters even though he may need help with complications;
> he should be able to understand most conversations on
> non-technical subjects and have a speaking vocabulary
> sufficient to express himself simply with some cir-
> cumlocutions; his accent must be intelligible; his
> control of the grammar, even though it may not be
> thorough or confident, should enable him to handle
> elementary constructions quite accurately.

The above descriptions are intended to be suggestive, but are not
recommended for adoption. Anyone who tries to use them in any
real situation will want to be much more specific in some respects,
but in many situations they will be inappropriate even as bases
for amplification.

    Coarse-grained specification comes before all other activities,
whether the project is a conventional one of writing materials for
distant and future students, or whether a lone Peace Corps Volunteer
is getting ready to find his/her own way through a hitherto unwritten language of the African savanna. Lack of such specifica-

tion leaves the team vulnerable to 'materials-writer's malaise,'
the symptoms of which are evident in the quotation on p. 132.
As we have said, it is the prospective materials developer who
asks the questions; the answers come from outside the language-
teaching community. This, then, is the first of a series of
interfaces.

Fine-grained Specification. Fine-grained specification is
the domain -- and the only domain -- over which the outside specialists hold unchallenged hegemony. Given that a trainee will
be operating within some general setting, an anthropologist or
other cross-cultural specialist is needed to preside over the
drawing up of a 'role model' (Wight and Hammons, 1970), which
lists the kinds of people with whom the trainee will interact,
and also shows how the culture preconditions his relationships
with each of them. Given that a trainee will be expected to help
others learn to drill wells or raise chickens, or that he will
have to arrange for getting his laundry done, someone with
authoritative knowledge must provide details of each of these
matters. Given that the trainee should have a particular level
of competence in a particular socio-cultural setting, the professional linguistic scientist can provide lists of verb tenses,
noun cases, stylistic levels, clause types, and grammatical
relationships that are indispensable. The items in each list
(sociocultural, topical, linguistic) may be marked to show relative frequency, importance and/or difficulty.

Here is the reason for separating coarse from fine specification. To have let the poultry raiser, anthropologist, and
linguistic scientist into the picture too soon would have led to
disproportionate influence of their theoretical preoccupations
and past experiences, and a disastrous loss in validity relative
to the interests of the future audience. To allow them to remain
in the picture after fine specification has been completed is

to invite those same professional preoccupations to distort the
teachability of the end product. But to ignore the specialists
altogether would be to stumble through the dark toward a distant
candle, or to build a house following only a floor plan.

A very rough, but full-scale example of the grammatical part
of fine specification for the linguistic aspect of an S-2 on the
FSI rating scale is the following, for Brazilian Portuguese. This
is primarily a list of contrasts that a student must learn to control as he speaks the language. The three main headings in the
list are <u>Sentence Patterns</u>, <u>Verbs</u>, <u>Substantives and Other Matters</u>.

<u>Sentence Patterns</u>

Affirmative vs. negative statements.
Statements vs. yes-no questions.
Yes-no questions vs. either-or questions.
Content questions with:

Que?	What? (adj.)
O que?	What? (pronoun)
Quem?	Who?
Quando?	When?
Quanto?	How much?
Onde?	Where?
Como?	How?
Qual?	Which?
Porque?	Why?

[English equivalents are only approximate.]

Short answers vs. long or yes-no answers.
Exclamations that emphasize:

Noun

Verb

Adjective

Verbs

Contrast between singular and plural, in the same endings that
    reflect person and tense.
Contrasts between first and third persons.
    [In Brazilian Portuguese, special second-person forms are
    very little used. The third person forms are used instead.]

Contrast among the most indispensable tenses:
        Present indicative.
        Preterite.
        Periphrastic future.
        Periphrastic progressive.
        Infinitive.

And limited exposure to:
        Imperfective.
        Present subjunctive.
        Past subjunctive.
        Future subjunctive.
        Personal infinitive.
        Future.

The above forms for the three 'regular' conjugations and for:

ser	be	querer	want
estar	be	poder	be able
fazer	do	saber	know
dar	give	ver	see
ter	have	vir	come
ir	go	trazer	bring
por	put	ha	there is

Substantives and Other Matters

Gender and number in:

>   Definite articles.
>   Indefinite articles.
>   Object pronouns.
>   Adjectives.
>   Demonstratives.
>   Possessive pronouns.

Demonstratives.   Distinctions among three series represented by:

>   este   this
>   ese   that
>   aquele   that

Pronominalization:

>   Subject pronouns.
>   Pronoun objects of prepositions.
>   Pronoun objects of verbs (direct and indirect).
>   Possessive pronouns.

Prepositions appropriate with assorted verbs and adjectives.

Contractions.

It should be emphasized that the above example of 'fine specification' is to be taken seriously only with regard to its size, and not in its details, even for Portuguese. For other languages, a comparable specification of major grammar points might vary greatly in its content, but probably somewhat less in its length.

The output of the fine specification function may be pictured as a three-dimensional matrix:

141

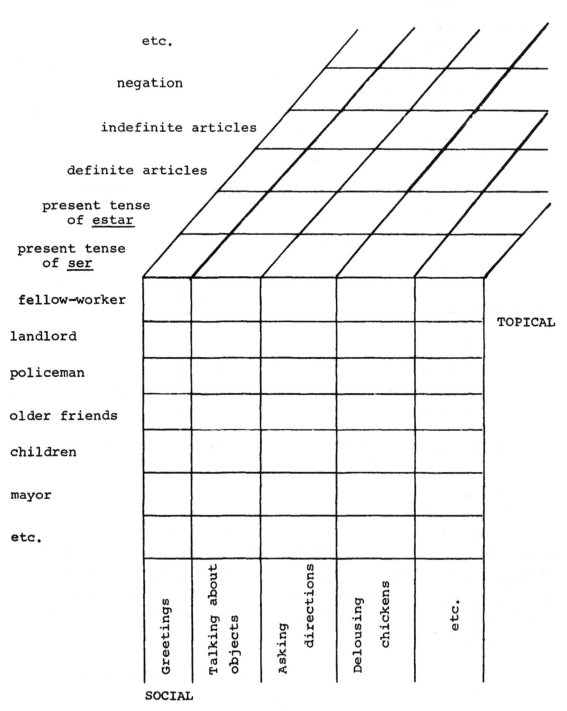

To recapitulate:

1. Specification begins outside the area of language-
   teaching, and relates to it facts from other areas:
   culture, law, work, requirements of the sending
   organization.

2. Given a particular set of external conditions,
   specification is relatively inflexible; that is, it
   does not depend on the preferences of the materials
   developer or of the prospective users.

3. Specification takes the form of a set of lists.

4. Linguistic scientists, anthropologists, poultry
   raisers, and other specialists from outside the area
   of language teaching are particularly useful in
   preparing these lists.

Coarse-grained Presentation. Here, the data which the
writing team elicited from the public, and which were cast by
the specialists into the form of detailed lists, must finally be
put onto paper and/or film and/or tape. Control has passed into
the hands of the language teaching specialist, and he must choose
among a wide array of formats, methods and approaches. It is at
this point of choice that the present proposal differs from the
practice of almost all materials developers. Most writers take
it for granted that they are called on to lay out for the student
some path which he is to follow, and which will lead to the desired
goal. The path may consist of conventional lessons or a self-
instructional program or a combination of live and canned instruction, and a self-instructional program may be linear, branching,
or cyclical. Any fixed set of materials, however, carries within
it the seeds of its own rejection: irrelevant content, inappropriate length, or uncongenial format. Furthermore, it fails to

tap the enthusiasm that comes when the users of a course feel that something of themselves is invested in its creation. This is one reason why some pedagogical monstrosities have produced good results, and why some well-constructed materials have fallen flat.

One way to go at coarse-grained presentation is the following:

HOW TO WRITE A $5000 (CHEAP!) SARKHANESE COURSE

1. <u>Prepare a sketch of the language.</u> Make it short enough so that an interested layman can read it at one sitting, and clear enough so that he won't get up and leave it. Make it long enough so that a student can relate to it most of the grammatical features that he finds in ordinary written or spoken texts, but don't try to make it exhaustive. Write from the point of view of the student, not of the linguistic scientist. (That is why the sketch is part of 'coarse presentation' rather than 'fine specification'!) If the sketch is well-written, it will also give to the student a convenient bird's-eye view of the language, to which he will be able to refer his own detailed experiences as they accumulate.

This kind of sketch is the subject of Chapter 5 ('Learner's Synopses'), and is illustrated in Appendices M (p. 235), N (p. 258), and O (p. 284).

2. <u>Present</u> within a small, lively and non-committal vocabulary, and in as foolproof a way as you can manage, <u>the main points of grammar.</u> These will be the same points that the linguistic scientist listed in his contribution to 'fine specification,' and that entered into the sketch in step 1 (above). Present them in at least two ways:

a. Identify each point and give simple directions for
demonstrating it with minimum dependence on the student's
native language or on other knowledge of the target
language. This is the 'enactive' mode of presentation
(Chapter 3, p. 61).

b. Give a brief, clear explanation of the structural
item. Make this explanation as independent as possible
from the explanations of the other points, or from the
sketch that you prepared in step 1, but include cross-
references to the sketch, and/or some more comprehensive
treatment of the grammar. Use charts and diagrams if you
think they will help. These are the 'symbolic' and 'iconic'
modes.

Put each point on a separate sheet of paper (or 5"x8" card).
This will make it easy for you or others to rearrange them.
Appendix K, p. 220, shows grammar points of Swahili that have
been treated as suggested above. Some excellent examples for
English are found in Harold Palmer's little book on The Teaching
of Oral English.

Just the output of this one step, if arranged in some appropriate order, would form a sparse set of lessons. The Swahili
materials in Appendix K have been used that way several times.
In the teaching of Eskimo, too, S. T. Mallon (1970) reports:

> One hundred and twenty three-by-five inch cards
> were prepared, one to a lesson. On the face of
> each was written a phrase or sentence illustrat-
> ing the structure for that lesson. No other
> formal lesson plan was prepared.(Last year in
> Ottawa the principal had written out a series of
> 120 fully detailed lesson plans: on arrival in
> Rankin Inlet he discarded them as being too re-
> strictive and inflexible.) Instead of written

lessons plans the instructor preferred to rely on
his own teaching experience, on the material at
hand, and on the spontaneous reactions of informants
and students. The instructor would enter the class
with a preconceived notion of how to conduct the
lesson, but prepared to adapt.

3.   Present, in as foolproof a way as you can manage, the main
question-types and virtually all of the interrogative words, with
sample answers. This is part of the 'grammar,' of course, but
its main purpose is to enable the student to explore the vocabulary
of the language for topics that he is interested in. One way of
presenting and exploiting questions is the 'Cummings device,'
discussed in Chapter 6 and exemplified in Appendices P (p. 331),
Q (p. 337), R (p. 346), G (p. 154) and elsewhere.

4.   Stop. Recognize that the course is incomplete. It is
incomplete for two reasons, but also for a third and a fourth:

   a. All students will need many more words than you have
   included so far. (But they will differ as to just what
   words they do need.)

   b. All students will need much more practice with the
   grammar than you have provided for. (But they will differ
   as to how often, how long, and how they should practice.)

But also:

   c. What is in the course has no connection with anything
   that really matters to the student. Words are connected
   to words (either Sarkhanese or English) and patterns are
   connected to patterns, but there is no feel or motion, no
   touch, no smell, no flavor and no joy. There are no people
   yet, only teachers and students. There is no flesh, but
   only dry bones.

d. You may have taught the student to speak the language a little, but you have not taught him to learn it for himself.

5. Although Steps 1-4 will produce only an incomplete course, yet what they do produce will be useful to almost anyone who undertakes to teach or learn Sarkhanese. If there is still money in the budget (and there should be), begin to complete the course for one reason, but also for a second:

a. You can give to teachers and students something to use in their work together.

But also:

b. You can give to teachers and students an example of how they can complete the course for themselves.

As you begin to complete the course, follow your own convictions and the needs of some moment. Aim more at effectiveness than at permanence. It is more important that your lessons should work than that they should last (or sell!). You may decide:

a. that the most foolproof way to present the essential structures (step 2, above) is through a fixed, self-contained 'program' which depends as little as possible on teachers, and as much as possible on books, tapes, and visual aids that you yourself will devise. This is the route taken by Spanish Programmatic Course (Appendix D), and by programmed self-instruction in general. Or you may decide:

147

b.   that the most foolproof way to present those same structures is through examples, explanations, and teacher-supervised drills. Here are the audiolingual courses (e.g. Appendix A), and also the pattern-practice courses (e.g. Appendix C). Or you may decide:

c.   that the most foolproof way to present the structures is through a series of activities in which talk agrees with action, action agrees with talk, and both go on together. The 'total response' experiments of Asher (1965), the 'Situational Reinforcement' of Eugene Hall, and the 'Silent Way' of Gattegno (1970) all emphasize this principle, though in quite different ways. Or you may decide:

d.   that there is some other way better than any of these.

You may also decide:

e.   that the 'dry bones' of structure should be stacked near the beginning of the course; or

f.   that they should be scattered throughout the course as a whole.

6.   Before you begin each lesson, <u>list a number of things that the student will be able to do</u> in Sarkhanese at the end of it. These may take any of several forms.

a.   things to learn through eliciting further information from instructors or from fellow students;

b.   games (including free conversation!) that are fun in themselves;

c. role playing situations that the student can imagine
himself being in someday;

d. printed or taped information in which the student is
interested, and which is not available to him otherwise;

e. doing things together (e.g. trading postage stamps,
gardening, assembling a bicycle) that involve language.

Have these objectives, or 'pay-offs,' in mind as you write the
lesson, and put them on the last page when you have finished.
Aim at a lesson that the student can finish in 1 - 4 class hours.

Examples of payoffs are found in Chapter 3, p. 54-57 ;
Appendix R, pp. 361- 364, Appendix G, p. 184f, and elsewhere.

7. Assemble structure points (step 2) and Cummings devices
(step 3) that seem appropriate for the objectives of step 6.
Put each on a separate sheet of paper -- not just a separate page.
Combine the Cummings devices into an exchange sequence[1] something
like the following:

> What is this?
> It's a book.
> Where is the book?
> It's on the table.
> Is the book red, or blue?
> It's blue.

---

[1]This term arises out of discussions with Carol Flamm, and
is approximately equivalent to what Eugene Hall has called
a 'response sequence.'

149

(This sort of stuff is called a 'dialog' in some textbooks. The difference is that a exchange sequence so emphasizes lightness and transparency (p. 47f) that it is credible only in a language classroom.) Put each exchange sequence on a separate sheet of paper.

If you think it expedient to do so, go on and write some genuine, lifelike dialog that incorporates the contents of the exchange sequence but goes beyond it. Either kind of dialog has certain advantages: it provides a change of pace from the very short Cummings devices or the situationally disjointed drills (see Newmark and Reibel, 1968, p.149); it provides a kind of transition from them to the connected discourse that the students will have to produce as they 'apply' their Sarkhanese at the end of the lesson; it provides a vehicle for introducing set expressions, sentence connectors, and other items that do not lend themselves to drills or Cummings devices.

8. <u>Write</u> whatever <u>drill materials</u> seem necessary. Put each drill on a separate sheet of paper, double-spaced, with plenty of white space around it. (For examples, see Appendix G, pp.165-182, and Appendix I, pp. 206-214).

9. <u>Leave room for additions and changes</u>, <u>and show that you expect them.</u> That, of course, was the reason for doublespacing the items in steps 7 and 8, and especially for putting each one on a separate sheet of paper.

If you have followed the instructions in steps 1-9, your lessons will be clusters of available items that support one another, rather than fixed sequences of activity. The users of your lessons will be able to modify or replace any item. Whatever items they choose, they can use in any of several orders:

one will want to begin with memorization of a dialog or an exchange sequence; another will want to build up to the dialog
or exchange sequence through drills and Cummings devices, and
then memorize it; a third will want to eschew dialog memorization
altogether. The same class may handle one such 'cluster' in one
way, and another in another way.

At this point, you have completed a Sarkhanese course that
is a least minimally usable, and that is at the same time maximally
adaptable. The options that you have left for users of your course
are more numerous and also more obvious than those provided in
most language-teaching materials. (For the sake of those who do
not want options, you can always arrange your 'clusters' in some
linear order and number them serially.)

Although we have written this section of Chapter 4 in terms
of a non-existent language, Sarkhanese, it is not merely a programmatic statement. Full-scale materials have been written in
this way and classroom tested for Spanish (Teacher Corps),
Mauritian Creole and Thai (Peace Corps). The same system has
been tested on a smaller scale for Portuguese, French and Swahili.
Appendix J describes how the cluster format was used in the
Spanish materials, and Appendix G gives examples for Thai.

Fine-grained Presentation. But the work of the writers is not yet
ended. In addition to general procedures, they should suggest a
number of superficial variations of technique which will be sufficient either to reduce or increase the pressure, as the need
arises. Examples are the change from fixed to random order in
calling on students; change of pace; racing against the clock;
exchange of roles between student and teacher. The essential
difference between these variations of technique and the steps
in a procedure is that the latter are relatively fixed, while

151

the timing and ordering of the former depend on clues that come
out of the moment-to-moment behavior of a particular class.

Coarse-grained Articulation. What Francis calls the 'articulation
function' is easy for writers to overlook or take for granted,
yet conscious attention to it can contribute greatly toward
teachability. The articulation function consists of two
'routines': a 'criterion routine' by which one decides that
it is time to move on to something else, and a 'selection routine'
by which one decides what that something else is to be. The
writers should make very explicit suggestions for the 'articulation'
of each part of each cluster, particularly with regard to the
criterion routine. These suggestions might be in some such form
as: 'Continue with this drill until the students can complete
it in 40 seconds or less, but in no case longer than 7 minutes.'
'Do this role play on at least two different occasions. Be sure
that each student has had a chance to take both parts. Do not
spend more than 20 minutes on the first occasion, or 15 minutes
on the second.'

Fine-grained Articulation. This consists of the decisions that
the individual teacher makes as he teaches. It governs the choice
of material from the lists of content, social roles, and linguistic features (Fine Specification), and also governs the choice of
minor variations of technique (Fine Presentation). Among them,
these choices determine what actually happens -- in Francis' terms,
'the course.' The course, in this sense, is what the student
encounters.

SUMMARY

On p. 135, we pictured the writing of language textbooks as a flow chart, and the process as a linear one. Seen in another way, the same activities we have described in this chapter are concentric: each successive procedure establishes a nucleus around which to fit what may be produced by later procedures. Writers of lessons may provide one layer of inner structure, or many. It would be a mistake, however, for them to assume that they can supply the final outer layer; only the users of the lessons can do that.

The remaining chapters of this book are about devices that we have mentioned as particularly useful in adapting materials or in making them adaptable: learners' synopses, Cummings devices, one kind of sample of language in use, and routine drills.

CHAPTER 4   MUTUALLY-DERIVABLE MATERIALS (THAI)

APPENDIX G

TO

CHAPTER 4

MUTUALLY-DERIVABLE MATERIALS IN
TECHNICAL SPECIALITIES (THAI)

THE PROBLEM

Thailand 33, a Peace Corps training program, was to prepare
Volunteers to work in three medical specialties: malaria control,
leprosy control, and laboratory technology. Training was to take
place during the period November 9 - January 27. A number of sets
of lessons for teaching elementary Thai were already available,
but none of them covered the technical areas of this program.
There was therefore a call for providing effective 'tech-specific'
materials. The first question was:

1. How quickly and how cheaply could they be written?

This part of the problem had come up in many programs in
dozens of languages, had been recognized, and had been dealt with
in one way or another. Two other aspects of the problem, however,
have usually received little or no attention. They were:

2. How readily will those in charge of later programs be
    able to change these materials without destroying them?

3. Will the existence of these materials make it any easier
    to write tech-specific materials in other specialties,
    such as tuberculosis control or vocational agriculture?

In general, the more specialized a set of lessons, the higher
their cost per student-hour. The goal of the project was to deal
with all three of these aspects of the problem: to write usable
materials on a relatively low budget; to write them in such a way

154

that subsequent users could change them as easily as possible to suit their own needs and pedagogical preferences; and to provide a basis from which to derive future courses in other technical specialties.

THE RESOURCES

Although the budget was very low, and the amount of lead time very small, the personnel available for this project were extraordinarily well-suited to undertake it. Professor Sutira Ariyapongse had participated, as language instructor or as coordinator, in Thai language training for over a dozen groups of Peace Corps Volunteers. In some of these programs she had also served as materials writer. She had also had some medical training, and had observed medical Volunteers at work in Thailand.

General supervision of the project was the responsibility of Dale P. Crowley, Chief of the Language Unit in the University of Hawaii's Center for Cross-Cultural Training and Research (CCCTR), at which the program was to take place. Besides having run dozens of Peace Corps language training programs for Thailand and elsewhere, Crowley had a personal command of Thai sufficient to enable him to monitor the project at all levels.

Less heavily involved, but of crucial importance in laying the groundwork, were two returned Volunteers: Carl Hirth, who had worked in Thailand for two years as a malaria control specialist, and Mark Brinkman, who had worked the same amount of time in leprosy control. Hirth and Brinkman served as spokesmen for the future 'audience' (Chapter 4, p.135) of Thai villagers and co-workers.

155

CHAPTER 4   MUTUALLY-DERIVABLE MATERIALS (THAI)

The project also depended heavily on Miss Surapha Rojanavipart, Keenan Eiting, and the language instructional staff for Thailand 33; on technical suggestions from other knowledgable CCCTR professional staff; and on the typing and reproduction facilities of CCCTR.

The principal textbook for the first part of the course was to be Marvin Brown's A.U.A. Language Center Thai Course, but two other sets of materials that had been developed in previous Thai programs were available to supplement it. In particular, this meant that:

1. Much non-technical (and very little technical) vocabulary was already presented in the existing materials.

2. Many but by no means all grammatical points were explained and drilled in the existing materials.

3. There would be a definite advantage in following Brown's format as closely as possible. In his books, each lesson consists of ten numbered parts:

   (1) Vocabulary and expansions.

   (2) [New] patterns.

   (3) Dialog.

   (4) Tone identification and production.

   (5) Tone manipulation.

   (6) Drills on vowels and consonants.

   (7) Grammar.

   (8) Numbers.

   (9) Conversation.

   (10) Writing.

THE PROCEDURE

The team spent the period November 10-13 in tooling up for the project. As a by-product of this activity they produced one complete lesson in malaria control and a parallel lesson in leprosy control. The sequence of the work is set forth below.

1. The team first drew up a list of question-types which they thought would enable the student to elicit the content vocabulary of a specialized field.

2. Within the general areas of 'malaria control' and 'leprosy control,' the team then listed several component activities in which Volunteers would spend much of their time. For the tooling-up period, they then selected one of these sub-specialties for malaria, and one for leprosy. The centers of interest that they selected were 'Spraying' and 'Examining Patients for Leprosy.'

3. The list of question-types was adapted for each sub-specialty. The results for 'Spraying' and 'Leprosy Examinations' are reproduced on pp. 161-164.

4. Hirth and Brinkman provided in English multiple answers to each question in the indices, based on their own experience of the needs of health Volunteers in Thailand. Their answers were then edited and translated into Thai. Parallel samples are found on pages 165-170. (Throughout the project, Thai and English were placed on consecutive pages. Because few of the readers of this account can be expected to read Thai, and in order to conserve space and the reader's time, most of the samples will be given in English only.)

5. For each sub-specialty, Professor Sutira wrote a number of· exchange sequences. Each consisted of three of the questions from the index, with one answer for each question.

6. She then placed the exchange sequences in order relative to one another and began to develop a lesson around each. The format was that of 'clusters' (Chapter 4, p. 150), in which each drill, exchange sequence, Cummings device, etc. was placed on a separate sheet of paper and punched for looseleaf binding. The order of components which most closely paralleled that of the A.U.A. Course (p. 156, above) was the following:

(0) Statement of 'objectives' for using Thai. On the same sheet were references to the question series, and to grammatical exposition in other textbooks. (This item is numbered 'O' because it precedes the items that correspond to numbered sections in the A.U.A. Course.) Examples are found on pp. 171-172.

(1) New vocabulary from the pages in the question series (see Step 3, above).

(2) Pattern drills for structures not covered in basic lessons. In the lessons from which these illustrations are being taken, the pattern that corresponds to English 'use something for some purpose' was in that category. It was treated as shown on pp. 173-177.

(3) The exchange sequence. The ones used in the two lessons on which we are concentrating our attention are found on pp. 179-180. A longer and more realistic one from a lesson on malaria surveillance, is found on p. 181.

158

(4)   Extra drills on the new structures introduced in
       (2), and also 'routine manipulations' (Chapter 8)
       on persistent grammatical problems covered in the
       basic lessons, but emphasizing vocabulary from the
       lesson. An example from the first malaria lesson
       is on p. 182. The parallel example from leprosy
       is obvious and will not be reproduced here.

(5)   Materials to be prepared outside of class. Some,
       but not all of these items contained new, genuine
       information. See pp. 183-184.

(6)   'Applications:' Suggestions for using Thai in class
       or outside, in ways that will be rewarding either
       esthetically (humor, competition, etc.), or in
       demonstrating attainment of objectives (0, above),
       or preferably both. See pages 185f for the
       examples from the first lessons on malaria and
       leprosy, and pp. 187-188 for corresponding pages
       from other lessons.

After the tooling-up period, work proceeded rapidly. Other
subtopics were covered within malaria and leprosy control, and a
new series of lessons were written for laboratory technologists.
Parallelism among the series was even closer than had been expected. Reception of the new materials in the training program
itself was encouraging.

SUMMARY

Quod erat demonstrandum. The team did in fact succeed in
writing materials with replaceable parts on a number of different
scales. The materials are in this sense highly 'modular'. They
seem, in fact, to have achieved that degree of modularity which

CHAPTER 4   MUTUALLY-DERIVABLE MATERIALS (THAI)

will permit <u>mutual derivability</u>: any one of the set of parallel units provides a basis for reconstructing any of the others, <u>or for constructing new units on topics yet to be selected</u>. This quality is obviously of great economic importance in training international Volunteers, or commercial, industrial and diplomatic personnel, where each trainee has some clearly defined technical specialty that he must be able to discuss in his new language. Possibly of equal interest, however, are the applications of mutual derivability in enhancing the strength, or socio-topical relevance of teaching in schools and colleges.

The question remains, however, whether this set of materials is merely a mildly interesting tour de force, with no wider significance. Could the same series of basic questions be applied to Thai cooking, or Thai boxing, or malaria control in Lingala, or French cuisine in French? Can the same 'cluster' format that seems to have worked in this program be applied to teaching by Quechua speakers in the Andes? Or to teaching of English by Thais in Thailand?

The answers are not apparent. The general approach of Chapter 4 is only general, and this specific case study describes only one ad hoc solution. Together, however, we hope that they represent a potentially fruitful trend in finding other ad hoc solutions to other problems. Writers of language lessons can do no more than that.

Malaria: Question Index: (Spraying)

Pages

(M1-2):   A. What is this?

(M3-4):   B. What is his work? (OR Who is he?)

(M5-6):   C. What does the sprayman use?

(M7-8):   D. Where is (thing) kept?

(M9-10):   E. What is (thing) used for?

(M11-12): F. What is wrong with (thing)?

(M13-14): G. Which spray can do you use?

(M15-16): H. What are the parts of a spraycan?

(M17-18): I. What is (thing)? (It's a kind of category or
                                          larger unit)

(M19-20): J. Whose (thing) is this?

(M21-22): K. What kind of furniture is that?

(M23-24): L. Where does he work?
               Where does he go to spray?

(M25-26): M. What all is in the house?
               (From point of view of spraying crew)

(M27-28): N. What does (person) do?

(M29-30): O. What does the squad chief have to do with the
                                          sprayman?

(M31-32): P. How much.....? (Answer with certain number.)

(M33-34): Q. How to make judgments (Criteria).

(M35-36): R. When does one do something (Verb)? (Cues)

(M37-38): S. Why does one have to do so (Verb)?

CHAPTER 4   MUTUALLY DERIVABLE MATERIALS (THAI)

(M39-40): T. How does one do something (Verb)? (Steps of doing)

(M41-42): U. What are the parts of a house?

(M43-44): V. Who are working at the zone office? (Spraying section) (OR what kind of people are at the zone
office)

(M45-46): W. Where is (place) or (person)?

(M47-48): X. Which one is (person)?

(M49-50): Y. What must one pay attention to when he is going to
spray?

Leprosy: Question Index: (Examination)

Pages

(L1-2): A. What is this?

(L3-4): B. What is his work?   (OR: Who is he?)

(L5-6): C. What does the leprosy worker use?

(L7-8): D. Where is (thing) kept?

(L9-10): E. What is (thing) used for?

(L11-12):F. What is wrong with (thing)?

(L13-14):G. Which one (thing) do you use?

(L15-16):H. What equipment and supplies are there in the UNICEF
                                                    bag?

(L17-18):I. What is (thing)? (It's a kind of category or larger
                                                    unit)

(L19-20):J. Whose (thing) is this?

(L21-22):K. What kinds of medicine does the leprosy worker have?
             What are the doses of DDS?
             What are the names of some skin diseases?
             What are the other names of leprosy?

(L23-24):L. Where does he work?

(L25-26):M. What is in an examination room?

(L27-28):N. What does the leprosy worker do?

(L29-30):O. What does the leprosy worker have to do with the
                                                    patient?

(L31-32):P. What does (person) have to do with (person)?

(L33-34):Q. How much.....? (Answer with certain number)

(L35-36):R. How to make judgments. (Criteria)

(L37-38):S. When does one do something (Verb)? (cues)

(L39-40):T. Why does one have to do so (Verb)?

(L41-42):U. How does one do something (Verb)? (Steps of doing)

(L43-44):V. What are the parts of the body?

CHAPTER 4   MUTUALLY-DERIVABLE MATERIALS (THAI)

(L45-46):W.   Who all are working at the sector office and
              Leprosy Control Division? (OR: What kind of people
              are at the sector office and Leprosy Control Divi-
              sion?)

(L47-48):X.   Where is (<u>place</u>) or (<u>person</u>)?

(L49-50):Y.   Which one is (<u>person</u>)?

(L51-52):Z.   What must one pay attention to when he is <u>working</u>?

(A)

malaaria: (kaan phôn DDT)

nîi ꞏaray

nîi   khrꞋanphôn

phŏŋ DDT

thăŋ

kapŏɔŋ

bàt pracam bâan

prɛɛŋ

sîi

khăykhuaŋ

khiim

kuncɛɛ lâan

kruay

phꞋenthîi

khrꞋaŋchâŋ

fέɛm

bὲep fɔɔm

M:1

165

CHAPTER 4   MUTUALLY-DERIVABLE MATERIALS (THAI)

Malaria (Spraying)   (A)

    What is this?

        This is a spray can.

                DDT powder

                mixing pail

                house card

                brush

                paint

                screwdriver

                pliers

                wrench

                funnel

                map

                scale

                folder

                forms

                        M:2

                        # # #

Malaria (Spraying)   (E)

What is a spray can used for?

        It is used for spraying DDT.

        mixing pail   mixing DDT
                                       keeping water
                                       carrying water

        DDT   killing mosquitoes

        water   mixing DDT
                                       washing the spray can

        scale   weighing DDT

        maps   finding the village
                                       finding the house

        funnel   pouring DDT into the
                                           spray can

        paint   writing on the house
                                           after spraying

        screwdriver   tightening the
                                           screws
                                       stirring DDT

                    M:10

                    # # #

CHAPTER 4   MUTUALLY-DERIVABLE MATERIALS (THAI)

(A)

rôokrúan: (kaan trùat ráksăa)

nîi ɂaray

        nîi mîitkoon
        pàakkhîip
        sămlii
        ɂɛɛlkoohɔɔ
        (kracòk)saláy
        phɛ̀ɛn saláy
        kracòk
        phâa kɔ́ɔs
        phâa yaaŋ pìt phlɛ̆ɛ
        pláatsatêe
        khɛ̆m mùt
        takiaŋ
        bɛ̀ɛp fɔɔm
        fɛ́ɛm
        yaa khîiphûŋ
        (yaa) DDS
        yaa bamruŋ lûat
        (yaa) wítaamin
        kapăw yuu ni séep
        kapăw yaa
        kapăw mɔ̆ɔ

            L:1

            168

Leprosy: (Examination)   (A)

What is this?

        This is a razor blade.

              forceps

              cotton

              alcohol

          a slide

          a cover slip

              gauze

              adhesive tape

              plaster (adhesive tape)

          a pin

          a lamp

          a form

          a folder

              salve

              DDS

              iron complex

              vitamins

              UNICEF bag

              UNICEF bag, or medical kit

              medical kit

                  L:2

                # # #

CHAPTER 4   MUTUALLY-DERIVABLE MATERIALS (THAI)

Leprosy (Examination)   (E)

What is a razor blade used for?

                    It is used for slitting the skin.

                              scraping the skin

    alcohol and cotton   sterilizing the razor blade

                              sterilizing the skin

                              wiping the blood

                              cleaning the wound

                              testing for anesthesia

                              flaming the slide

    gauze   covering the wound

    pin   checking for anesthesia

    DDS   treating leprosy

    cover slip   covering the smear on the slide

    Vitamin B   helping the nervous system

                         L:10

                         # # #

MALARIA

TECH LESSON 1

(Spraying)

I. Objectives:

> To identify items used in spraying
> To tell what each item is used for
> To tell to whom each item belongs

II. Basic Functional Questions: A (Pages 1-2)
                                     E (Pages 9-10)
                                     J (Pages 19-20)

III. Grammatical references to materials used earlier in the course.

> Basic Lessons 4, Pages   9-10
> "   10, "   30-31
> "   12, "   37
> "   20, "   72
> "   21, "   81
>
> Microwave Cycle XII
> "   XV
>
> AUA Book I, Lesson 8, Page 83
> "   13, " 137-145

ML:1

# # #

CHAPTER 4   MUTUALLY-DERIVABLE MATERIALS (THAI)

LEPROSY

TECH LESSON 1

(Examination)

I. Objectives:

To identify items used in examination.
To tell what each item is used for
To tell to whom each item belongs

II. Basic Functional Questions: A (Pages 1-2)
                                    E (Pages 9-10)
                                    J (Pages 19-20)

III. Grammatical references to materials used earlier in the course.

Basic Lessons 4, Pages 9-10
       "   10,   "   30-31
       "   12,   "   37
       "   20,   "   72
       "   21,   "   81

Microwave Cycle XII
       "   XV

AUA Book I, Lesson 8, Page 83
             "   13, "   137-145

LL:1

# # #

172

Pattern Drill: (AEJ)

(a) Listen to the whole drill. Try to get the meaning by watching
    your instructor. If you don't get it by the third time, the
    instructor will tell you the meaning in English.

(b) Repeat in unison after the instructor one sentence at a time.
    Then repeat individually.

(c) Try to give the entire sentence when the instructor gives you a
    cue word, phrase, or gesture.

(d) Give one or more sentences that you remember, with no cue from
    the instructor.

cháy sǎmràp tham ʔaray

cháy sǎmràp phasǒm DDT

cháy sǎmràp khon DDT

cháy sǎmràp phôn DDT

What do we use that for?

We use that for mixing DDT.

We use that for stirring DDT.

We use that for spraying DDT.

ML:3

173

<u>Drills</u> on "cháy ..X.. sămràp ..Y.."

(a) Repeat if necessary.
(b) Make substitutions from cues.
(c) Answer the questions.
(d) Make substitutions AND answer the questions.
(e) Students do both questions and answers with no cues.

I. cháy preeŋ   sămràp khâa yuŋ máy

        bàtpracambâan

        khăykhuaŋ

        sĭi

        khiim

        kuncɛɛ lûan

        dii dii thii

II. cháy preeŋ sămràp khâa yuŋ   máy

                khăn tapuu khuaŋ

                phasŏm DDT

                phŏn DDT

                khon DDT

                thaa sĭi

III. cháy preeŋ   sămràp khâa yuŋ   máy

        kuncɛɛ lûan

                    khon DDT

        khăykhuaŋ

                    laleeŋ sĭi

        khrûaŋphŏn

                    phasŏm DDT

IV. cháy preeŋ sămràp khâa yuŋ rɛ́ thaa sĭi

     cháy khăykhuaŋ sămràp khăn tapuukhuaŋ rɛ́ khon DDT

     cháy thăŋ sămràp chăŋ DDT rɛ́ phasŏm DDT

174

Drills on "Use__x__for__y__"   (AEJ)

(a) Repeat if necessary.
(b) Make substitutions from cues.
(c) Answer the questions.
(d) Make substitutions AND answer the questions.
(e) Students do both questions and answers with no cues.

I.   Do you use a brush   for killing mosquitoes?

              housecard

              screwdriver

              paint

              pliers

              wrench

              DDT

II. Do you use a brush for killing mosquitoes?

                    tightening screws

                    mixing DDT

                    spraying DDT

                    stirring DDT

                    painting

III. Do you use a brush   for killing mosquitoes?

              wrench   stirring DDT

              screwdriver   spreading paint

              spraycan   mixing DDT

IV. Do you use a brush for killing mosquitoes, or for painting?

     Do you use a screwdriver for tightening screws, or for stirring DDT?

     Do you use a pail for weighing DDT, or for mixing it?

ML:5

# # #

Pattern Drill: (from Leprosy series)   (AEJ)

(a) Listen to the whole drill. Try to get the meaning by watching
     your instructor. If you don't get it by the third time, the
     instructor will tell you the meaning in English.

(b) Repeat in unison after the instructor one sentence at a time.
     Then repeat individually.

(c) Try to give the entire sentence when the instructor gives you a
     cue word, phrase, or gesture.

(d) Give one or more sentences that you remember, with no cue from
     the instructor.

          cháy sămràp tham ʔaray

          cháy sămràp krìit phǐwnǎŋ

          cháy sămràp khùut phǐwnǎŋ

          cháy sămràp chét phǐwnǎŋ

What do we use that for?

We use that for slitting the skin.

We use that for scraping the skin.

We use that for sterilizing the skin.

               LL:3

              # # #

<u>Drills</u> on "cháy ..X.. sămràp ..Y.."

   (a) Repeat if necessary.
   (b) Make substitutions from cues.
   (c) Answer the questions.
   (d) Make substitutions <u>AND</u> answer the questions.
   (e) Students do both questions and answers with no cues.

I. cháy mĭitkoon   sămràp chét phĭwnăŋ máy

      paakkhĭip

      kracòk saláy

      khĕmmùt

      (yaa) DDS

      sămlii

      ʔɛɛlkɔɔhɔɔ

II. cháy mĭitkoon sămràp chét phĭwnăŋ   máy

          chét phlĕɛ

          pìt phlĕɛ

          thótsɔɔp khwaamrúusàk

          ráksăa rôokrɤan

          khùut phĭwnăŋ

          krìit phĭwnăŋ

III. cháy mĭitkoon   sămràp chét phĭwnăŋ   máy

      khĕmmùt

               krìit phĭwnăŋ

      sămlii

               ráksăa rôokrɤan

      paakkhĭip

               thótsɔɔp khwaamrúusàk

IV. cháy mĭitkoon sămràp chét phĭwnăŋ rɤ́ krìit phĭwnăŋ

    cháy sămlii sămràp chét mĭitkoon rɤ́ khùut phĭwnăŋ

    cháy (yaa) DDS sămràp thótsɔɔp khwaamrúusàk rɤ́ ráksăa
                                   rôokrɤan

CHAPTER 4   MUTUALLY-DERIVABLE MATERIALS (THAI)

Drills on "...use ,X.. for ..Y."   (ACFG)

    (a) Repeat if necessary.
    (b) Make substitutions from cues.
    (c) Answer the questions.
    (d) Make substitutions AND answer the questions.
    (e) Students do both questions and answers with no cues.

I. Do you use a razor blade for sterilizing the skin?

               forceps

               slide

               pin

               DDS

               cotton

               alcohol

II. Do you use a razor blade for sterilizing the skin?

                         cleaning the wound?

                         covering the wound?

                         testing for anesthesia?

                         treating leprosy?

                         scraping the skin?

                         slitting the skin?

III. Do you use a razor blade for sterilizing the skin?

      pin   slitting the skin

      cotton   treating leprosy

      forceps   testing for anesthesia

IV. Do you use a razor blade for sterilizing the skin, or for slitting the skin?

Do you use the cotton for cleaning the razor blade, or for scraping the skin?

Do you use DDS for testing for anesthesia, or for treating leprosy?

LL:5

# # #

178

malaaria: (kaanphôn DDT)

bòtsõnthanaa thiam I   (AEJ)

A: nîi ʔaray kh.

  B: thăŋ kh.

A: cháy thăŋ sămràp tham ʔaray kh.

  B: cháy thăŋ (sămràp) phasõm DDT kh.

A: thăŋ bay nîi khõŋ khray kh.

  B: khõŋ khun suphát kh.

Malaria   (Spraying)

Pseudo-dialog I   (AEJ)

A.   What is this?

  B: It's a pail.

A: What do you use it for?

  B: For mixing DDT.

A: Whose pail is this?

  B: It's Khun Suphat's pail.

ML:2

# # #

rôokrâan: (kaantrùat ráksăa)

bòtsŏnthanaa thiam I   (AEJ)

A: nîi ʔaray kh.

    B: mîitkoon kh.

A: cháy mîitkoon sămràp tham ʔaray kh.

    B: cháy mîitkoon (sămràp) krìit phĭwnăŋ kh.

A: mîitkoon ʔan nîi khɔ̆ŋ khray kh.

    B: khɔ̆ŋ khun chaan kh.

Leprosy (Examination)

Exchange Sequence I   (AEJ)

A: What is this?

    B: It's a razor blade.

A: What do you use it for?

    B: For slitting the skin.

A: Whose razor blade is this? (Whose is this razor blade?)

    B: It's Khun Chaan's razor blade.

LL:2

# # #

(BbZc)

<u>Malaria</u>: (Surveillance)

<u>Dialog 4</u>:
    P -- Peace Corps Volunteer
    V -- Villager
    S -- Sick person

P: Hello. I'm a house visitor. I came from the Malaria
    Eradication Center.

    Is there anyone sick with fever in this house?

    V: Yes, there is. He is in the room. Please go in.

P: How do you feel?

    S: I have a terrible headache, and am also very cold.

P: Does he have a fever every day?

    S: No, he does not. He is feverish every other day.

P: May I take your blood sample?

    S: O.K. Where will you prick?

P: Any finger (is all right). It won't hurt.

ML:61

CHAPTER 4   MUTUALLY-DERIVABLE MATERIALS (THAI)

(c) Making negative by using "mây chây + N".
     [See Basic Lesson 10]

1. This spray can is the squad chief's.

2. This pliers is the assistant zone chief's.

3. This scale is the sector chief's.

4. This screwdriver is the sprayman's.

5. This folder is the zone chief's.

6. This form is Khun Suphat's.

7. This brush is the mop-up sprayman's.

8. This pail is the doctor's.

9. This funnel is the chief's.

10. This DDT is Khun Prasong's.

ML:10

# # #

Out-of-Class Research   (Spraying: AEJ)

I.   This is a stick. It is used for stirring DDT. It is Khun
     Suphat's stick.

     Questions: [Questions are not necessarily in the same order
                  as the facts.]

     1.   What is this?
     2.   Whose is it?
     3.   What is it used for?

II. This is a pencil. It is used for filling out the form. It is not
     Khun Suphat's pencil.

     Questions:

     1.   What is this?
     2.   Whose is it?
     3.   What is it used for?

                         ML:16

                        # # #

CHAPTER 4   MUTUALLY-DERIVABLE MATERIALS (THAI)

Out-of-Class Research   (Examination)   (AEJ)

I.   These are <u>scissors</u>.   They are used for cutting the gauze.

     They are Khun Chaan's <u>scissors</u>.

     <u>Questions</u>:   (Questions are not necessarily in the same order
                     as the facts.)

     1. What is it?

     2. Whose is it?

     3. What is it used for?

II. This is a pencil.   It is used for <u>filling out</u> the form.

     It is not Khun Chaan's pencil.

     <u>Questions</u>:

     1. What is it?

     2. Whose is it?

     3. What is it used for?

LL:16

# # #

Applications of the Lesson   (Spraying: AEJ)

1. See who can name all the spraying gear in good Thai in the shortest time.

2. One person points to an object. The other person tells all he knows about it. He should bring in materials that he remembers from the Basic Lessons and AUA Book. (One-minute limit.)

3. Trade instructors for the last 5-10 minutes of class, and let the students try to impress the visiting instructor.

4. Outside of class, learn the name of one object and what it is used for.

5. Each student is given a different word to find the meaning of.

ML:84

# # #

CHAPTER 4   MUTUALLY-DERIVABLE MATERIALS (THAI)

<u>Applications of the Lesson:</u>   (kaantrùat ráksăa)   (AEJ)

1. See who can name all the examination gear in good Thai in
    the shortest time.

2. One person points to one object. The other person tells all he
    knows about it. He should bring in materials that he remembers
    from the Basic Lessons, AUA Book.   (One-minute limit)

3. Trade instructors for the last 5-10 minutes of class, and let the
    students try to impress the visiting instructor.

4. Outside of class, learn the name of one object and what it is
    used for.

5. Each student is given a different word to find out the meaning of.

ML:17

# # #

(cUf)

Application of the Lesson:

1. (From Out-of-Class Research No. I) Identify the different
    parts of various objects such as bottles, cans, boxes, etc.

2. (From Out-of-Class Research No. II) Describe a situation
    in which you would feel:
    (a) cayklâa
    (b) khêɛŋcay
    (c) caykhêɛŋ
    (d) fǔuncay
    (e) camcay

3. See who can tell all that he has to pay attention to when:
    (a) he releases blodd from the blood bank.
    (b) he performs the CSF test.
    (c) he performs a fecal examination.
    (d) he performs a urinalysis.

4. Let each student describe some activities from his daily
    work in which there could easily be a mix-up. Then he
    should suggest ways of avoiding them.

5. Have one person name as many abbreviations as he can that
    are used in the lab report, and have the other students
    explain each abbreviation in Thai.

MTL:116

Application of the Lesson: (BbZc)

1. (From Out-of-Class Research No. II) Identify the different parts
   of various objects such as bottles, cans, boxes, etc.

2. In <u>one-minute limit</u>, each student tells the symptoms of malaria
   fever.

3. Each student is given the titles of people who work in the M.E.
   project or Malaria Zone Office and asked to describe their jobs.

4. Have each person pantomine some action from his daily work, and
   have other class members guess what he is doing and the time of
   day that it is usually done. They must then give the reasons why
   they guessed as they did.

5. Have each person take a turn to be a house owner or surveillance
   worker. On a house-visiting trip, the surveillance worker interviews
   the house-owner. (<u>Three-minute limit</u>)

6. Have each person take a turn to be a patient or a surveillance
   worker having a conversation during the house visit. (<u>Three-minute limit</u>)

ML:84

# # #

APPENDIX H TO CHAPTER 4

MUTUAL COMPLEMENTATION OF ENGLISH AND
SWAHILI MATERIALS IN TRAINING FOR EAST AFRICA

I.   THE PROBLEM

In January, 1971, the East African training staff of the
Foreign Service Institute undertook a project the purpose of
which was to answer the question 'Can a team of language
materials developers be responsive to "specification" in the
form of a scholarly article, provided by an area studies
specialist who has no connection with the linguistic dimension
of training?' In particular, could the response of the language specialists be rapid enough to be economic, and interesting enough to be worthwhile? Favorable answers to this
question would in turn point ways to closer integration of
the two principal aspects of the training given to Foreign
Service Officers bound for East Africa.

II. THE PROCEDURE

The article used for demonstration purposes was R. G.
Hollister 'Manpower problems and policies in Sub-Saharan
Africa.' (International Labour Review, 1969, pp. 515-32).
Miss Ann Reid, African area training specialist at the
Foreign Service Institute, suggested it as typical of the
articles that she asks her students to become familiar with.
The response of the language team was in three phases: (1)
to begin collecting materials in Swahili which relate to the
content of the article; (2) to show how these materials can
become the basis for language study; (3) to list questions

189

arising out of these materials which might be answered by
further English-language resources to be provided by the
area specialist. The objective, then, was not merely to
catch the ball, or merely to catch it and run with it, but
to catch it, run with it, and return it.

Phase 1: Swahili counterpart materials.

Swahili-language materials to support the English-
language article were drawn principally from East African
newspapers, for four reasons:

1. They are authentic, in the sense that they
were written by East Africans for East Africans.

2. They are inexpensive, and dependably available
to classes of trainees for East Africa at the
Foreign Service Institute.

3. They cover a wide, though not unlimited, range
of topics.

4. There is a variety of style: news stories,
advertisements, letters to the editor, cartoons,
even occasional fiction. (There is not in Swahili,
as there is in some languages, a drastic difference
in vocabulary or syntax between spoken and published
styles. If there were, the items might have had to
be recast into colloquial style before being used.)

By only scratching the surface of the available newspaper files, the language team quickly assembled 60 items
on manpower, ranging in length from 50 to 500 words. About half
of these related directly to the major points of the Hollister
article; most of the rest had to do with the structure and
operation of East African labor unions.

The English-language article and the Swahili-language
newspaper items complement one another in four respects:

1. An article in a scholarly journal gives a broad
and comprehensive view; a newspaper item is a glimpse
of a fragment.

2. An article is the result of organizing data and
abstracting from them; a newspaper item is, in a
sense, itself a datum.

3. An article may be higher in intelligibility
than a single news item, but the news item is
often higher in immediacy and interest.

4. Examples given by the author of an article
can be expected to illustrate his thesis, and
are therefore suspect of being self-serving.
A newspaper story that agrees (or disagrees) with
the article is in effect a second, unprejudiced
witness.

Some of the principal points of the original article,
paired with their corresponding newspaper items, are the
following:

1. 'There remains the problem of developing adequate
indigenous sources to fulfill the natural desire
to Africanise the skilled labour force.'

TECHNICAL SKILLS ARE IMPORTANT FOR PROGRESS OF
TANZANIA

[The above headline is quoted from a speech by
a Junior Minister delivered at the opening of
a course to prepare 139 members of the national
youth service corps (Jeshi la Kujenga Taifa) to
take tests in trades. After 12 months of technical
training, they will serve an additional 12 months
in factories. The trades include mechanics,
welding, plumbing, electricity, and construction.

The special goal of this experiment is to
establish standards of competence which will be
useful to employers and workers alike. Anyone
who does not meet these standards will be denied
a certificate. The government now recognizes
three levels of examinations. A total of 925
craftsmen have been tested in Dar es Salaam in
the last six months. Formerly, tests were given
only in Dar, but this worked to the disadvantage
of those who could not afford the trip to Dar,
and so temporary examining stations were set up
at six inland sites.]

UHURU, 11 July 70

KENYANS SHOULD RECEIVE RESPONSIBLE POSITIONS
IN HOTELS.

[Mr. J. M. Kariuki, Junior Minister of Tourism
and Wild Life, reproached the executive committee
of the East African Hotel Keepers Association in
Nairobi. He charged that they were unwilling to
train Africans, and that they had replaced African
degree-holders with Europeans. Anyone caught doing
so will lose his license. He hopes that efforts to
correct this situation are sincere.

Tourism should attract not only Europeans,
but people from all over Africa as well.

Hotel employees should be given good clothing
and living quarters.

The president of the association replied that
not all hotels are guilty of discrimination against
African employees. He also said that when Africans
have time off from their jobs, they prefer farming
to travelling.

There was discussion of the practice of
ordering some items from abroad. Mr. Kariuki
said that the practice must stop.]

TAIFA LEO, 5 March 70

[A representative of the Tanzanian Labor Office said
that it is important to allow entrepreneurs to run
their businesses without interference, and that many
employers had already initiated plans to train Africans
for responsible posts, and had hired Africans at lower,
middle and higher levels. The government is grateful
for this, and intends to help the employers by making
available a larger pool of skilled labor, both Tanzanian
and foreign.]

BARAZA, 11 August 66

DISCRIMINATION

[A full-length editorial describing and condemning
wage differentials between Asian and African employees
who do the same work. A six-man commission is looking
into this problem.]

UHURU, 15 August 70

2.   'The development of a modern sector has generally
       been accompanied by an increasing drift of the
       population from rural areas to urban centres.'

'ZAMBIANS SHOULD NOT RUN OFF TO THE CITIES.'

[The annual report of the Bank of Zambia states that
the practice of moving from rural areas to urban
centres in search of work is endangering the progress
of Zambia. This hurts agriculture, on which the country
depends. If the government does not take steps, this
danger will soon become critical.]

UHURU, 9 July 70

RETURNED TO THEIR HOMES

[Thirty unemployed young men were rounded up in Mwanza
and returned to their homes. They had been loitering
around, and were reported to have robbed people in the
area, including bus passengers.]

UHURU, 1 September 70

CHAPTER 4 MUTUALLY COMPLEMENTARY MATERIALS (SWAHILI)

ROUNDUP OF UNEMPLOYED TO BEGIN ON MONDAY

[An announcement by the head of Dar es Salaam region in remarks addressed to 195 people who were leaving to begin agricultural work in a bush area. These were some of 600 people who had enrolled for this work because they were unable to find work in the city.

Some of the people who will be rounded up have no land or parents, and it is for this reason that the government has prepared the new settlement at Mkata.]

UHURU 30 March 68

Phase 2: Use of newspaper materials for language acquisition.

A number of ways to develop language skills based on short newspaper stories had already been illustrated in the Foreign Service Institute's unpublished Active Introduction to Newspaper Swahili (Appendix T, pp. 387-390). These included such ordinary devices as sentence translation, blank filling (to focus attention on various classes of features), substitution and transformation drills, and instructions to use certain words in sentences. The same devices could obviously have been applied to the items that had been collected for this project, but to have done so would have only partly met the objective of Phase 2. It remains to be demonstrated:

(1) that these materials can lend themselves to dealing with day-to-day needs that arise in the linguistic dimension, particularly with regard to structural problems.

194

(2) that they are a suitable basis for further
     exploration of the lexicon.

(3) that their linguistic content can be used in
     ways that appeal to the student's interests
     other than his interest in language mastery
     per se.

(4) that keeping materials of this kind up to
     date does not require a prohibitive amount
     of time.

The team attempted to demonstrate these four proposi-
tions in relation to one rather routine item which reported
the results of a local union election:

> The Eldoret Branch of the Transport and Allied
> Workers Union has elected its officers. The
> following were elected: Mr. _____; assistant
> chairman, Mr. _____; secretary, Mr. _____;
> assistant secretary, Mr. _____; treasurer,
> Mr. _____; assistant treasurer, Mr. _____.

It seems clear that if favorable results could be obtained
with this item, then longer and more interesting stories, or
groups of stories, would _a fortiori_ pass the tests.

As a test of adaptability to unforeseen structural drills,
the team first made two inventories of the news item:

<u>Inventory of nouns</u>:

chama (KI-VI class)	association, union, party
tawi (LI-MA class)	branch
afisa (MA personal class)	officer

bwana (MA personal class)	gentleman
katibu (" " ")	secretary
makamu (" " ")	assistant, vice-
mwenye kiti (MU-WA class)	chairman
mtunza hazina (" ' ")	treasurer

Inventory of simple sentences:

Chama hiki kina matawi mengi.	This union has many branches.
Tawi hili limewachagua maafisa wapya.	This branch has elected new officers.
Wafuatao walichaguliwa.	The following were elected.
Bw. _____ alichaguliwa kuwa mwenyekiti.	Mr. _____ was chosen to be chairman.

Next, the team selected at random three units from Swahili Basic Course (Units 32, 60, 75), noted the structure drills in each, and tried to write new drills on the same points as the existing ones. Content was drawn either from the two inventories, or from other closely-related vocabulary that the students could be counted on to know. This proved to be possible for all drills except those on very minor and specialized points.

Two examples will suffice. The first, from Unit 32, is a completely ordinary substitution-correlation drill involving concords with the adjective stem -zuri 'good':

muhogo	Mkulima huyu apanda muhogo mzuri sana. (or: ...anapanda...)	This farmer plants very good cassava.

196

mimea	Mkulima huyu apanda mimea mizuri sana.	This farmer plants very good plants.
mpunga	Mkulima huyu apanda mpunga mzuri sana.	This farmer plants very good rice.
vitunguu	Mkulima huyu apanda vitunguu vizuri sana.	This farmer plants very good onions.

The adapted drill is as follows:

chama	Chama hiki ni kizuri.	This union is good.
vyama	Vyama hivi ni vizuri.	These unions are good.
tawi	Tawi hili ni zuri.	This branch is good.
matawi	Matawi haya ni mazuri.	These branches are good.
mwenyekiti	Mwenyekiti huyu ni mzuri.	This chairman is good.
wenyeviti	Wenyeviti hawa ni wazuri.	These chairmen are good.
afisa	Afisa huyu ni mzuri.	This officer is good.
maafisa	Maafisa hawa ni wazuri.	These officers are good.

The second example, from Unit 75, requires the student to respond to an affirmative question with a negative answer. (Formation of negatives is one of the most troublesome habits for beginning Swahili students to get into.) The original drill consists of pairs of sentences:

kupalilia	Umepalilia mahindi yako?	Have you weeded your maize?
	Bado sijapalilia.	Not yet, I haven't.

197

kupanda	Umepanda muhogo wako?	Have you planted your cassava?
	Bado sijapanda.	Not yet, I haven't.
kupeleka	Umepeleka kalamu yako kwa fundi?	Have you taken your pen to the repair-man?
	Bado sijapeleka.	Not yet, I haven't.

The replacement begins:

Mwenyekiti amechaguliwa?	Has the chairman been elected?
Bado hajachaguliwa.	He hasn't been elected yet.

The team concluded that, while the new drills are not particularly brilliant, they at least are no less so than the originals were. There appears, then, to be no reason at this point why the newspaper items should not be suitable for dealing with a random series of structure points.

Further exploration of Swahili vocabulary may be carried out using such questions as:

Viongozi wa chama ni nani?	Who are the officers of the organization?

This question will elicit answers like the words for president, committee member, public relations man.

(Mwenyekiti) hufanya nini?	What does the (chairman) do?

Answers to this question will enable the student to talk about the principal duties of the various officers.

Inafaa kuchagua mtu gani   what kind of person
  kuwa (mwenyekiti)?   should be chosen
                                     to be (chairman)?

Answers to this question will elicit words and phrases of a
generally 'adjectival' nature.

This news item thus fulfills the second desideratum
(p. 195) by serving as a suitable basis for lexical exploration.

The content of these materials may be related to the
student's extralinguistic interests in at least three areas:

(1) A Foreign Service Officer is concerned to show
     common courtesy to all people with whom he deals.
     One aspect of courtesy is getting people's names
     right. The following exercises provide experience
     in remembering and handling names:

     (a) Students quiz one another on what position
          is occupied by each person mentioned in the
          article, competing to see who can be first
          to get all six pieces of information right.

     (b) As above, except that the students give
          personal names to match position titles.

     (c) Simulated social function. Students practice
          introducing themselves, or one another,
          mentioning both name and position. The
          instructor should of course pay attention
          to linguistic correctness, but should also
          coach them in non-linguistic matters such
          as when, how, and how long to shake hands.

(2) Foreign Service Officers need to be alert to more
than the superficial information contained in what
they read and hear. A surname is a partial guide to
the ethnic background of its bearer.

    (d) Find out from the instructor what might be
the ethnic origin of each of the six elected
officers.

    (e) Discuss such questions as: Are the officers
from a single ethnic group, or do they represent a cross-section of Kenya? How do
the origins of the officers correspond to
the geographical location of their branch
of the union?

(3) A Foreign Service Officer is often called on to
deal tactfully with a wide variety of questions,
where he is in fact, though perhaps not officially,
representing his country.

    (f) Students and instructor pose to one another
questions that they think can be answered
briefly with the Swahili at their disposal.
For example, one of the team members was
asked by a Nairobi taxi driver, 'What do
Americans think of Tom Mboya?'

Since the new materials were not in actual classroom
use, there was no direct way of demonstrating how much time
would be required in order to update the file. There are
however reasons to believe that this time would be very
short if we can assume that the teacher is reasonably adept
at improvising routine manipulative drill if he is given

the principle of the drill (e.g. present affirmative changed
to present negative, or singular changed to plural) and a
set of content words and sentences. (For more on this
process, see Appendix U, p. 403ff.) All that remains is to
find the article, cut it out, mount it, place it in a looseleaf binder, decide what lexical areas to explore, and devise
ways of relating its content to the extralinguistic interests
of the student. All of these steps except the last are highly
mechanical.

It appears, therefore, that the four questions of Phase 2
(p. 194f) can all be answered favorably with respect to the very
pedestrian news item chosen. Items that are more interesting
ought to be even easier to handle.

Phase 3: Questions that arise from the Swahili items.

The questions raised by the 60 news items that were
assembled for this project are innumerable. A few, taken
from the stories cited in this paper, are following:

What is a new settlement, or 'ujamaa village'?

When were the 'new settlements' begun, and why?

How does the statement that entrepreneurs should be
able to run their businesses without interference
conform to other actions of the Tanzanian government?

To what extent have USAID and Peace Corps contributed
directly toward training East Africans in technical
skills? What is US Government policy in this respect?

III. SUMMARY.

The results of this project tend to increase the plausibility of the following assertions:

1. It is possible to find recent, authentic and plentiful Swahili-language materials on an arbitrarily selected non-linguistic theme.

2. These materials lend themselves to grammatical drill, lexical exploration, and realistic communication.

3. Work with Swahili-language materials in turn generates initiatives to which an area studies expert can respond.

In the project, Swahili was not reduced to translation of ideas from the area studies curriculum, and the English-language materials were not limited to trivia. Rather, the two languages played different and complementary roles.

It therefore appears that technical or mechanical obstacles to integrated area training are not insuperable.

APPENDIX I TO CHAPTER 4

CLUSTERS AS SUPPLEMENTS (PORTUGUESE)
(with Guaraciema Dorsey)

In the summer of 1970, the Center for Research and Education trained a group of agricultural Volunteers for work with the Peace Corps in Brazil. The project had, in Hoge's <u>Oral Brazilian Portuguese</u>, an excellent general text, but that book of course had no direct reference to the work that these trainees were preparing to do. Yet one of the distinctive features of the program was its emphasis on trying to make the language program an integral part of the training design, rather than a separate enterprise concerned only with imparting basic language skills.

In this situation, the staff decided to use the cluster format (Chapter 4, p. 150 ff) as a tool for integrating language instruction with the rest of the program. During the phase of the training which took place in the United States, clusters made up approximately the last 25% of each day's language study beginning with the second week. They were also used in the Brazil phase, where their usefulness was even greater because it was there that the Volunteers received most of the cultural and technical part of their training.

Coarse-grained specification for the content of the clusters (Chapter 4, p.135) presented no problem, since most of the Portuguese instructors were in fact specialists not in language teaching but in the occupational specialties for which the Volunteers were being trained. Fine-grained specification in its linguistic dimension was taken from the basic textbook, and in its socio-topical dimensions from the experience of the staff as organized in a matrix similar to the one on p. 142.   Actual

CHAPTER 4   CLUSTERS AS SUPPLEMENTS (PORTUGUESE)

writing was done by the instructors and the cultural coordinator, and then polished by the language coordinator.

The experience of this training program demonstrated certain advantages of the cluster format:

1. It was fairly easy to coordinate the presentation of a particular cluster with the ongoing cross-cultural or technical program.

2. The language coordinator felt that clusters ·could as easily have been devised for most other kinds of basic material with which she was familiar.

3. Clusters made the staff confident and aware of how much of the culture and the technical details they could explore even as early as the second week (i.e. after 50 hours of instruction).

4. Use of clusters at the end of the day aroused the attention and enthusiasm of the trainees for something they were curious about and interested in.

5. The very loose format helped the instructors to see how they were able to use different clusters or parts of clusters with different groups or single trainees.

There were also a few caveats:

6. Since the matrix (p.142) provides so many possible combinations of linguistic, social and topical content, writers must decide on some way of establishing priorities.

7. Insofar as the devices used in the clusters differ from those in the basic textbook, they require some extra staff training.

8. Actual preparation of the clusters (or of any supple-
    mentary material) should be in the hands of a full-time
    person experienced in those matters, with the expert
    contributions of other staff members being used on a
    consultant basis. (This was done in writing the materials
    described in Appendix J.)

One of the early clusters is reproduced below, with English
translations added. Socially, it concerns an interview between
a Volunteer and a mayor. Its topic is an appeal for help. The
linguistic constraints under which it was written were not
recorded, and so can only be inferred.

This cluster does not have an explicit list of occasions for
use of the language (Chapter 3, p. 54). In the U. S. phase of
the training, these generally consisted of role playing, sometimes
with the help of videotape. In the Brazil phase, they more commonly took the form of group discussion or individual reports
about the trainees' real interactions with local people, for which
the other parts of the cluster had helped to prepare them.

DIALOG

(Continued from a previous lesson)

Prefeito: Qual é o problema,
seu João?

[What's the problem, John?]

Voluntário: As galinhas dos
vizinhos estão entrando
na horta.

[The neighbors' chickens
are getting into the garden.]

Prefeito: Isso é uma coisa seria.
Ja estragou muitas
hortaliças?

[That's a serious matter.]
[Has it already ruined
many vegetables?]

Voluntário: Até agora o
estrago foi pequeno.
Mas queremos
evitar mais prejuizo.

[So far, the damage
has been slight.]
[But we want to avoid
any more.]

Prefeito: Como vamos
resolver esse problema,
seu João?

[How are we going to
solve this problem,
John?]

DIALOG, Part 2

Vol: É por isso que estou   [That's why I'm here.]
      aquí, seu Manoel.

          O senhor pode nos ajudar?   [Can you help us?]

Pref: Com muito prazer, seu João.   [With great pleasure.]

          Em que posso ajudar?   [How can I help?]

Vol: Precisamos de arame   [We need wire to
      para cercar a horta.   fence in the garden.]

Pref: Nós vamos tentar a   [We'll try to help.]
      ajudar, seu João.

Vol: Que bom, seu Manoel.   [How nice!]
      Êste problema e de   [This is a very
      grande urgência.   urgent problem.]

CUMMINGS DEVICE

O que é isso?   [What is that?]

Isso é   [That's]

    uma coisa seria   [a serious matter]

    uma cerca   [a fence]

    um inseticida   [an insecticide]

    um tomate   [a tomato]

    um repôlho   [a cabbage]

    adubo químico   [chemical fertilizer]

       etc.   etc.

CUMMINGS DEVICE

Qual foi o estrago?   [What was the damage?]

Houve estrago   [There was damage to]

    no tomate   [the tomatoes]

    no alface   [the lettuce]

    nas hortaliças   [the vegetables]

    na horta   [the garden]

       etc.   etc.

CHAPTER 4   CLUSTERS AS SUPPLEMENTS (PORTUGUESE)

CUMMINGS DEVICE

Em que posso ajudar?   [How can I help?]

O senhor pode ajudar com   [You can help with]

        arame   [wire]

        sementes   [seeds]

        adubu químico   [chemical fertilizer]

        mudas   [seedlings]

        cêrca   [a fence]

        etc.   etc.

210

CUMMINGS DEVICE

Qual é o problema?   [What is the problem?]

O problema é   [The problem is]

    as galinhas   [the chickens]

    os porcos   [the pigs]

    o gado   [the cattle]

    os animais   [the animals]

    os vizinhos   [the neighbors]

      etc.   etc.

CHAPTER 4   CLUSTERS AS SUPPLEMENTS (PORTUGUESE)

DRILL WITH ATÉ AGORA ('UP TO NOW')

Cues

O estrago foi pequeno?	Até agora foi pequeno.
Plantaram o tomate?	Até agora não plantamos.
Resolviu o problema?	Até agora não resolví.
etc.	etc.

Has the damage been small?	So far, it has.
Have you (pl.) planted the tomatoes?	So far, we haven't.
Have you (sg.) solved the problem?	So far, I haven't.
etc.	etc.

DRILL WITH <u>POR ISSO</u> ('FOR THIS REASON')

Precisamos de cêrca.	Por isso estou aquí.
O tomate está fraco.	Por isso está caro.
As hortaliças estao fracas.	Por isso precisamos de adubo.

etc.   etc.

We need a fence.	That is why I'm here.
Tomatoes are delicate.	For that reason they're expensive.
The vegetables are in poor condition.	For that reason we need fertilizer.

etc.   etc.

DRILL ON PERSON-NUMBER

AGREEMENT IN PRESENT TENSE

Eu [I]	evito [avoid]	falar inglês
Você [you]	evita	[speaking English]
Êle, ela [he, she]	evita	prejuízo
Nós [we]	evitamos	[damage]
Vocês [you (pl.)]	evitam	filhos
Êles, elas [they]	evitam	[children]

Eu	resolvo	o problema
Você	resolve	
Êle, ela	resolve	
Nós	resolve	

etc.

APPENDIX J TO CHAPTER 4

RELEVANCE   UNDER   STRESS   (SPANISH)

> ...Time is of the essence. The staff,
> exhausted as they are, still are asking for
> a specific task, and we can no longer lead
> them blind. They must be given the tools to
> perform their task, whether it be the clusters
> or a textbook adaptation.,... The clusters...
> are not conclusive in that they are not
> sequentially prepared nor culturally approved,
> and they are insufficient to make the staff
> feel adequately prepared for the coming weeks.
> Therefore, it is by necessity that we turn
> to the adaptation of [an existing] textbook....

This honest statement came from the director of a program
in which the staff, together with an experienced materials
developer, had been trying to prepare project-specific
materials in a 'cluster' format (see Chapter 4, p. 150 , and
Appendix G). With only two weeks' lead time, the staff tried
valiantly to cooperate, then lost heart and, as recorded in
the director's statement (above), abandoned the attempt. The
following day, however, they returned to the cluster format
and produced the materials cited in this appendix.

The reactions to the resulting lessons, in the third
week of instruction, are given below. They are the unedited
and complete notes on interviews with eight of the trainees--
about 20 % of the total group, selected at random. Only the
names have been deleted. The trainees knew that the inter-
viewer was 'an evaluator from Washington,' but not that he
had participated in designing the materials.

215

CHAPTER 4   RELEVANCE UNDER STRESS (SPANISH)

#1   H.d studied 6 lgs., including a little Spanish
      a long time ago. Entirely favorable on materials.
      Says that she is finally getting to speak Sp.,
      but that the ones who arrived 2 weeks ago with no
      Sp. are speaking more than she is.

#2   Had studied other lgs. and gotten A's, but had
      never learned to speak any of them. Likes these
      for relevance and because she is learning to
      speak. No neg. comments, she says. Feels she is
      learning 20 times as much as she expected to.
      More Sp. now than in 4 yrs. of Fr. Went shopping
      yesterday evening. Found some Sp. phrases came
      naturally.

#3   Spanish minor in college, but didn't speak it
      then. Very enthusiastic about these materials.
      'Tremendous.'

#4   No previous Sp. Feels she can speak more/knows
      more than after 1 yr. of Fr. Has 'visual hangup.'
      Other student comments that #4 can always find
      some way to speak.

#5   Former Spanish tchr. in jr. hi: Beginners know
      more Sp. after 2 weeks than I was able to teach
      in 1 yr. with [widely used textbook series].
      Very relevant. [Interviewer said these materials
      are sloppy.] 'Not sloppy!'

#6   32 hrs. of Sp., but lang. coordinator says she
      can't talk. (Actually, she can, but not very
      well.) Likes materials, but as basis for impro-
      vising, would be bored if she had to stick to
      them alone. Has learned some new words from them.

#7   [Older than most, not a member of the group, but
      been taking Sp. with them.] Feels self weakest
      stdt. in the bldg. But feels he can go out,
      strike up a conversation and maintain it for
      'quite a while.' Has noted that his Sp-speaking
      colleagues' eyes light up when he does so. Thinks
      these clusters have gotten the class 'sensitized
      to each other' thru Sp.

#8   Enthusiastic.

The contrast between the director's statement of mid-
July and the trainees' statements of early August shows
dramatically and frankly what kinds of tension, excitement,
risk--and reward--may attend the writing of on-the-spot
materials.

In comparison with the reactions of people to them, the
materials themselves look tame. They consisted of 14
'clusters.' Lesson 2, quoted below, is based on a six-line
sample of Spanish in use; the sample can be treated either
as a basic dialog or as an 'exchange sequence' (Chapter
4, p. 149). The names of the speakers are those of actual
members of the group: one instructor and or · trainee.

        Señora S____: ¿De dónde es usted?
        Señor T____ ·   Soy de San Antonio.
        Señora S____: ¿Es casado?
        Señor T____: No, no soy casado. Soy soltero.
        Señora S____: ¿Cuántos hermanos tiene?
        Señor T____: Tengo tres.

        [Where are you from? I'm from S. A. Are you
        married? No, I'm not. I'm a bachelor. How
        many brothers do you have? I have three.]

Related to this sample are three Cummings devices
(Chapter 3, p. 59 , and Chapter 6), drills, and suggestions
for use. The first Cummings device used the question ¿De
dónde es usted? 'Where are you from?' and three answers:

Nací en (Pueblo) 'I was born in (Pueblo),'

Soy de (San Antonio) 'I'm from (San Antonio),'

and Vivo en (San Antonio) 'I live in (San Antonio).'

The second built on the question ¿Es casado? 'Are you
married?' and taught the replies 'No, I'm (a bachelor,

widowed, divorced, not married), and 'Yes, I'm married.'

Drills on the very important matter of person-number agreement for three common verbs was provided by substitution drills based on sentences taken either from the basic sample or from Cummings devices. In these drills, the cue words are underlined; the expected replies are the entire sentences:

Yo vivo en Taos.	I live in Taos.
El vive en Taos.	He lives in Taos.
Nosotros vivimos en Taos.	We live in Taos.
etc.	

Yo tengo un hermano.	I have one brother.
etc.	

Yo soy de San Antonio.	I'm from San Antonio.
etc.	

The occasions for use lie both within the content of the lesson and outside it. Similarly, the uses that are suggested take place both inside and outside the walls of the classroom:

1. In class, find out as much as you can about your instructor and about each other by using the questions learned in this lesson.

2. Stand up in front of the class and talk about yourself as long as you can. Begin by using the material in this lesson, but go on from there if you can.

3. Outside of class, ask the following people
   questions based on what you have learned in
   this cluster: 5 other trainees, 3 other
   instructors, 1 Spanish-speaking neighbor.

4. Outside of class, learn to count from 5 to
   15 by asking your instructors to count
   various objects for you. [Numbers from 1-5
   had been taught in this lesson. These
   materials do not provide for teaching any
   further numbers in class.]

In summary, the favorable reactions of the users cannot
be explained in terms of clever, innovative features of the
materials themselves, for there were none. They depended,
rather, on the extent to which the staff forced each of the
'suggestions for use' to yield both practical and psychological satisfactions: the student was of course glad to
to find out 'What I can do' with Spanish, but he also had
frequent opportunities to be pleased with himself at 'What
I can do!'

APPENDIX K TO CHAPTER 4

UNSEQUENCED PRESENTATION OF STRUCTURES

(SWAHILI)

Freedom is not following a river.
Freedom is following a river,
    though, if you want to.
It is deciding now by what happens now.
It is knowing that luck makes a difference.

                                        William Stafford

Freedom for a language teacher may mean not following someone else's structural sequence, or following it. Of the materials which a writer can place at the disposal of a teacher, the Learner's Synopsis (Chapter 4, p. 144; and Chapter 5) should flow as smoothly as possible from the beginning to end. The subject of this appendix, however, is the presentation of structural points not as continuity but as chunks, so that they are maximally independent of each other in two ways: in their wording, and in their physical existence on paper or cardboard.

The material which follows illustrates the second point made in the directions for writing an adaptable Sarkhanese course (Chapter 4, p. 144ff). It is based on cards numbered 1, 2, 3 and 5 in a series of 62 5"x8" cards. This series has been used for two years, by four different instructors, in presenting the rudiments of Swahili grammar to beginning students. To emphasize mutual independence, however, the cards are given here in an order different from the one in which they have been used in the past. As in Chapter 4, p. 145, the suggestions for presentation are placed before the explanation, but the cards need not be used in that order. (The students with whom these cards have been used have in fact not seen the explanations in this form at all.)

Concord: singular 'near me' demonstratives

    Have available in the classroom a number of objects, at
least one from each of the following classes:

               M-WA
               M-MI
               LI-MA
               KI-VI
                 N

Pick up or touch one item at a time, and say Hiki ni kiti, or
whatever the object is. Have the students do the same. Be sure
that they touch the item they are talking about, so as to preserve the difference between hiki and hicho or kile. Then begin
to use the question Hii ni nini? or, if you prefer, Hiki ni
kitu gani?   When the students can reply to this question, let
them question and answer each other. Answer their questions about
names of objects that you have not yet talked about. Finally,
fall silent and let them use this new material in their own way.

    If a demonstrative word (this, that, these, those)
accompanies or refers to a noun, its form depends on the noun.
This can be seen in the 'near me' demonstratives for singular
nouns:

meza table	hii this	'this table'
mlango door	huu this	'this door'
kitu thing	hiki this	'this thing'
mtu person	huyu this	'this person'
dirisha window	hili this	'this window'

(See Synopsis, par.   18.)

Concord: <u>plural 'near me' demonstratives</u>.

Have available a number of objects, two or more of each kind, to represent each of the following classes:

> M-WA
>
> M-MI
>
> LI-MA
>
> KI-VI
>
> N

Pick up or touch one pair of items at a time, and say <u>Hivi ni viti</u> , or whatever the objects are. Have the students do the same. Be sure that they touch the items they are talking about, so as to preserve the difference between <u>hivi</u> and <u>hivyo</u> , <u>vile</u>. Then begin to use the question <u>Hivi ni vitu gani?</u> When the students can reply to this question, let them question and answer each other. Answer their questions about names of objects that you have not yet talked about. Finally, fall silent and let them use this new material and/or earlier material in their own way.

If a demonstrative word (<u>this</u>, <u>that</u>, <u>these</u>, <u>those</u>) accompanies or refers to a noun, its form depends on the noun. This can be seen in the 'near' demonstratives for plural nouns:

meza tables	<u>hizi</u> these	'these tables'
milango doors	<u>hii</u> these	'these doors'
vitu things	<u>hivi</u> these	'these things'
watu people	<u>hawa</u> these	'these people'
madirisha windows	<u>haya</u> these	'these windows'

(See <u>Synopsis</u>, par.   18 .)

Concord: Singular 'near you' demonstratives.

Have available a number of movable objects, at least one from each of the following classes:

                         M-WA

                         M-MI

                         LI-MA

                         KI-VI

                          N

Put one object near a student, move away, and say <u>Hiyo ni kalamu</u> , or whatever the object is.   Then take the object away from him, and have him say the same thing to you.   Then hold the object and ask <u>Hiki ni kitu gani?</u>   Have him reply <u>Hicho ni kitabu</u> , or whatever the object is.   Be sure that there is agreement between the location of the object and the use of <u>hii</u>, <u>hiki</u>, <u>hili</u>   or <u>hiyo</u>, <u>hicho</u>, <u>hilo</u> .   Let the students use these questions among themselves, and in getting new vocabulary from you.   Do not require them to remember the new words that they get from you in this way.

If a demonstrative word (<u>this</u>, <u>that</u>, <u>these</u>, <u>those</u>) accompanies or refers to a noun, its form depends on the noun. This can be seen in the 'near you, or otherwise already identified' demonstratives for singular nouns:

meza table	hiyo that	'that table near you, or already mentioned'
mtu person	huyo that	'that person'
dirisha window	hilo that	'that window'
mlango door	huo that	'that door'
kitu thing	hicho that	'that thing'

(See <u>Synopsis</u>, par.   18 .)

Concord: _subject prefixes_

Have available a number of small, movable objects, at
least one from each of the following classes:

M-WA

M-MI

LI-MA

KI-VI

N

Using appropriate actions, substitute each in the sentence:

Kalamu	iko	mezani.
pen	is-located	on-table

Have the students do the same until this becomes easy for them.
Then teach them a few place expressions to replace _mezani_.
Finally, teach the question _Kalamu iko wapi?_ and let them use it.

When a noun is the subject of a locative word '_am_, _is_, or
are located,' the subject prefix of the locative word depends
on the choice of noun:

Meza	iko	wapi?	Where is the table?
Table	is-located	where?	
Meza	ziko	wapi?	Where are the tables?
Kitu	kiko	wapi?	Where is the thing?
Vitu	viko	wapi?	Where are the things?
Mtu	yuko	wapi?	Where is the person?
Watu	wako	wapi?	Where are the people?
Dirisha	liko	wapi?	Where is the window?
Madirisha	yako	wapi?	Where are the windows?
Mlango	uko	wapi?	Where is the door?
Milango	iko	wapi?	Where are the doors?

(See _Synopsis_, par. 23, 62 .)

224

APPENDIX L TO CHAPTER 4

INCOMPLETE MATERIALS FOR DISCUSSION (FRENCH)

With two exceptions, the appendices in this report are intended to be, on some scale, complete illustrations of points that were made in the chapters that they follow. It is hoped that they will provoke some discussion, but they do not demand it. This appendix and Appendix F, however, are deliberately incomplete. Instead of suggesting answers, they raise questions.

Material for this appendix is drawn from materials prepared at the Virgin Islands Training Center of the Peace Corps, under the direction of Allen Brooks, in late 1970.

The starting point for this series of problems is an exchange sequence of six lines, which the student might meet after perhaps 50-100 hours of study:

Qu'est-ce que c'est?	What is this?
C'est la suspension.	It's the suspension.
Où est la suspension?	Where is the suspension?
La suspension est fixée au chassis.	The suspension is attached to the chassis.
Quelle est la fonction de la suspension?	What is the function of the suspension?
La suspension est pour absorber les chocs.	The suspension is for absorbing the bumps.

1. To what degree would this exchange sequence have 'strength' (Chapter 3, p. 46) for:

    a. Adult students already familiar with automobile mechanics in their own language, who plan to

225

teach that subject in French?

b. Adult trainees who know little about auto
   mechanics, but who will need a knowledge of it
   in their future work?

c. Junior high school boys with an interest in
   mechanical things?

2. The sequence obviously calls for use of visual aids.
   What would be the advantages and the disadvantages
   of two-dimensional aids (diagrams, etc.) and three-
   dimensional aids (models, or an actual car)?

3. What 'payoffs' (p.23ff) might this exchange provide,
   either practical or psychological?

4. Are any parts of the exchange prohibitively 'heavy'
   (p. 47) or 'opaque' (p. 48)?

The object of the game in writing a lesson that will
include this exchange sequence is to find ways of increasing
the payoffs, or strength, with a smaller increase in
weight and opacity. In the materials from which this
example is taken, parallel sequences cover the names,
locations and purposes of a chain of items: the axles are
attached to the suspension, the brakes and the wheels to the
axles, and the tires to the wheels. A total of five
substitution tables provide some of the routine vocabulary
needed for talking about these parts of a car. They may be
summarized as follows:

A.   Qu'est-ce que c'est?

B.

C'	est	le chassis.	chassis
Ce	sont	la suspension	suspension
		l'essieu avant	front axle
		l'essieu arrière	rear axle
		les roues	wheels
		les freins	brakes

C.

Où	est	la suspension?
	sont	l'essieu avant
		etc.

D.

La suspension	est	fixé(e)(s)	au	chassis.
Les roues	sont		a la	suspension
etc.			aux	essieux

E.

Quelle est la fonction	de la	suspension?
	du	chassis
	des	roux
		etc.

F.

La suspension	est	pour	absorber les chocs.
etc.	sont		fixer les roux a la
			suspension
			rouler
			arrêter le véhicule

The possibility of talking about five (literally)
interconnected sub-topics more than quintuples the strength
of the original exchange sequence.

227

5. Or does it??

    At the same time, the 16-word vocabulary of the
    first sequence has been increased to only 25, an
    increase of only 50 %, and the structural additions
    are either nil or very slight, depending on one's
    point of view.

6. How would the above exchange sequence have to be
    modified in order to incorporate basic facts about
    (a) mechanic's tools?   (b) kitchen utensils?
    (c) equipment used in stamp collecting?

7. In the following drill, the cue words are under-
    lined.   What is the purpose of the drill?

> C'est   le   chassis.
> C'est   la   suspension.
> C'est   l'essieu arrière.
> C'est   la   fonction du chassis.
>   etc.

8. Given the material quoted above, and given the
    desirability of 'drilling the negative,' what
    would be two ways of writing such a drill? What
    circumstances--or what theoretical convictions--
    would make one of these ways preferable to the
    other?

        What would be two ways of administering each
    drill in class? What circumstances--or what
    theoretical convictions--would make one of these
    ways preferable to the other?

9. The correct placement of object pronouns causes
    trouble for most students of French. How, prin-
    cipally within the vocabulary of the above example,

could students be led to improve their speed and accuracy in the use of this feature of the language?

10. Write another exchange sequence, in French or in some other language, which would reflect other basic facts on this or some other topic.

CHAPTER 5

LEARNER'S SYNOPSES

The mythological antagonist of 'modern' systems of
language teaching was the 'grammar and translation method.'
By this method, students were given words to memorize, and
rules to operate. Having done so, they at once demonstrated
and developed their knowledge of the language by translating
lists of sentences, and finally by translating authors. The
crucial element, however, was mastery of grammar. It was
not for nothing that grammar schools were called 'grammar
schools.' The crowning achievement in language study by
this method was to read, mark, learn and inwardly digest
an entire reference grammar.

It is not surprising that in reacting against the grammar
and translation method, many language teachers became impatient
either with translation, or with instruction in grammar, or
with both. Rules, they said, if presented at all, should be
ad hoc, derived inductively by the students from their own
recent experiences with the language. This approach produced
large numbers of courses with individual 'grammar notes'
scattered throughout their contents. Sometimes the notes
were of minimal quality, and sometimes they were brilliantly
written, but they were never easy for the student to relate
to one another.

More recently, as we noted in Chapter 1, there has
been a revival of willingness to appeal directly to the
full range of the student's intellectual powers. Teachers
who are of this persuasion believe that they may properly
explain structure on any scale or any level of abstract-
ness that suits their purposes, and that they may do so
before, during, or after the student's direct experience
with examples, and that they may expect the student to
make some deductive application of the rules.

The fifth assumption that underlies the modular
approach is 'pluralism': 'If a thing is worth doing at
all, it is worth doing in at least two ways.' In fact,
it seems to be the case that if a word or a sound or a
grammatical relationship is to be retained at all, it
must be met with and studied from at least two points of
of view. The coherent picture of structure afforded by a
reference grammar, and the immediate linkage of individual
grammar points with individual instances in meaningful
discourse, both should be available. The problem is how
to combine them.

One solution to this problem may lie in a 'learner's
synopsis' of the language. Like a reference grammar, a
learner's synopsis presents an organized view of the total
grammar of the target language. It differs from a reference
grammar in that it is shorter and less detailed. A student
requires so much time to go through an ordinary reference
grammar that he cannot form a general view ('syn-opsis') of
the whole. The proposed format is therefore limited to
perhaps 3000 running words (exclusive of examples), and

covers only enough of the details to account for perhaps $95^{\circ}/o$
of the problems (by text frequency) that the student will
meet. A good reference grammar aims at $99^{\circ}/o$ coverage, but
the extra $4^{\circ}/_{o}$ may quadruple the length and difficulty of
the treatment, and the 'reference' grammar may be too cumber-
some for ordinary students to refer to.

Gage (1970, p.3) recognizes that 'a compact overview
can serve as...a sort of road map to orient the more sophisticated learner to what to expect in his studies,' and goes
on to suggest (p.5) that 'the development of students'
structural synopses is perhaps the most rewarding direction
for efforts to supply aid to students of neglected languages
in the near future....Considerable benefit for the learners
can be expected from a project of rather manageable scope...
In spite of the great need for dictionaries, it is at least
questionable that the benefit to students per man-year
invested in one is as great as that obtainable from
structural synopses.'

Another advantage of the synopsis format is that it
lends itself to pseudo-self-instructional treatment. It
need not stop with presenting examples for each point, as
a reference grammar does. It can provide opportunities,
within a very limited vocabulary, for the student to test
his understanding of what he has read, and it can do this
at the end of every paragraph. It may do so by matching
each set of examples with one or more self-testing frames.
In the Swahili synopsis (Appendix N, pp.272-283) the self-
testing frames are on the right-hand pages, opposite the
corresponding sections of the synopsis on the left-hand pages.

232

In the Kirundi synopsis (Appendix O, pp. 284-309), they
are enclosed in boxes.

A suggested procedure for constructing a learner's
synopsis is the following:

1. Write a connected essay on the structure
    of the language, with no examples. There
    are two reasons for omitting examples at
    this step: (a) It is easier to be sure of
    the continuity of the exposition, and (b)
    the exposition will be less dependent on
    specific examples.

2. Break this essay up at every point where
    examples ought to be inserted. Assign a
    number to each such section. These section
    numbers will be available for cross-referenc-
    ing from lesson materials of various kinds.
    (A Swahili synopsis that has been brought to
    this stage is found in Appendix N, pp. 261-271.)

3. Choose some one field of interest from which
    to draw a small amount of content vocabulary.
    One might in fact choose two or more such
    fields, and produce two or more parallel
    versions of the same synopsis, each within
    its own small vocabulary. (In the Swahili
    example on p.389, the principal topic is
    'meetings, as reported in the press.')

4. Prepare a full set of examples for each
    field chosen in Step 3.

5. Insert the examples into the essay at the
    points marked in Step 2, and type the
    result onto what are to be the left-hand
    pages of the finished synopsis. (The Thai
    example [Appendix M , pp. 235-256] has been
    carried to this point.

6. For each section, prepare self-testing
    frames of approximately the same length
    in column-inches as the section itself.
    Put these on the right-hand pages. (The
    Swahili example on pp. 272-283 illustrates
    this format.)

7. Add any interpretive material that seems
    desirable. (An example is the opening
    paragraphs of the Thai synopsis [Appendix M,
    pp. 235-237].)

APPENDIX   M
TO
CHAPTER 5

A LEARNER'S SYNOPSIS OF THAI
(with Warren G. Yates)

1.   Any English speaker who wants to communicate with Thais
will find that his problems lie in two areas: his perception of
the world, and his inability to handle the mechanics of the Thai
language.   In the first of these areas lie such questions as What
should I have for breakfast? Who am I? What kinds of deference
are expected of me by whom? What does it mean to be 'punctual'?
What is 'honesty'? What of importance has happened today? What
of importance was happening 500 years ago? Of the two areas,
this is the one in which lie the most serious obstacles to
communication.

2.   Yet in training Americans--including Peace Corps
Volunteers--for work in other countries, the second area is the
one that has usually claimed most attention.   There are at least
six reasons why this has been so:

   1.   Language facts are easier to write down as
        separate items on sheets of paper.

   2.   It is easy to know when (verbal) language is
        being performed and when it is not.

   3.   Some ability in handling the language normally
        goes hand in hand with ability in the first area.

4. People react to mistakes in either area, but
    they are more likely to react verbally to
    mistake in the verbal area.

5. Unfamiliarity with the non-verbal code often
    leads   misunderstanding, while unfamiliarity
    with the verbal code inevitably leads to total
    (verbal) unintelligibility.

6. Language learning is time-consuming.

3. Whenever we limit our attention only to the cultural
area or only to the linguistic area, or to only one of them
at a time, we do so at our peril. There is no language without
meaning, and there is no culture without words. Nevertheless,
this synopsis will violate that principle by concentrating
entirely on the mechanics of speaking Thai. It is addressed
primarily to native speakers of English who expect to live in
Thailand, and gives a bird's-eye-view of the tasks they will
encounter in their study of the language.

4. Why a Synopsis? There already exists at least one
reference grammar of Thai, as well as courses which contain
detailed grammatical notes. But people learn things when they
are ready to learn them. They also need to have the same facts
available on more than one scale. Experience with basic courses
in other languages suggests that most students need a connected
summary of the main points of structure, in addition to and not
instead of the notes that are scattered among the lessons. A
reference grammar, of course, does just that, but if it is as
detailed as it ought to be, it is necessarily too long to be
accessible to many students until after they have completed
most of their study. A Synopsis, on the other hand, should be
short enough and general enough so that a person who has not yet

begun to study the language can follow it; it should also contain
cross-references to existing sources of further detail,
so that the student may use it as a rough map, to be looked at
and added to from time to time as he plods (or jogs) through
the hundreds of individual side streets and alleys of Thai
structure. <u>Its purpose is to help him establish and maintain
perspective.</u>

5.   The persistent difficulties that we have in learning
Thai fall into three general categories: pronunciation, sentence
structure, and vocabulary.

I.   PRONUNCIATION PROBLEMS.

6.   The most conspicuous--though not the largest--unit of
Thai pronunciation is the syllable. In spite of some similarities, Thai syllables differ drastically from English syllables
in the way they are organized. The most striking difference is
that each Thai syllable has one or two of three possible 'tones,'
and that the vowels and consonants of a syllable make up either
one or two tone-bearing elements ('moras'). Among the consonants,
where English has only a two-way distinction between <u>p</u> and <u>b</u>, or
between <u>t</u> and <u>d</u>, Thai has a three-way distinction that causes
trouble for English speakers. Finally, though many Thai vowels
and consonants have similar-sounding counterparts in English,
there are many differences in the details of pronunciation. <u>The
key sentences of this paragraph will now be amplified in sections</u>
7-22 , <u>below.</u>

   7.   '<u>Each Thai syllable has one or two of three possible
        tones.</u>'

It is more usual to say that a Thai syllable may have <u>one</u>
of <u>five</u> possible tones: three 'level' tones (low, mid, high)

and **two** glides (high falling and low rising). But the glides **are** found only on syllables that have two moras (see 12, below). Either way of describing the tones will work, but the one we have chosen here seems to us to highlight the physical aspects of pronunciation better. (For further details on what the tones sound like, see Noss, pp. 18-20; Yates and Tryon, p. xli.)

8. The 'tone' of a syllable is related to its 'pitch,' but the two are not identical. 'Pitch' means the note or notes on a musical scale which are heard with one particular occurrence of a syllable. Different speakers may pronounce the same word with the same 'tone,' and even a single speaker may use quite different pitches on different occurrences of the same word, but again with constant 'tone.' 'Tone,' then, refers to how the pitch of a syllable sounds relative to its neighbors: relatively high, relatively low, relatively level, or relatively long glide, and so forth.

9. In producing acceptable approximations to the five tone-combinations of Thai, it is not necessary for us to do anything that even the most tone-deaf of us does not do every day in speaking English. The problem lies not in the mechanics of controlling the pitch, but in the uses to which we are accustomed to put pitch distinctions. In English, we employ pitch to show where a given word is in the sentence, or to signal that we are asking a question, or to convey attitudes and emotions. Furthermore, we learned to use pitch in these ways very early, and these matters have very deep roots in our linguistic personalities. In Thai, on the other hand, the <u>tone</u> of a word remains relatively constant, no matter where it is in the sentence or how the speaker feels about what he is saying.

10. '<u>The vowels and consonants of a Thai syllable make up either one or two tone-bearing elements ('moras').</u>

Before talking about Thai syllable structure, it will be
worthwhile to take a quick look at the surface structure of
English syllables. In English, every syllable has a 'nucleus,'
and most also have 'onsets' or 'codas' or both. A 'nucleus'
may either be a simple vowel (as in bet), or a diphthong (as in
bite or bout). The 'onset' is the consonant or group of consonants that comes before the nucleus (s, p, l, sp, sl, pl, m, sm,
br, etc.), and the 'coda' is the consonant or group of consonants
that comes after it. (s, t, st, ts, sts, mp, etc.). The number
of possible onsets and codas in English is very great, and some
of them are quite long and complex.

11. One fact is of the utmost importance in understanding
the differences between Thai and English syllables: y-glides
(as in buys, boys), and w-glides (as in knows, cows) are part of
the nucleus in English. This means (1) that the same codas that
can follow a simple vowel in English can also follow a diphthong
that ends with a w-glide or a y-glide, and (2) that the t in cat
counts as a coda, but the w of cow is part of the nucleus: cow
has no coda.[1]

12. In Thai syllables that consist of two moras, the first
half consists of a vowel and whatever consonant(s) (if any) stand
before it. The second half consists of (1) a repetition of the
same vowel, plus whatever one consonant (if any) stands after it,
or (2) the vowel a, plus whatever one consonant (if any) stands
after it, or (3) one of the 'sonorant' consonants j, w, m, n, ŋ,
Examples are:

---

[1](Non codam sed caudam!)

239

(1)	ma		a
	tɛ		ɛ
	thi		i
	khy		y
	lɛ		ɛw
	ka		at
	tha		an
(2)	klu		aŋ
	klu		aj
	khry		aŋ
	khu		ap
(3)	khu		j
	khu		n
	kha		w

Notice that unless there is a vowel in the second half of the
syllable, a sonorant (m̲, n̲, ŋ̲, j̲, w̲) carries tone just the way
a second vowel does. It also occupies about as much time, so that
a sonorant after a single vowel sounds stronger and longer than
after a double vowel (Noss, p. 9; Yates and Tryon. p.xxxiii). Notice
also that two sonorant consonants cannot occur together. This is
why Thais who find it easy to approximate the pronunciation of
English T̲im, T̲om and t̲ie may still tend to say t̲ie when they mean
t̲ime.

13. A one-mora syllable in Thai therefore cannot end with a
sonorant consonant. It consists of a single short vowel, which
may be preceded by consonants and may be followed by a non-sonorant
consonant (p̲, t̲, k̲ or glottal stop and in loan words f̲, s̲).

14. In a two-mora syllable, the tone of the first half may
be low and the tone of the second half high, or the first half
may be high and the second half low, or the tones of the two
halves may be identical. These possibilities provide for four
of the five combinations that exist for long Thai syllables:

1. low rising
2. high falling
3. high level
4. low level

The fifth combination is pronounced in at least two different ways.
When a syllable with this combination is pronounced by itself,
both of its halves are high, but there is a very noticeable downstep of pitch between the first and second halves. When such a
syllable is preceded by a syllable with high tone, its own tone
is level, but there is a downstep between the two syllables. The
fifth combination may therefore be described as

5. high with downstep

(It is usually called mid tone.)

15. 'Where English has a two-way distinction between p and b,
     Thai has a three-way distinction that causes difficulty
     for English speakers.'

English speakers find it hard to hear and produce consistently
the differences among the three Thai sounds that are romanized as
p, ph, b. Of these sounds, b is fully voiced, as in English samba.
The sounds ph and p are not voiced. The former is followed by a
puff of air ('aspiration') and the latter is not. The trouble is
that while both aspirated and unaspirated p occur in English, the
choice between them depends on position in the word, and so the
difference cannot be used for distinguishing between two different

English words. Accordingly, we have learned to ignore it. In Thai, on the other hand, many pairs of words differ only in this respect.

16. Just as English p may be either aspirated or unaspirated, so English b may be voiced or unvoiced. This choice depends less on position in the word than on the identity of the speaker: some people almost always voice b in English, but many others virtually never do. The result, however is the same as for p-ph: because the difference between voiced and unvoiced b never carries a difference of meaning in English, we have learned to ignore it.

17. English speakers therefore may have considerable difficulty in hearing the difference between Thai b and p, or between p and ph, or both. Comparable problems exist in dealing with Thai d, t, th; c, ch; k, kh.

18. One logically minor but in practice troublesome fact is that the consonant ŋ which occurs only at the ends of English syllables (e.g. sing) is hard for English speakers to pronounce when it begins a word, as it often does in Thai.

19. 'Though many Thai vowels have similar-sounding counterparts in English, there are differences in the details of pronunciation.'

If we compare a chart of the simple vowel contrasts of the surface structure of English with a chart of the vowels of Thai, the two charts look virtually identical:

ENGLISH
(Trager and Smith's analysis)

	Front Unrounded	Central Unrounded	Back Rounded
High	i (pit)	ɨ	u (put)
Mid	e (pet)	ə (putt)	o (as in coat, but no w-glide)
Low	a (pat)	a (pot, American)	ɔ (pot, Standard British)

[The high central vowel sound ɨ is very frequent
in speech, but is only rarely in contrast with
other English vowel sounds, and is therefore
hard to illustrate for non-phoneticians.]

20.   THAI
(Symbols as in Yates and Tryon)

	Front	Central-Back Unrounded	Back Rounded
High	i (pii)	y (khyy)	u (duu)
Mid	e (thee)	ə (pə̀ət)	o (too)
Low	ɛ (jɛ̂ɛ)	a (sǎa)	ɔ (tɔ̀ɔ)

21. By far the most important difference between these two
vowel systems is that in Thai the vowel y is in full contrast
with all other vowels, while in English the vowel ɨ can almost
always be replaced by some other vowel without a change of meaning. There are however certain noticeable differences between
the Thai vowels and their closest English counterparts. (For
details, see Noss, pp. 15-17.)

22. 'Though many Thai consonants have similar-sounding
     counterparts in English, there are differences in
     the details of pronunciation.' For details, see
     Noss, pp. 10-14.

II.   Problems of Sentence Structure

23.   In the way they are put together, even the simplest Thai
sentences bear little resemblance to their English counterparts.
True, the subject does ordinarily come before the predicate, as
in English, and the verb does stand before its object, but almost
everything else is different. The following are nine of the differences that cause English speakers the most trouble.

24.   (a) Every English statement must have a subject, even if
the subject is only a personal pronoun (I, etc.) In Thai, the
subject may be omitted if no ambiguity would result:

jùu	(He)'s in.
rɔ́ɔn mâak	(It)'s very hot.
dii máj	Is it good?
chɔ̂ɔp máj	Do (you) like it?
mâj sâap	(I) don't know.

25.   (b) In English, we must show the gender for third person singular pronouns (he, she, it), but not for the first person singular pronoun (I). In Thai there is no he-she-they distinction but I has separate translations for men and women:

phǒm	I (male speaker)
dichǎn	I (female speaker)
khǎw	he, she, they

For a female Thai speaker to refer to herself by the masculine pronoun (phǒm) I instead of the feminine I (dichǎn) would be as great a blunder as to refer to an English speaker's mother as he. (There is a distinction between he-she-they and it, but the latter is rarely used. (khǎw) he, she, they; (man) it.)

26.   (c) English sentences must show the time of an action (goes, went, will go, etc.), while Thai sentences are often noncommittal in this respect.

khǎw paj talàat	He goes (is going, went) to the market.
phǒm mâj chɔ̂ɔp	I (don't, didn't) like it.
mii thahǎan jùu máj	(Are, were) there soldiers there?
khǎw khuj kan	They converse(d).

When time is indicated in a Thai sentence, it is sometimes shown by the choice of a sentence particle which has no direct relation at all to the verb.

paj rýplàaw	Did you go?
paj máj	Do you (want to) go?

245

27.   (d) Most English nouns must show by their form whether they are singular (cow, child, man) or plural (cows, children, men). They must do so even if the matter is obvious or not important in a particular context: I snapped my fingers, I bumped my head, The light came through the window(s). In Thai, there is no singular-plural indication in the nouns themselves, though the concept can be put across in other ways when the need arises.

khruu khon nyŋ	one teacher (teacher person one)
phûujǐŋ 2 khon	two women (woman 2 person)
nǎŋšyy dii dii	good books (book good good)
dèk dèk	children (child child)

The temptation for English speakers here as in the other examples is to overuse the available mechanisms in Thai for specifying plurality and to specify in Thai what Thai speakers leave unspecified.

28.   (e) Corresponding to English sentences with be as the main verb, Thai has at least six different constructions. The choice among these constructions depends partly on the subject and partly on the expression that follows be.

Subject	Verb	Complement	
nîi[1]	(khyy)	phŷan kháw	This is his friend.
khun cɔɔn	pen	khruu phǒm	John is my teacher.
kháw	chŷy[2]	cɔɔn	His name is John.
aahǎan	dii[3]	_____	The food is good.

---

1. Demonstratives only.   2. Only with names.   3. Stative verbs only.

kháw	jùu	bâan	He's at home.
thɛ̌ɛwníi[4]	mii	ráantàtphǒm	In this area there is a barber shop.
kháw	(mii)	aajú 6 khùap	He's eight years old.
wanníi	(pen)	wansǎw	Today (is) Saturday.

29. (f) The part of the simple sentence that is most likely
to arouse comment from foreigners is the system of 'classifiers'.
A 'classifier' is one of a special list of about 200 nouns which
are used in constructions to enumerate or specify other nouns.

naŋsy̌y lêm diaw
book clf. one   one book

rót khan nyŋ:
car/clf/one   one car

nákrian sǎam khon
student 3 people   3 students

Each classifier is normally used with a large number of nouns of
very different meanings, and there is frequently no observable
connection between the classifier and its noun.

takraj 2 lêm   2 pairs of scissors

nǎŋsy̌y 2 lêm   2 books

mîit 2 lêm   2 knives

khûumyy 2 lêm   2 manuals

Fortunately, for limited purposes there are about 50 very common
classifiers that will take care of most of our needs. Some of
these are of very high frequency: <u>khon</u>, <u>tua</u>, <u>an</u>, etc.
    an   khan   khrŷaŋ   lûuk   baj   hὲɛŋ   lêm

---

4. Locatives only.

30.   (g) Questions based on even the simplest statements provide new complications. The interrogative words do not usually occur at the beginning of questions as they do in English.

kháw ca paj m<u>ŷaraj</u>	<u>When</u> will he go?
tham <u>jaŋŋaj</u>	<u>How</u> do you do it?
kháw bɔ̀ɔk wâa <u>araj</u>	<u>What</u> did he tell?
kháw pen <u>khraj</u>	<u>Who</u> is he?

The sentence particle, and not the verb, may indicate something about the time of an action.

kháw paj rýplàaw	<u>Did</u> he go?

The sentence particle may also show something about what the speaker expects from his hearers.

khun pen thahǎan <u>rɣ̌y</u>	You're a soldier? (expecting confirmation)
paj kin khâaw <u>máj</u>	Do you (want to) go eat? (an invitation)

Knowing how to reply to a question depends on noticing what its structure was. Even as simple (to us) a concept as 'yes' has different translations after various kinds of question.

(1) Q: paj rýplàaw   Did you go?
    A: paj/mâjdâj paj   Yes (or) No.

(2) Q: khun pen thahǎan rɣ̌y   You're a soldier?
    A: khráp/plàaw khráp   Yes (or) No.

(3) Q: paj mǎj   Want to go?
    A: paj/mâj paj   Yes (or) No.

(4) Q: kin khâaw lɛ́ɛw rýjaŋ   Have you eaten yet?
    A: kin lɛ́ɛw   Yes, I have' (or)
        jaŋ khráp   No, not yet.

248

31.   (h) Negation of simple sentences is likewise accomplished in several different ways, depending largely on the way the affirmative sentence is constructed.

kháw mâjdâj chŷy prasə̀ət	His name isn't Prasert.
nân mâjchâj tó	That isn't a table.
mâj dii	(It) is no good.
mâj paj	I don't (want to) go.
jaŋ mâj paj	(He has)n't gone yet.
jaŋ mâj dâj kin khâaw	(They) hadn't eaten yet.
jàa paj	Don't go.
phǒm mâj dâj pen chaawnaa	I'm not a farmer.

32.   (i) Some of the aspects of simple Thai sentences appear strange and arbitrary to foreigners, and the classifier system is formidable, but all these can be understood and mastered one-by-one through hard work. Possibly the most confusing features of Thai structure are the ways in which one sentence can be embedded in another to form a more complicated sentence. Sentence embedding is in itself nothing new to us. We do it in English all the time. Embed <u>The exam was hard</u> in <u>She took an exam</u> and we get <u>She took a hard exam</u>. Embed <u>The model works</u> in <u>This is a model</u> and we may get <u>This is a working model</u> or <u>This is a model that works</u>.

33.   We have two problems with Thai embedding in Noun Phrases and Noun Compounds: (1) The word order is frequently wrong, since the main noun precedes its modifiers instead of following them as in English:

khruu phûujiŋ	(teacher woman)	woman teacher(s)
maa sii dam	(dog color black)	black dog(s)
mɛɛw tua jàj	(cat body large)	a large cat
ŋaan mâj khɔ̌ɔj mâak	(work not hardly much)	hardly any work

34. (2) The connectors (-ing, that, which, etc.) that help us keep track of embeddings in English are virtually always missing in Thai. Stative verbs, other verbs, and even whole clauses may stand between the main noun and its classifier or determiner, with no change in their form.

mii bâan bɛ̀ɛp thaj chán diaw than samǎj wâaŋ châw jùu lǎŋ nyŋ

There is house style Thai storey single modern vacant rent classifier one.

'There is one vacant, modern one-storey Thai style house for rent.'

news relate to this matter	news relating to this
person propose resolution request....	the proposer of a resolution requesting...
matter not break law beginning	a matter that was not initially illegal

35. Similarly, English has several verb forms that may function as nouns or as adjectives. For example, driving is a verbal noun in I like driving cars; to drive is a verbal noun (sometimes called an 'infinitive') in I like to drive cars. Compare maintain:maintenance, proceed:procedure, and many others. In barking dogs and frozen food, barking and frozen are verbal adjectives derived from bark and freeze. There are only two noun formatives that are used to form nouns like those above:

<u>kaan</u>	and	<u>kwaam</u>
kaantàtsŷa		tailoring
kaan sùup burìi		smoking cigarettes
kaan wîŋ		running
kwaam rúu		knowledge
kwaam khawrópthoŋ		respect for the flag

36. We have just seen why English speakers may have difficulty keeping track of noun expressions in Thai. Verb expressions may also create bewilderment because of (1) the lack of connectors, and (2) the number of verbs that may be stacked next to each other.

take	gentle	stuff	back	enter	go	keep	further

'Gently stuff it back in some more.'

III. Problems of Vocabulary

37. Except for a few borrowings (which may be unrecognizable with Thai pronunciation) Thai words sound entirely different from their English equivalents. They not only sound different from English words, they frequently resemble each other in ways that make it difficult for the English speaker to distinguish them. For example, these three words differ only in tone:

khǎaw	white
khàaw	news
khâaw	rice

These pairs of words are identical except for length of vowel:

khǎaw	white
khǎw	he, she
khàaw	news
khàw	knee

These pairs of words differ only in the type of initial consonant (one is aspirated; the other isn't):

kâaw	step, pace
khâaw	rice

and

pàa	forest
phàa	to cut

Since these particular types of contrast are not present in English, the student may find it hard to keep them in mind in Thai.

38. Since the experience area covered by a particular word in Thai will usually differ from that in English, the student will usually not know the range of meaning of the word in Thai and may extend it into areas where it is not used. An example of this would be the word hǔu 'ear', which the student might extend to ear of corn or grain where the word ruaŋ is used. In some areas where it might be extended, such as khîihǔu (excretion of the ear) 'earwax', or tàaŋhǔu 'earring', the student may feel afraid to extend it, although the 'basic' meaning of 'ear' is kept. Frequently the student will understand compounds in which a somewhat extended meaning of the word is used, such as hǔuthoorasáp (ear telephone) 'telephone receiver', although he would be unable to orginate a compound of this sort.

39. The meaning of a word as used in a compound may be quite different from the 'basic' meaning learned by the student. In these cases the student will find the compound difficult to understand. An example of this is h̆uukrapǎw (ear bag) 'handle of a bag (suitcase, etc.).'

40. The way that Thai words are put into categories differs from English. For example, wheat, corn, millet, oats, and different varieties of rice all contain the word khâaw:

khâaw	rice, grain
khâawnǐaw	glutinous rice
khâawfâaŋ	millet
khâawsǎalii	wheat
khâawphôot	corn
khâaw	rice, food, grain

In a similar fashion, pocket, pouch, purse, handbag, briefcase, glasses case, and suitcase are all considered as (krapǎw). When a number of Thai words are subsumed under one category, the only problem for the student is recognizing what is being referred to.

A more serious problem arises when one English word has many Thai translations. An example is the word 'carry', which is translated according to how things are carried:

1. h̆am: two people carry with a pole between them

2. h̀aap: two people carry something on a pole on their shoulders

3. h̆ɔɔp: carry on the arm, like a package

253

255

4. hɔ̂ɔj: to carry hanging, on the arm for example

5. thy̌y: to carry in the hands

6. hîw: to carry by the handle, like a basket, bag, etc.

7. bὲɛk: to carry on the back

8. ûm: to carry in one's arm, like a baby

9. banthúk: to carry in a vehicle, like a truck, etc.

10. saphaaj: to carry with a strap over the shoulder

11. kradlat: to carry against the hip or waist, like a
                basket

12. khǒn: to carry or transport large objects

13. phók: to carry wrapped in a cloth

14. thuun hǔa: to carry on the head

41. Another problem that students have in learning Thai
words is that frequently what is expressed as one word in English
may require two or more in Thai. Compare the word 'fetch' with
Thai (paj aw maa) (literally: 'go take come'). Other examples
are: 'store up' (kὲp aw wáj) (literally: collect take keep) or
'squeeze it out' (khán aw ɔ̀ɔk maa) (literally: squeeze take out
come).

APPENDIX N TO CHAPTER 5

LEARNER'S SYNOPSIS OF SWAHILI

(with John Indakwa and John Thiuri)

The content of this appendix is taken from materials prepared for use at the Foreign Service Institute. The original experimental edition was completed in 1967, but the material has been completely rewritten in 1971.

The general purpose of the synopsis is to enable people to retain some orientation to the forest while they are contemplating several of the larger trees. To this end, we have given the same description twice: once in continuous prose form (reproduced here in its entirety), and once with examples and self-testing frames. Only a few selections of this second, rather bulky presentation are given here.

A LEARNER'S SYNOPSIS OF SWAHILI STRUCTURE

TO THE STUDENT

   This Learner's Synopsis of Swahili Structure is an active
introduction to the language. It assumes no prior knowledge
of Swahili. In its present form, the entire synopsis with no
examples is given in continuous, paragraphed form on pp. 261-
271 . Numbers within this version refer to the interrupted
exposition on pp. 272 - 283. The latter consists of pairs of
pages. The left-hand page of each pair repeats the exposition,
adding examples. On the right-hand page opposite each section,
there are simple 'frames,' of the kind found in many self-
instructional programs, by means of which the student can
check his comprehension of the material on the left-hand
pages. Some of these frames will be quite easy. Some, however, will require reflection, and rereading of the left-hand
page. It is hoped that, by providing some kind of intellectual
challenge, and thus involving the reader, this introduction
will qualify as 'active.'

   Because Swahili pronunciation offers comparatively little
difficulty to speakers of English, it is not treated here.

   The vocabulary in each version of the synopsis has intentionally been kept very small. The words in this version are
chosen from among those that the student is most likely to
encounter in reading newspaper accounts of meetings.

   The synopsis contains many internal cross-references. In
addition, it contains references to further information in
E. O. Ashton, Swahili Grammar (1944) and E. C. Polomé, Swahili
Language Handbook (1967).

CHAPTER 5   SYNOPSIS OF SWAHILI

CONTENTS OF SYNOPSIS

OVERVIEW   Par.   1-5

NOUNS AND OTHER SUBSTANTIVES   6-27

   The system   6-7
   The classes   8-16
   The concords   17
   Sets of words showing concord   18-27
      Demonstratives   18
      Possessives   19
      Adjectives   20-21
      Relative amba-   22
      Verbs   23-26
   Pronouns   27

VERBS   28-

   Prefixes   29-
    Tenses   29-41
    Relatives   42-47
    Infinitives   48-50
    The meaningless ku   51-52
    Negation   53-61
    Locative enclitics   62
    'To have'   63-65
    Abbreviated forms of -w- 'be'   66
    Emphatic copula   67
    Compound tenses   68-70
    Concords without antecedents   72-76
   Extensions   77-82

1/ The most common type of sentence in Swahili contains an 'inflected verb phrase.' This phrase may consist of a single verb (par. 29 - 35), or of two verbs (par. 68 - 69).

2/ The sentence may or may not contain a subject expression, 3/ and it may or may not contain object expressions. 4/ It may also contain references to time, manner, etc., but these will give the learner relatively little difficulty.

5/ The parts of Swahili grammar that require most effort from speakers of European languages are (1) the requirements of 'concord' which exist between nouns and other words (including verbs) that are related to them in the sentence, and (2) the internal structure of the verb phrase. 'Concord' is treated in sections 17 - 26 of this synopsis; the verb phrase is covered in sections 28 - 70.

6/ Historically, the concord system is basically alliterative; that is, the same prefix is repeated with all of a set of words that are in agreement with each other. On this basis nouns are divided into a number of 'classes.' The alliterative relationship still shows up clearly in one of the noun classes. 7/ In most classes, however, sound changes that have taken place over the centuries have obscured the alliteration, and made the picture more confusing.

8/ All nouns in the MU-WA class stand for people. All verb infinitives (par. 48f) have the prefix ku- and take concords of the KU class. Almost all members of the U class are abstract nouns with no plural, but some nouns in this class stand for concrete objects and have plurals in the N class. 9/ None of the other classes has any obvious overall meaning, although certain tendencies are worth remembering. 10/ Diminutive nouns are sometimes in the KI-VI class, and

augmentative nouns are sometimes in the LI-MA class. 11/ Many
nouns are derived from verbs by putting them into the MU-MI
class or into the MA class, often with a change of the final
vowel to o. 12/ Names of plants are often in the MU-MI class,
and the corresponding fruits are often in the LI-MA class.
13/ Many nouns borrowed from English or Arabic are in the N
class.

14/ Three of the concordial classes have meanings that
relate to location. These classes are unlike the other classes
in that they contain no nouns, except for mahali 'place' in the
PA class. The PA class has to do with definite place or position, the KU class with direction or indefinite or wider
place, and the MU class with location inside something. If a
noun is put into any of these three classes, it takes the
suffix -ni instead of a prefix. Whether it is in the PA, KU
or MU class must be determined by looking at the words that
agree with it, if any.

15/ Some nouns that stand for people or animals exhibit
some characteristics of one class, but other characteristics
of another class. Thus, some personal nouns have the prefixes
of the KI-VI class, but words that agree with them have concords appropriate for the personal (MU-WA class). 16/ Some
nouns denoting close kin have no prefix in the singular (as
in the N class) and either no prefix (N class) or ma (LI-MA
class) in the plural. The words that agree with these nouns
may have prefixes of the N class or of the MU-WA class.

17/ The actual form of a concordial prefix changes according to the stem or other element to which it is attached.
Table 1 is a summary of the principal variations. The full
forms of some of the most important word types are given in
sections 18 - 26. 18/ The words that agree with nouns include

TABLE 1

Class	NOUN MARKERS Bef. Cons.	Bef. Vowel[1]	CONCORD MARKERS Bef. Cons.	Bef. Vowel[1]
1	m(u)[5]	mw		w
2	wa	w[4]	wa	w[4]
3	m(u)[5]	mw	u	w
4	mi	mi	i	y
5	ji,# [2]	j	li	l
6	ma	m[4]	ya	y
7	ki	ch	ki	ch
8	vi	vy	vi	vy
9	N[3]	ny	i	y
10	N[3]	ny	zi	z
14	u	w	u	w
15	ku	kw	ku	kw
16	(suffix) ni	(suffix) ni	pa[4]	p
17	(suffix) ni	(suffix) ni	ku	kw
18	(suffix) ni	(suffix) ni	m(u)[5]	mw

1   Under certain circumstances, the markers that occur before consonants also are found before vowels:

Nilikiona.   'I saw it (Cl. 7).'

viatu   'shoes'

2   The symbol # stands for the fact that most nouns of Class 5 have no overt marker at all when the stem begins with a consonant.

3   Classes 9 and 10 have no special prefix syllable for nouns, but many nouns in this class begin with a nasal sound (/m, n/etc.).

4   When a stem begins with the vowel /i/ (e.g. /ingi/ 'many') and the prefix ends with /a/, the vowel that is pronounced is /e/: /wengi, mengi, pengi/, instead of the nonexistent */waingi, maingi, paingi/.

5   Coastal standard pronunciation of these prefixes is with syllabic /m/, but the pronunciation /mu/ is often heard also.

demonstratives, 19/ possessives, 20/ adjectives with stem-
initial consonants 21/ and with stem-initial vowels, 22/ and
the relative word amba- (par.47). 23/ Within the verb,
agreement with nouns is required for subject prefixes (par.
28), 24/ object prefixes (par. 28), 25/ and relative prefixes
(par. 28, 42). 26/ Present locative forms (par. 66), though
they are related to the verb -w- 'be,' have a different
subject prefix for the singular of the MU-WA class.

27/ There are non-possessive personal pronouns for first,
second and third person, singular and plural. These refer
only to people, not to things.

28/ A simplified diagram of the verb phrase is in
Figure 1.

SUBJECT PREFIX (23)	TENSE PRFX (29-41)	The verb /-w-/ (70)	FINAL VOWEL (36, 56)	SUBJ. PRFX (23)	TENSE PRFX (29, 34, 68-71)	[OBJ. PRFX] (24)	STEM (77-82)	FINAL VOWEL (36)

The [ ] stands for the fact that the object prefix is often
optional. The arrow stands for the fact that in any given
verb phrase, both of the subject prefixes must be the same.

Figure 1

29/ The principal tenses of Swahili are indicated by
means of prefixes. Certain of these tenses are 'independent.'
This means that if a verb is the only verb in a sentence, it
must be in one of these tenses. Five independent tenses have
prefixes that begin with a consonant. These are the na
tense (present), the li tense (past), the ta tense (future),

the me tense (perfective) and the nge tense (potential).
30/ One independent tense prefix consists of the vowel -a- .
This is one kind of 'general present' tense, and is partially
interchangeable with the na tense (above, par. 29). 31/ A
third 'present tense ' which is used only in talking about
regular, characteristic or permanent actions and states. It
begins with hu-, and is unique in having no subject prefix.

32/ Two important tenses are 'dependent.' This means
that a verb in one of these tenses cannot be the only verb in
the sentence. For some reason, speakers of English generally
neglect these tenses, resorting instead to paraphrases of
what they are accustomed to in their native language. 33/ One
of the dependent tenses has the prefix -ki- . It is sometimes translatable as 'if,' sometimes as 'when,' sometimes as
'while.' A good first approximation to its translation is
'...ing.' 34/ The ki tense is often used instead of the na
tense as the second verb in an inflected verb phrase (see
par. 68 - 70). 35/ It may also be used as the only verb in a
subordinate clause.

The ka tense is used for one or more actions that are
subsequent to some other action in the past. The first verb
in such a series is in the li tense.

36/ One tense functions sometimes as a dependent tense,
but sometimes as an independent tense. This is a noncommittal
tense, which does not specify time, nor even whether the action
will take place at all. It has no tense prefix. For verbs
whose present tense forms end in -a , the noncommittal tense
ends in -e . 37/ For other verbs, there is no vowel change.
38/ The noncommittal tense may be used by itself in making a
suggestion. 39/ It is also used after -taka 'want,' -omba
'request' and many other verbs where the subject of the first

verb is not the same as the subject of the second. 40/ It is also used after a number of individual words, such as lazima 'necessary' and afadhali 'it were better that... '   41/ The noncommittal tense is usually called the 'subjunctive.' It is in fact partly similar to the tenses that go by that name in some European languages. There are differences, however, the most important of which is that the Swahili 'noncommittal tense' is much easier to handle than a French or Spanish 'subjunctive.'

42/ Relative verbs are dependent also, but in a different way. They may be in any of several tenses (par. 29), and take the places normally occupied by verbs or adjectives. The characteristic affixes (except one) have the vowel -o- . 43/ In relative verbs that correspond to the a tense, the relative affix stands at the end of the word. 44/ In all other tenses, it stands between the tense prefix and the object prefix (if there is one). 45/ The future relative has the tense prefix -taka- instead of -ta- . 46/ The present relative of the verb -w- 'be' is irregular. The relative affix stands at the end, as for the a tense (par. 43), and the stem is -li- instead of -w- . 47/ One-word relative forms exist in the affirmative only for the na , li , ta , and a tenses, and in the negative only for the present. For the other tenses (and optionally for these also), relative constructions consist of amba- plus relative affix, followed by the non-relative verb.

48/ The form by which a Swahili verb is usually cited is called the infinitive. It begins with the prefix ku , and may have an object prefix, but no subject or tense prefixes. 49/ In its use, the infinitive resembles European 'infinitives,' but when it is used as a noun it takes its own special

266

concord (see par. 8, 17).

50/ When two verbs are in consecutive independent clauses and have the same tense and the same subject, the second may be put into the infinitive. (Speakers of European languages seldom catch on to this useful trick.)

51/ What is historically the ku of the infinitive shows up in yet another way in affirmative tenses when the stem of the verb is monosyllabic (-pa 'give,' -wa 'be, become,' -ja 'come,' -fa 'die,' -la 'eat' etc.). The word stress always falls on the next-to-last syllable of a word. But there are certain prefixes which never take word stress. They are -na- , -li- , -ta- , -me- and -nge- (par. 29), and the relative prefixes (par. 42). If one of these would otherwise be the next-to-last syllable of the verb, then the meaningless syllable ku is inserted (from a historical point of view, 'retained,' and not 'inserted'). 52/ In the same tenses, if there is an object prefix, the meaningless ku is not needed.

53/ The most troublesome thing about Swahili verbs is the way they form the negative. There are two different problems connected with negatives. One is that the negative tenses don't correspond exactly to the affirmative tenses. There is only one negative to go with the na , a , and hu tenses (par. 29, 30, 31, 56). 54/ The negative of the me tense may be formed with -ja- or with -ku- , depending on the meaning. In this latter case, it is identical with the negative of the li tense.

55/ The other problem with negatives is that the learner should be prepared to find that each negative tense is formed in its own peculiar way. (It isn't quite that complicated, but if one starts with that assumption, then the similarities

among the tenses will stand out as welcome relief.) 56/ The
change of the final vowel from -a to   -i is used in the
negative present, and only there. This is also the only
negative tense that has no negative prefix after the subject
prefix. 57/ The negative prefixes -ja- and -ku- are
found in only one tense apiece. 58/ The prefix -si- is
found in the noncommittal tense (par. 36 - 41), the negative
relative of the present tense, and in one way of making the
negative of the nge tense. 59/ Negative infinitives are
unique in using -to- . 60/ The negative that corresponds
to the ki tense (par. 34, 35) contains the prefix combination -sipo- . It is thus a present negative relative
form (par. 58) with the concord of the PA class (par. 74).
As is explained in par. 74, the use of this concord without
an antecedent refers to time or place. 61/ The pre-prefix
ha- stands before the subject prefix in most tenses, but ha
plus the first person singular subject prefix ni- (par. 23)
comes out si- .

62/ Verbs that have to do with location may have
locative 'enclitics' representing any of the three locative
classes (par. 14, 23). These stand at the very end of the
verb, after everything else.

63/ The Swahili construction that most often corresponds
to the English main verb 'have' consists of -w- 'be'
plus na 'with.' 64/ When the subject prefix is in one of
the locative classes, this construction is usually translated
'there is, was, etc.'

65/ In place of the relative phrases aliye na 'who has'
or palipo na ('where there is' (par. 46,64), Swahili often
uses a concordial prefix with the stem -enye 'having.'

66/ The verb -w- 'be, become' differs from all other Swahili verbs in that certain of its present tense forms are, in most of their uses, drastically abbreviated.

67/ The forms ni 'is, are, am' ·and si 'is, are, am not,' which we have described as optional abbreviated forms of -w- 'be' (par. 66), are usually called respectively the affirmative and the negative 'copula.' Swahili has a construction that is like these copular constructions except that it is emphatic. In this construction, instead of ni or si, we find ndi- or si- with the relative affix (par. 42).

68/ Swahili has a very handy and very logical way of making time relationships more precise by using inflected verb phrases with two words (par. 28). In any such phrase, the first of the two words sets the time generally: past, present or future; the tense of the second verb is relative to the time established by the first. 69/ If the second verb is future in relation to the first, then the noncommittal tense (par. 36 - 41) is used, and not the ta tense (par. 29). 70/ In the construction of these phrases, certain things are always true: (1) the first word is a form of -w- 'be, become;' (2) the second word may contain any root, including -w- ; (3) no other word may stand between the two; (4) the subject prefixes of the two verbs are identical. When the second verb in this construction is also a form of -w- , it may turn up as the abbreviated form ni (par. 66-7). But parallel to each of these sentences is another, identical except for the absence of ni , which is virtually synonymous with it.

71/ A two-word inflected verb phrase in which -w- 'be' has its stem form -li (cf. par.   46) preceded by the

prefix -nga- conveys the idea that an action is still going
on.

72/ The only frequently-occurring feature of verb prefixes that remains to be covered is the way certain class
concords are used with no noun of that class to refer back to.
This can be mystifying at first, but once learned it is highly
useful. 73/ When the subject of a verb is an infinitive or a
noun clause, it usually follows the verb, and when such a
subject follows, the subject prefix is i- , as for the
singular of the N class (par. 13, 17). This in some ways
corresponds to one use of 'it' as the subject of certain
English sentences.

74/ When the PA-class relative concord is used with no
locative noun to refer back to, it usually refers to time and
is translatable as 'when.' This may be true even with a
subject noun like wakati 'time,' which is in the U-N class.

75/ When the VI-class concord is used with no VI-class
noun to refer back to, it usually refers to the manner in
which something was done. This may be true even when the
VI-class word refers to a noun like jinsi 'manner,' which
is in the N class.

76/ The concords of the MA class are sometimes used
where the MA-class noun mambo 'matters' may be said to be
understood in the context.

77/ But the Swahili verb has suffixes (or 'extensions')
as well as prefixes, Students, teachers and textbook writers
sometimes slight the extensions, for at least three reasons:

1. Extensions don't have to do with matters like time,
   affirmation and negation, or who is doing the action.

270

2. Most of them lack a simple English equivalent. A root plus one extension may be translated quite differently from the same root with another extension.

3. Unlike the prefixes, some of the extensions vary markedly in their form.

78/ Nevertheless, extensions are in some ways of as much potential value to a student as the prefixes are. Familiarity with them will do more than anything else (except possibly a knowledge of Arabic) to increase vocabulary, particularly in reading and oral comprehension.

79/ A verb stem may contain no extensions, or one, or more than one. Some of the most common are the passive, 80/ the causative, 81/ the applicative, 82/ and the reciprocal

1.   The most common type of sentence in Swahili contains an
'inflected verb phrase.' This phrase may consist of a single
verb (par. 29 - 35), or of two verbs (par. 68 - 69). In the
following examples, the inflected verb phrases have been
underlined.

Viongozi <u>walikutana</u>.	The leaders <u>met one another</u>.
Mkutano <u>umemalizika</u>.	The meeting <u>has ended</u>.
Viongozi <u>walikuwa wamekutana</u>.	The leaders <u>had met one another</u>.
<u>Ulikuwa umemalizika</u>.	<u>It had ended</u>.
<u>Alikuwa ameanzisha</u> mkutano.	<u>He had opened</u> the meeting.

2.   The sentence may or may not contain a subject expression.
In these examples, the subject expressions are underlined:

Walikutana.	They met.
<u>Wanachama</u> walikutana.	<u>The members</u> met.
<u>Wanachama hao wote</u> walikutana.	<u>All those members</u> met.

(Polomé, 159)

272

1.   In the following sentences, which word is probably the inflected verb?

>   Viongozi walifika.

>> [walifika]

>   Raís aliondoka.

>> [aliondoka]

>   Chama kitaongozwa.

>> [kitaongozwa]

Which is the most likely translation for each of these inflected verb phrases?

>   walishauriana: they consulted?   they had consulted?

>> [they consulted]

>   walikuwa wame-   they consulted?
>   shauriana: they had consulted?

>> [they had consulted]

Which of the following is more likely to be translated into Swahili by two words: they have escaped? they had escaped?

>> [they had escaped]

2.   Pick out the subject expressions in these sentences:

>   Chama kitaundwa.

>> [chama]

>   Ushirika mkubwa utaundwa.

>> [ushirika mkubwa]

>   Wengi wameuawa.

>> [wengi]

3.   The sentence may or may not contain an object expression.
In these examples, the object expressions are underlined:

    Walianzisha mkutano.   They began the meeting.

    Kiongozi aliwahutubia   The leader addressed
        wanachama.   the members.

    Wanachama hawakukutana.   The members didn't meet.

                                        (Polomé, 159)

4.   The sentence may also contain references to time, manner,
etc., but these will give the learner relatively little
difficulty.   Such expressions are underlined in the following
examples:

    Mkutano ulifanywa jana.   The meeting was held yesterday.

    Wote walikutana ofisini. All met in the office.

    Mkutano ulifanywa kwa   The meeting was held in a
        moyo wa kusikilizana.   harmonious spirit.

                          (Ashton 18, 125-32, 158-77, 195-200.
                          Polomé 128-9, 145-47)

3. Pick out the object expressions in these sentences:

Walianzisha majadiliano.

[majadiliano]

Tulimaliza masomo yetu.

[masomo yetu]

The normal place for subject expressions seems to be ____ the verb, and the normal place for object expressions seems to be ____ it.

[before, after]

In this respect, Swahili (resembles? differs from?) English.

[resembles]

4. In the sentence:

Mkutano utafanywa kesho.

a good guess at the meaning of kesho would be: chairman? tommorrow? this?

[tomorrow]

The word ofisini has to do with: time? manner? place?

[place]

The reason why this Synopsis does not go into more detail about expressions of time, place and manner is that:

they are too complicated?
they will not cause great trouble?

[both]

5. The parts of Swahili grammar that require the most effort
from speakers of European languages are (1) the requirements
of 'concord' which exist between nouns and other words
(including verbs) that are related to them in the sentence,
and (2) the internal structure of the verb phrase. 'Concord'
is treated in par. 17 - 26 of this synopsis; the verb phrase
is covered in par. 29 - 70.

                    *   *   *   *   *

19. Demonstratives must agree with the nouns to which they
refer. There are three series of demonstratives, typified by
huyu, huyo, and yule. The huyu series corresponds closely to
many of the uses of English 'this, these:'

    mwanachama huyu   this member

    wanachama hawa   these members

    chama hiki   this organization

The huyo series corresponds to 'that, those' when the noun is
already sufficiently identified either by having been mentioned before, or by being near to the hearer:

    kiongozi huyo   the aforementioned leader
    kalamu hiyo   that pen near you, or
                       the aforementioned pen

The yule series corresponds to 'that, those' when the noun is
in need of further identification either through pointing, or
through use of words:

    jumba lile   that building over yonder

    kiongozi yule   that leader who called the
      aliyeita mkutano   meeting

5. The parts of Swahili grammar that require most study are:

    (1) the internal structure of _____,
    [the verb phrase]

and (2) the requirements of 'concord' between _____

    and _____.
    [nouns, other words related to
    them]

* * * * *

18. In the following English sentences, choose the Swahili demonstrative that would be needed in translating it:

Do you see that bridge?	hili?	hilo?	lile?
			[lile]
What was that name?	hili?	hilo?	lile?
			[hilo]
What was that address?	hii?	hiyo?	ile?
			[hiyo]
These people are waiting for you.	hawa?	hao?	wale?
			[hawa]
That meeting yesterday was long.	huu?	huo?	ule?
			[huo]
Come <u>here</u>!	hapa?	hapo?	pale?
			[hapa]
He's <u>over yonder</u>.	hapa?	hapo?	pale?
			[pale]

The actual forms of the demonstratives are given below, with
the concordial part of each underlined:

CLASS	huyu series		huyo series		yule series	
	sg.	pl.	sg.	pl.	sg.	pl.
MU-WA	huyu	hawa	huyo	hao	yule	wale
MU-MI	huu	hii	huo	hiyo	ule	ile
LI-MA	hili	haya	hilo	hayo	lile	yale
KI-VI	hiki	hivi	hicho	hivyo	kile	vile
N	hii	hizi	hiyo	hizo	ile	zile
U	huu		huo		ule	

Locatives:

PA	hapa	hapo	pale
KU	huku	huko	kule
MU	humu	humo	mle

(Ashton 327, 58-9
Polomé 106-7)

278

If you can say <u>mji huu</u>, then you can also say <u>mji huo</u> and <u>mji</u> ____.

[ule]

If you can say <u>kitu hicho</u>, then you can also say _____ and _____ .

[kitu hiki, kitu kile]

Fill in the blanks by referring to the left-hand page:

mtu huyu	mtu ____	mtu ____
mto huu	mto ____	mto ____
mito hii	____ ____	____ ____
watu ____	watu hao	____ ____
jimbo ____	____ ____	jimbo lile
____ ____	kitu hicho	____ ____
maongozi haya	____ ____	____ ____
kiti ____	____ ____	kiti kile
vyama ____	____ hivyo	____ ____
nyumba hii	____ ____	____ ____
nyumba hizi	____ ____	____ ____
kugoma huku	____ ____	____ ____
umoja ____	____ huo	____ ____

The plural of <u>kile</u> is <u>vile</u>. What is the plural of:

ule?

[ile]

hicho?

[hivyo]

hili?

279

[haya]

*   *   *   *   *

29. The principal tenses of Swahili are indicated by means of
prefixes. Certain of these tenses are 'independent.' This
means that if a verb is the only verb in a sentence, it must
be in one of these tenses. Five independent tenses have prefixes that begin with a consonant. In these examples, the
tense prefixes are underlined.

    Wan_a_kutana.   They are meeting.

    Wal_i_kutana.   They met.

    Wat_a_kutana.   They will meet.

    Wam_e_kutana.   They (have) met.

    Wan_ge_kutana.   They would meet (if ...).

                              (Ashton 35-8, 187
                                Polomé 115-7, 120)

*   *   *   *   *

53. The most troublesome thing about Swahili verbs is the way
they form the negative. There are two different problems
connected with negatives. One is that the negative tenses
don't correspond exactly to the affirmative tenses. There is
only one negative to go with the _na_, _a_, and _hu_ tenses (par.
29, 30, 31, 56).

    Wan_a_kutana.   They meet/are meeting. (_na_ tense)
    Wakutana.   They meet.   (_a_ tense)
    Hukutana.   They regularly/characteristically
                      meet.   (_hu_ tense)

    Hawakutani.   They aren't meeting/don't meet.
                    (Ashton 70-2   Polomé 114)

*　　*　　*　　*　　*

29.　State whether each of the following verbs is FUTURE, PAST, PRESENT, PERFECTIVE or POTENTIAL in its tense:

wamehudhuria	[PERFECTIVE]
tumehudhuria	[PERFECTIVE]
tutaonekana	[FUTURE]
ataonekana	[FUTURE]
angeonekana	[POTENTIAL]
angehudhuria	[POTENTIAL]
tulihudhuria	[PAST]
vitahusiana	[FUTURE]
ningejaribu	[POTENTIAL]

One of the dependent tenses, to be discussed in a later paragraph, is represented by /wakihudhuria/. What is the prefix that marks this tense?　　　　　　　　　　[-ki-]

*　　*　　*　　*　　*

53.　Construct the negative forms that correspond to the following affirmatives:

wanaondoka　　　　　　　　　　＿＿＿＿＿＿＿＿＿[hawaondoki]

kinajulikana　　　　　　　　　＿＿＿＿＿＿＿＿＿[hakijulikani]

Which could **not** be an affirmative counterpart of the negative form in the left-hand column?

hakijulikani:　kinajulikana?　kilijulikana?　hujulikana?
　　　　　　　　　　　　　　　　　　　　　　　　[kilijulikana]

hatuoni:　　　huona?　　　　twaona?　　　　tungeona?
　　　　　　　　　　　　　　　　　　　　　　　　[tungeona]

hawawezi:　　waweza?　　　huweza?　　　　hutoka?
　　　　　　　　　　　　　　　　　　　　　　　　[hutoka]

54. The negative of the <u>me</u> tense may be formed with -<u>ja</u>-
or with -<u>ku</u>- , depending on the meaning. In this latter
case, it is identical with the negative of the <u>li</u> tense.

Wa<u>me</u>kutana.	They met/ have met.
Wa<u>li</u>kutana.	They met.
Hawa<u>ja</u>kutana.	They haven't met yet.
Hawa<u>ku</u>kutana.	They didn't meet.
I<u>me</u>vunjika.	It has gotten / is broken.
Hai<u>ku</u>vunjika.	It isn't broken.
Hai<u>ja</u>vunjika.	It hasn't gotten broken yet.

(Ashton 70-2)

54. Which is the more likely translation?

hayakumwagika: it isn't spilt? it isn't spilt yet?
                                [it isn't spilt]

hayajamwagika: it isn't spilt? it isn't spilt yet?
                                [it isn't spilt yet]

If jana means 'yesterday,' then which of the following
makes sense? Hawajakutana jana. Hawakukutana jana.
                        [Hawakukutana jana.]

The word sijala probably (means? does not mean?)
'I didn't eat.'

                        [does not mean]

283

APPENDIX O TO CHAPTER 5

PART OF <u>A LEARNER'S SYNOPSIS OF KIRUNDI STRUCTURE</u>
(with Raymond Setukuru)

The Thai synopsis (Appendix M) was written in 1970-71, and the Swahili synopsis (Appendix N) was first drafted in 1967. The Kirundi synopsis, of which this appendix contains a part, was written still earlier, in 1963, as an unexpected consequence of a decision to try to teach students to use tone in speaking the language. Kirundi tones are not numerous, but the tone on any given syllable, particularly in the verb forms, changes in ways that are both puzzling to the foreigner and grammatically significant to native speakers. A series of individual grammar notes, distributed among the 30 units of the course, simply would not have been effective.

What is reproduced below is the grammatical section of the synopsis. Vowels, consonants and tones are treated in other sections. These materials illustrate a physical arrangement of examples which is different from that used in Swahili synopsis (pp. 272 ff.), and also show how a synopsis can deal with a type of structural problem which tends to elude the student because tone is not as real for him as vowels and consonants are.

A LEARNER'S SYNOPSIS OF KIRUNDI STRUCTURE:

Kirundi is the principal language of Burundi. It shares a
high degree of mutual intelligibility with Kinyarwanda, the language of Rwanda. Considered together, the cluster Kirundi-
Kinyarwanda ranks third among Bantu languages, after Swahili and
Lingala, with respect to number of speakers. There are however
two important differences between Swahili and Lingala on the one
hand and Kirundi-Kinyarwanda on the other: (1) Swahili and Lingala
are spoken over very wide areas, and a high proportion of their
speakers have some other Bantu language as the mother tongue;
Kirundi-Kinyarwanda is spoken in a relatively small area, as the
first language. (2) Swahili and Lingala are relatively free of
troublesome complexities for the learner; Kirundi and Kinyarwanda
are full of them. The two books in this series which are concerned with Swahili and Lingala set out the grammar of those languages in the form of a series of individual notes, distributed
throughout the units of the course. The present volume presents
the details of Kirundi grammar in the same way. In addition,
however, this synopsis has been prepared, first of all to provide
orientation for those who plan to use the entire book, and sec-
ondarily for the student whose desire is to learn as much as possible about the language in the shortest time. Only the most
important features of the grammar are mentioned at all, and the
vocabulary used in the examples has intentionally been kept small.
The exercises, with answers given in square brackets at the right,
are not intended to make this synopsis into an auto-instructional
program, but only to give the reader an opportunity to participate
if he desires to do so, and to keep constant check on his understanding of the text.   285

CHAPTER 5 A LEARNER'S SYNOPSIS OF KIRUNDI STRUCTURE

The analysis on which this synopsis is based is found in
Essai de Grammaire Rundi, (Tervuren: Musée Royal, 1959) by A.E.
Meeussen. Certain key ideas concerning style of treatment have
been acquired over the years from many teachers and colleagues,
especially William E. Welmers.

The problems which are faced by a non-Bantu student of
Kirundi may be classified under the three traditional headings of
phonology, morphology, and syntax. 'Phonology' has to do with all
aspects of pronunciation, but without consideration for the grammatical function or the dictionary meaning of what is pronounced.
'Morphology' is a description of the meaningful units of the language (prefixes, roots, stems, etc.) and of the ways in which
they combine with one another within single 'words'. 'Syntax'
continues this description up to the levels of what are usually
called 'phrases' and 'sentences'.

This synopsis concentrates on two of the most complex parts
of Kirundi structure: (1) the morphology of the verb, and (2)
the pronunciation of the vowels and consonants.

I. PRINCIPAL FEATURES OF KIRUNDI GRAMMAR

Subject prefixes, object prefixes, roots and stems. The
kinds of meaningful elements which may be found in any one Kirundi
verb form are both numerous and highly diverse. There are three,
however, at which the student should look first, both because
they serve as useful landmarks in the description of complicated
verb forms, and because they correspond closely with familiar
categories of Indo-European grammar. These three kinds of elements
are (1) subject prefixes, (2) object prefixes and (3) roots.

The order in which these components of the verb have been named is the order in which they occur within a word. The most central of the three is the root:

        tu<u>duu</u>ga...   'we climb ...'
          tu<u>gee</u>nda...   'we go ...'

These two words differ in meaning in a way which is apparently close to the difference between English 'climb' and 'go'. They differ in form by the difference between /-duug-/ and /-geend-/. The forms /-duug-/ and /-geend-/ may thus be identified with approximately the same meanings as those for which 'climb' and 'go' are used in English. Further investigation of Kirundi would disclose no basis for recognizing any more divisions within either of these forms; they are therefore what the linguist calls ROOTS. Every language has a large stock of roots.

What is the root in each of these verb forms:

        tubona...   'we see...'   [-bon-]

        tugura...   'we buy...'   [-gur-]

        tugoroora...   'we iron...'   [-goroor-]

Each Kirundi verb form has one and only one root. A root may have any of several shapes, some of which are:

    -C- (single consonant)   -v-   'to go from'
    -VC- (vowel and consonant)   -íg-   'to study, learn'
    -CVC- (one short vowel)   -kór-   'to work, do'
    -CV$_1$V$_1$C- (one long vowel)   -duug-   'to climb'
    -V$_1$CV$_2$C- (two vowels, which   -andik-   'to write'
          may or may not be
          alike, separated
          by a consonant)

What is the root in each of these forms?

tuva...	we go from...	[-v-]
bava...	they go from...	[-v-]
baja...	they go...	[-j-]
baba...	they live...	[-b-]
bakora...	they do...	[-kor-]
baandika...	they write...	[-andik-]

In each group of three words, state which two have roots of the same general shape (i.e. -CVC-, -VC-, etc.):

ba<u>gur</u>a	
ba<u>goroor</u>a	[-goroor-]
Ba<u>mesuur</u>a	[-mesuur-]
ba<u>b</u>a	[-b-]
ba<u>bon</u>a	
ba<u>v</u>a	[-v-]

By far the most common shapes for roots are -CVC- and $-CV_1V_1C-$.

In Kirundi, a verb root is always followed by one or more suffixes:

-som-	'to read'
-som-a	(used in certain verb forms)
-som-ye	(used in certain other verb forms)
-som-e	(used in still other forms)

288

-som-eesh-   (a non-final suffix with causative
                        (meaning) to cause to read)

-geend-   'to go'

-geend-eesh-   'to cause to go'

What is the final suffix in each of these forms?

tugoroora	'we iron'	[-a]
bagura	'they buy'	[-a]
bagure	'that they may buy'	[-e]
tugeende	'that we may go'	[-e]

The second of each of these pairs of verb froms contains
one non-final suffix. What is it?

babona	'they see'	
babonana	'they see each other'	[-an-]
turima	'we cultivate'	
turimiisha	'we cause to cultivate'	[-iish-]

Except in the simplest imperative forms, the root is preceded by one or more prefixes of various kinds:

som-a	'read!'
ba-som-a	'they read'
nti-ba-som-á	'they don't read'

Verb prefixes will be dealt with more fully below.

In discussion of Kirundi verbs, it is expedient to use, in
addition to 'root', the terms STEM and BASE. The STEM of a
Kirundi verb form is defined as the root plus all suffixes.

289

CHAPTER 5 A LEARNER'S SYNOPSIS OF KIRUNDI STRUCTURE

The BASE of a Kirundi verb is defined as the root plus all suffixes except the final suffix.

Most kinds of Kirundi verb forms must contain, in addition to the stem, a subject prefix:

m-vuga	'I speak'
u-vuga	'you (sg) speak'
a-vuga	'he/she speaks'
tu-vuga	'we speak'
mu-vuga	'you (pl) speak'
ba-vuga	'they speak'

It will be noted that the subject prefixes stand for combinations of person (first, second, third) and number (singular, plural):

	Singular	Plural
1.	n- (or m-) 'I'	tu- 'we'
2.	u- 'you (sg)'	mu- 'you (pl)'
3.	a- 'he, she'	ba- 'they'

If /asoma/ is translated 'he, she reads', what is the translation of /musoma/?

['you (pl.) read']

/basoma/? ['they read']

/nsoma/? ['I read']

If /bageenda/ is one translation is equivalent of 'they go' write the corresponding translation equivalent of:

'I go'	[ngeenda]
'you (pl.) go'	[mugeenda]
'we go '	[tugeenda]
'he/she goes'	[ageenda]

290

Differentiation of person and number are familiar from the study of non-Bantu languages. But these six prefixes are used only when the subject is personal. For nonpersonal third person subjects (and for some personal ones) Kirundi uses other subject prefixes. Just which one is chosen depends on the identity of the noun that is the subject:

<u>inyama</u> <u>zi</u>raziimvye   'meat is expensive'
<u>umukaáte</u> <u>u</u>raziimvye   'bread is expensive'
<u>ibiríibwa</u> <u>bi</u>raziimvye   'foodstuffs are expensive'
<u>imicuúngwa</u> <u>i</u>raziimvye   'oranges are expensive'

For this reason, it will be necessary in this discussion of verb forms, to glance briefly at the nouns of the language.

In some, but not all cases, the student will soon learn to perceive an alliterative relationship between the subject prefix of a verb and the prefix that begins the noun subject of that verb.

After each of the words in the list, write either /iraziimvyye/ or /uraziimvye/ or /biraziimvye/:

Umukaáte _____.	'Bread is expensive.'	[uraziimvye]
Imikaáte _____.	'Breads are expensive.'	[iraziimvye]
Ibiintu _____.	'Things are expensive.'	[biraziimvye]
Imidúga _____.	'Cars are expensive.'	[iraziimvye]
Ibitabo _____.	'Books are expensive.'	[biraziimvye]
Umudúga _____.	'The car is expensive.'	[uraziimvye]

Generally, about half of the prefixes are used with singular meaning, and most of the rest are used with plural meaning. Most noun stems, then, occur with at least two prefixes——one

291

CHAPTER 5 A LEARNER'S SYNOPSIS OF KIRUNDI STRUCTURE

singular and one plural:

<u>umuc</u>uúngwa	'orange'
<u>imic</u>uúngwa	'oranges'
<u>ikii</u>ntu	'thing'
<u>ibii</u>ntu	'things'
i<u>zí</u>na	'name'
ama<u>zí</u>na	'names'
etc.	

In general, non-personal noun stems that have /umu-/ in the singular have /imi-/ in the plural, stems that have /iki-/ in the singular have /ibi-/ in the plural, and so forth, but there are some exceptions.

What is the plural form that corresponds to each of the following singular nouns:

umutí	'drug'	_____	'drugs'	[imití]
ikiintu	'thing'	_____	'things'	[ibiintu]
umushuumba	'servant'	_____	'servants'	[abashuumba]
umutéetsi	'cook'	_____	'cooks'	[abatéetsi]
igituúngwa	'domestic animal'	_____	'dom. animals'	[ibituúngwa]
umudúga	'car'	_____	'cars'	[imidúga]

What is the singular form that corresponds to each of these plurals?

ibiintu	'things'	_____	'thing'	[ikiintu]
abashuumba	'servants'	_____	'servant'	[umushuumba]
abakáraáni	'clerks'	_____	'clerk'	[umukáraáni]

ibiraato	'shoes'	_____	'shoe'	[ikiraato]
iminwe	'fingers'	_____	'finger'	[umunwe]
imipaka	'boundaries'	_____	'boundary'	[umupaka]

Matching of the subject prefix of the verb with the prefix of the noun subject is called CONCORD. 'Concord' affects the prefixes of several other kinds of words also. Nouns that are alike with respect to the concordial prefixes that go with them are said to be in the same CLASS. There are eighteen such 'classes' in Kirundi. (Remember that in this sense the singular form /ikiintu/ 'thing' and the plural /ibiintu/ 'things' are in different 'classes'.)

In the following pairs of sentences, the concordial prefixes have been underlined. State whether the two nouns (double underlining) are in the same class, or in different classes:

Ikiraato	caanje	kirǐhe?	'Where is my shoe?'	[same class]
Ikigóori	caanje	kirǐhe?	'Where is my maize?'	

Ikiraato	caanje	kirǐhe?	'Where is my shoe?'	[same class]
Igitabo	caanje	kirǐhe?	'Where is my book?'	

Ikiraato	caawe	kirǐhe?	'Where is your shoe?'	[different
Ikiínga	ryaawe	rirǐhe?	'Where is your bicycle?'	classes]

Umugeenzi	waawe	arǐhe?	'Where is your friend?'	[different
Umudúga	waawe	urǐhe?	'Where is your car?'	classes]

Impuúzu	yaanje	irǐhe?	'Where is my cloth?'	[different
Impuúzu	zaanje	zirǐhe?	'Where are my clothes/ cloths?'	classes]

CHAPTER 5 A LEARNER'S SYNOPSIS OF KIRUNDI STRUCTURE

An object prefix, unlike a subject prefix , is never required in a Kirundi verb, but it is optional in most forms. The
object prefix reflects the class of the object of the verb, just
as the subject prefix reflects the class of the subject. For
most classes, the subject and object prefixes are identical in
shape. The object prefix follows the subject prefix and stands
immediately before the stem:

tubiroónke	'that we should receive them' (e.g. /ibiintu/ 'things')
babiroónke	'that they should receive them'
bakiroónke	'that they should receive it' (e.g. /ikiintu/ 'the thing')
baziroónke	'that they should receive them' (e.g. /impuúzu/ 'clothes')

The most striking difference in the use of subject and object
prefixes is that the subject prefix must be used whether or not
there is an explicit noun subject, while the object prefix is
not often used unless the noun object itself is omitted. In
this respect the object prefix of a Bantu verb is similar to the
object pronouns of many European languages. A list of subject
and object prefixes is found below. The numbers are those which
are customarily assigned to these classes in the study of Bantu
languages generally, and which will be used throughout this course.

	Basic form of subject prefix	Basic form of object prefix
reflexive		-íi-
1 sg.	n-	-ny-
1 pl.	tu-	-tu-
2 sg.	u-	-ku-
2 pl.	mu-	-ba-

Class 1 (3 sg. personal)	a-	-mu-
Class 2 (3 pl. personal)	ba-	-ba-
3	u-	-wu-
4	i-	-yi-
5	ri-	-ri-
6	ya-	-ya-
7	ki-	-ki-
8	bi-	-bi-
9	i-	-yi-
10	zi-	-zi-
11	ru-	-ru-
12	ka-	-ka-
13	tu-	-tu-
14	bu-	-bu-
15	ku-	-ku-
16	ha-	-ha-
18	mu-	

Choose the correct object prefix for the second sentence in each pair. The class number for the noun object is given in parentheses.

Baguriisha ibitooke. (8)   Ba____guriisha.   [Babiguriisha.]
'They sell bananas.'   'They sell them.'

Baguriisha ibitabo.   Ba____guriisha.   [-bi-]
'They sell books.'

Baguriisha imiduga. (4)   Ba____guriisha.   [-yi-]
'They sell cars.'

Baguriisha impuúzu. (10)   Ba____guriisha.   [-zi-]
'They sell clothes.'

Baguriisha amǎgi. (6)   Ba____guriisha.   [-ya-]
'They sell eggs.'

CHAPTER 5 A LEARNER'S SYNOPSIS OF KIRUNDI STRUCTURE

What is the grammatical term for the underlined part of each word?

Ba<u>bi</u>gura.	[object prefix]
<u>Ba</u>bigura.	[subject prefix]
Babi<u>bona</u>.	[stem]
Babigur<u>iisha</u>.	[non-final suffix]
<u>Tu</u>bikeneye.	[subject prefix]
Tu<u>yi</u>keneye.	[object prefix]
Bazigoroor<u>a</u>.	[final suffix]
Babig<u>uriisha</u>.	[base]

Pick out the part of each word that is named by the grammatical term:

The subject prefix in /bagura/. 'they sell'	[<u>ba</u>gura]
The object prefix in /tubibona/. 'we see them'	[tu<u>bi</u>bona]
The stem in /tuyarimiisha/. 'we cause them to cultivate'	[tuyar<u>imiisha</u>]
The base in /tuyarimiisha/.	[tuya<u>rimiisha</u>]
The non-final suffix in /tuyarimiisha/.	[tuyarim<u>iisha</u>]
The root in /tuyarimiisha/.	[tuya<u>rim</u>iisha]

The separate verb forms which may be constructed on a single verb base in Kirundi number in the thousands. Fortunately, the system by which they are formed is not so complicated as this might suggest. Many of them differ from one another only in the identity of the subject and/or object prefixes which they contain. In general, the choice of one of these prefixes rather than another does not have any effect on the meaning of the remaining part of the verb form, or the grammatical structures in which it may be used. For this reason, it is possible to make a preliminary division of the thousands of forms into about 60 'sets'. A SET of forms is defined for purposes of this discussion as including all verb forms which differ from one another only with respect to their bases and their subject and object prefixes.

Which two in each of these groups of three verbs are in the same 'set'? (The base of each verb has been underlined.)

bazoot<u>aang</u>ura	'they will begin'	[bazootaangura]
bazoo<u>kor</u>a	'they will do'	[bazookora]
ba<u>kor</u>a	'they (will) do'	

n<u>doond</u>era	'I'm looking for'	[ndoondera]
n<u>dor</u>a		[ndora]
nzoo<u>geend</u>a	'I will go'	

ntibame<u>súur</u>a	'they don't launder'	[ntibamesúura]
nda<u>b</u>a	'I live'	
ntitu<u>vug</u>á	'we don't speak'	[ntiduvugá]

ba<u>geend</u>a	'they go'	
ba<u>geend</u>é	'that they should go'	[bageendé]
mut<u>aang</u>úre	'that you should begin'	[mutaangúre]

There are 21 subject prefixes and 21 object prefixes, plus the possibility of the absence of an object prefix, so that for any given base the number of forms in one set is as large as 21 x 21 or 441. There are over 60 such sets, which means a total of over 25,000 forms with any one stem.

The sets of verb forms may most clearly be described in terms of six dimensions. These will be described in order of the number of contrasting sets in which they are involved.

Dimension 1: <u>Affirmative vs. negative</u>. This is a two-way contrast. The overt representation of the contrast is either the initial prefix /nti-/, or the non-initial prefix /-ta-/. The former is used with all indicative forms (see Dimension 2), the latter with all non-indicative forms. All 60 sets are committed on this dimension. That is, it is possible to say definitely of any set either that it is affirmative or that it is negative. The meaning difference is affirmation vs. negation.

For each verb form two proposed translations are given. Pick the correct one:

ntibaboná	ꞌthey seeꞌ ꞌthey donꞌt seeꞌ	[they donꞌt see]
tumesuura	ꞌwe launderꞌ ꞌwe donꞌt launderꞌ	[we launder]
bátageenda	ꞌthey having goneꞌ ꞌthey not having goneꞌ	[they not having gone]
ntidukورá	ꞌwe workꞌ ꞌwe donꞌt workꞌ	[we donꞌt work]

Dimension 2: <u>Mood</u>. This is a four-way contrast. The overt representation of three of the four categories is found in the tones; the fourth is characterized by a vowel before the subject prefix. All 60 sets are committed on this dimension. The four categories differ with respect to the syntactic positions in which they are used: indicative forms are used in main clauses, relative forms as modifiers of substantives, autonomous forms as substantives, and participial forms in other dependent verb positions.

Most typically, the relative form has a tone on the syllable after the beginning of the root.

Choose the better rough translation for each verb, and say whether it is INDICATIVE, or RELATIVE:

baboná	'they see' '... who see'	['who see': REL.]
babona	'they see' '... who see'	['they see': IND.]
ageenda	'he goes' '... who goes'	['he goes': IND.]
ageendá	'he goes' '... who goes'	['... who goes': REL.]
bamesúura	'they launder' '... who launder'	['... who launder': REL.]
bataangura	'they begin' '... who begin'	['they begin': IND.]
ziziimvye	'they are expensive' '... which are expensive'	['they are expensive']
ziziimvyé	'they are expensive' '... which are expensive'	['which are expensive']

| biziimbúutse | 'they are cheap'
 '... which are cheap' | ['which are cheap'] |

Participial forms have a tone on the first vowel after the first consonant. Choose the better rough translation for each verb, and say whether it is INDICATIVE or PARTICIPIAL:

bábona	'they see' 'they seeing'	['they seeing':PART.]
amesuura	'he launders' 'he laundering'	['he launders':IND.]
amésuura	'he launders' 'he laundering'	['he laundering':PART.]
ushobora	'you are able' 'you being able'	['you are able':IND.]
ushóbora	'you (sg.) are able' 'you being able'	['you being able':PART.]
múshobora	'you (pl.) are able' 'you being able'	['you (pl.) being able': PART.]

Choose the nearest translation, and say whether each verb form is INDICATIVE, RELATIVE, or PARTICIPIAL:

| bábona | 'they see'
 '... who see'
 'they seeing' | ['they seeing':PART.] |
| baboná | '... who see'
 'they see'
 'they seeing' | ['... who see':REL.] |

300

babona	⌐... who see⌐ ⌐they see⌐ ⌐they seeing⌐	[⌐they see⌐: IND.]
izíimbuutse	⌐it is cheap⌐ ⌐... which is cheap⌐ ⌐it being cheap⌐	[⌐it being cheap⌐: PART.]
bashobóra	⌐they are able⌐ ⌐... who are able⌐ ⌐they being able⌐	[... who are able⌐: REL.]

The autonomous mood has an extra vowel before the subject prefix. Choose the better translation, and state whether each form is RELATIVE, or AUTONOMOUS:

baboná	⌐... who see⌐ ⌐ones who see⌐	[⌐... who see⌐:REL.]
ababóna	⌐... who see⌐ ⌐ones who see⌐	[⌐ones who see⌐:AUT.]
ziziimvyé	⌐... which are expensive⌐ ⌐ones that are expensive⌐	[⌐... which are expensive⌐ REL.]
izizíimvye	⌐... which are expensive⌐ ⌐ones that are expensive⌐	[⌐ones that are expensive⌐ AUT.]
abaróondera	⌐... who seek⌐ ⌐ones who seek⌐	[⌐ones who seek⌐:AUT.]
bagoróora	⌐... who iron⌐ ⌐ones who iron⌐	[⌐... who iron⌐:REL.]

CHAPTER 5 A LEARNER'S SYNOPSIS OF KIRUNDI STRUCTURE

State whether the words in each pair differ according to
NEGATION, (Dimension 1) or as to MOOD (Dimension 2):

bágeenda, bátageenda	[NEG.]
bageenda, ntibageendá	[NEG.]
bageenda, bageendá	[MOOD]
zítazíimvye, zitazíimvye	[MOOD]

Dimension 3: Time relations. This is treated in Meeussen's
tables as a seven-way distinction. The morphs which represent
the members of the contrast are prefixes made up of vowels and
consonants except that the hodiernal-hesternal distinction depends
on tone. These prefixes stand just before the object prefix or before
the stem if there is no object prefix. All 60 sets are committed
on this dimension. The meanings have to do with matters some of
which are usually classified as 'tense', some as 'aspect' and one
as 'mood' (in a sense different from that in which we have named
our 'Dimension 2'). The tenses have to do with the placement of
an action along the time axis. Kirundi distinguishes four of
these: immediate (past, present or future), past-today (also
called the 'hodiernal'), past-before-today (also called the
'hesternal' tense) and non-immediate future.

The aspectual time relations are those which have to do with
the shape of an action in time. One of these is the inceptive,
which is used for an action that is just beginning; the other is
the persistive, which calls attention to the fact that an action
is still going on.

The form with modal meaning that is included in Dimension 3
is the conditional, which is roughly equivalent to English verb

phrases with <u>would</u> or <u>might</u>.

All seven of these forms are classed together within a
single dimension because they are mutually exclusive with one
another. Also, as has already been pointed out, they are all
represented by prefixes (or, in the case of the immediate tense,
lack of a prefix) in one and the same slot in the verb structure.

The tense that refers to past actions within the present
day (the 'hodiernal' tense) is characterized by an /-a-/ immediately after the subject prefix:

nkora...   'I do....'
nakoze...   'I did.... (sometime today) '

Most subject prefixes have a slightly different form when they
stand before a vowel:

<u>a</u>soma...   'he/she reads....'
<u>y</u>asomye...   'he/she read....(sometime today)'
<u>tu</u>geenda...   'we go....'
<u>tw</u>agiiye...   'we went....(sometime today)'
<u>mu</u>geenda...   'you (pl.) go....'
<u>mw</u>aagiiye...   'you (pl.) went....(sometime today).'
<u>u</u>geenda...   'you (sg.) go....'
<u>w</u>agiiye...   'you (sg.) went....(sometime today).'

Choose the better approximate translation, and state whether
the verb is IMMEDIATE tense, or HODIERNAL tense:

Nataanguye....   'I began...(sometime today).'   [hodiernal]
                    'I begin...'
Nkora kazi.   'I work.'   [immediate]
                    'I worked...(sometime today).'

Twakoze kazi.	ʿWe work.ʿ ʿWe worked...(sometime today)ʿ	[hodiernal]
Naboonye....	ʿI see.ʿ ʿI saw...(sometime today)ʿ	[hodiernal]
Nkoze....	ʿI've just done...ʿ ʿI did...(sometime today).ʿ	[immediate]
Baasomye....	ʿThey've just read...ʿ ʿThey read...(sometime earlier today).ʿ	[hodiernal]
Basomye....	ʿThey've just read...ʿ ʿThey read...(sometime earlier today).ʿ	[immediate]

The hesternal or ʿyesterdayʿ, tense differs from the hodiernal in having a tone on the subject prefix.

Choose the appropriate time expression, and state whether each of the following verb forms is HESTERNAL or HODIERNAL:

Baáboonye ikí?   ʿWhat did they see {(today) / (before today)} ?ʿ   [HESTERNAL]

Baaboonye ikí?   [HODIERNAL]

Mwaariiye ikí?   ʿWhat did you (pl.) eat {(today) / (before today)} ?ʿ   [HODIERNAL]

Baávuuyěhe?   ʿWhere did they come from {(today) / (before today)} ?ʿ   [HESTERNAL]

The immediate tense may be used in talking about the immediate future, but verbs that refer to more remote future actions are characterized by the prefix /-zoo-/.

State whether each of these verbs in IMMEDIATE, or (non-immediate)   FUTURE:

    bageenda   [IMM.]

    bazoogeenda   [FUT.]

    tuzooshika   [FUT.]

For purposes of this synopsis, the persistive, inceptive, and conditional forms will be omitted.

Dimension 4: Imperfective vs. perfective aspect. This is a two-way contrast. The overt representation of the contrast is found at the very end of the verb form: each imperfective ends in some consonant plus /-a/, while the corresponding perfective ends in /-e/; this /-e/ is preceded either by a consonant different from that of the imperfective, or by the imperfective consonant plus /y/. Some verbs have irregularly formed perfectives, however. Perfective forms are used when the action is regarded as being complete, imperfectives are used for actions in progress, or actions mentioned without regard to completeness, but the English translation is not a reliable guide as to which actions are 'considered complete' in Kirundi. In all, 44 sets are committed on this dimension; the sets that are not are the inceptives and the futures (Dimension 3), which have the consonants and final vowels of the imperfectives.

State whether each of these verbs is PERFECTIVE, or IMPERFECTIVE:

ndahageze	'I've arrived here'	[PERF.]
urakeneye	'you need'	[PERF.]
uzootaangura	'you will begin'	[IMPERF.]
ndoondera	'I'm looking for'	[IMPERF.]

bararima	¹they cultivate¹	[IMPERF.]
sinuumviise	¹I don't understand¹	[PERF.]

Notice that the English equivalent of a perfective form may <u>or</u> <u>may not</u> sound as though it refers to a completed action or process.

Dimension 5: <u>Tone Class.</u> Virtually all verbs in Kirundi fall into one of two tone classes. The overt difference between the two is found in the presence of a high tone in certain forms of one verb, and the absence of high tone in the corresponding forms of other verbs. Only 13 sets are committed with respect to this dimension, 8 of which are the affirmative and negative inceptives. The difference is completely without grammatical meaning.

Given below are three forms of a high verb, and the corresponding forms of a low verb. State which verb is in the HIGH tone class, and which is in the LOW tone class.

naboonye	¹I saw (today)¹	
kubóna	¹to see¹	[HIGH]
baboná	¹...who see¹	
narimye	¹I cultivated (today)¹	
kurima	¹to cultivate¹	[LOW]
barimá	¹...who cultivate¹	

Do the same for the two verbs /-taangura/ and /-goroora/:

abatáangura	¹those who begin¹
twaagoroorá	¹we ironed (today)¹
bazóotáangura	¹...who will begin¹
twaatáanguye	¹we began (today)¹
abagóroora	¹those who iron¹
bazóogóroora	¹...who will iron¹

306

Is the stem /-taangura/ in the HIGH class, or the LOW?   [HIGH]
Is the stem /-goroora/ in the HIGH class, or the LOW?   [LOW]

Dimension 6: Linkage. This is a two-way distinction. Its
most characteristic mark is the prefix /-ra-/, which is used with
'disjunct' forms. Forms that are not disjunct are 'conjunct'.
Only ten sets are committed with respect to this dimension. The
significance of the distinction is grammatical: the conjunct
must be followed by some kind of object or other word to which it
is closely tied. The disjunct may be used without a following
object, or with a following object where there is no close connection between verb and object.

Place a period after each disjunct form, to signify that it
can be the last word in a sentence. Place three dots (...) after
the conjunct forms, to signify that it must be followed by something further.

navúze	'I spoke (before today)'	[...(conjunct)]
narávuze	'I spoke (before today)'	[.(disjunct)]
turiiye	'we've eaten'	[...(conjunct)]
turaríiye	'we've eaten'	[.(disjunct)]

The intersection of these six dimensions with one another
accounts for over 90 per cent of the forms of any Kirundi verb.
There are however a few sets of forms which lie outside this
framework. Most important are the subjunctive, the infinitive,
and the imperative. These are differentiated for Dimension 1
(affirmative vs. negative), and the infinitive shows the tone
class of a verb (Dimension 5), but they are not marked for mood,
tense, aspect, or linkage. These sets need not be discussed
further in a brief synopsis.

307

CHAPTER 5 A LEARNER'S SYNOPSIS OF KIRUNDI STRUCTURE

The discussion of subject and object prefixes
showed one important role which concordial agreement plays in
the operation of the Kirundi language. A list of concordial
classes was given on p. x , together with a list of the prefixes which represent those classes where the subjects of verbs
are concerned.

Class concords also appear in many other parts of the
language:

Class 8:   Ibiriíbwa mufisé ni ibiki? ('Foods that-you-have
                                              are which?')

Class 10: Impuúzu mufisé ni inkí? ('Clothes that-you-have
                                           are which?')

Class 8:   Zana ibiriíbwa.   'Bring foodstuffs.'
           Ngiibi.   'Here they are.'

Class 10: Zana impuuzú.   'Bring [articles of] clothing.'
           Ngiizí.   'Here they are.'

Class 3:   Umudúga waawe ni   'Your car is good.'
           mwiizá.

Class 12: Akazi kaawe ni   'Your work is good.'
           keezá.

Compare these two short dialogues, which are identical
except for the first noun and the concords that depend upon it.

Barafíse impuúzu?   '[Do] they have [articles of] clothing?'

Eegó, barazífise.   'Yes, they have them.'

Bafise nyiínshi?   'Do they have many?'

Oya, bafise nké.   'No, they have few.'

Ni ziingáahé?   'How many are there.'
                                 ('[They] are how-many?')

Zitaanu gusa.   'Five only.'

308

Barafíse <u>ibitabo</u>?	¹Do they have books?¹
Eegó, bara<u>bí</u>fise.	¹Yes, they have them.¹
Bafise <u>vyi</u>ínshi?	¹Do they have many?¹
Oya, bafise <u>ba</u>ké.	¹No, they have few.¹
Ni <u>bii</u>ngáahé?	(¹[They] are how-many?¹)
<u>Bi</u>taanu gusa.	¹Five only.¹

Now underline the concordial prefixes in the following conversation:

Bafise <u>amakáraamú</u>?	¹Do they have pens/pencils?¹	
Eegó barayáfise.		[-ya-]
Bafise meénshi?		[m-]
Oya, bafise maké.		[ma-]
Ni aangáahé?		[aa-]
Ataanu gusa.		[a-]

This concludes the portion of the synopsis which is devoted to grammar.

CHAPTER 6

CUMMINGS DEVICES

HISTORY

> In the year of our Lord 1219, and the
> thirteenth year of his conversion, Brother
> Francis held a general chapter at Santa
> Maria della Porziuncola, and sent brethren
> to France, Germany, Hungary, Spain, and
> those provinces of Italy which the brethern
> had not yet reached.... The German mission
> was led by Brother John of Parma with some
> sixty or more brethren. When they were
> come into Germany, not knowing the language,
> and when men asked whether they desired
> lodging or meat or any such thing, they
> answered Ja, and thus received kindly wel-
> come from some folk. Seeing therefore that
> this word procured them humane treatment,
> they resolved to answer Ja to all questions
> whatsoever. Wherefore, being once asked
> whether they were heretics, come now to
> infect Germany after the same fashion where-
> with they had already perverted Lombardy,
> they answered Ja; so that some were cast
> into prison, and others were stripped of
> their raiment and led to the common dancing-
> place where they were held up for a
> laughing-stock to the inhabitants. The
> brethren therefore, seeing that they could
> make no fruit in Germany, came home again;
> and this deed gave the brethren so cruel a
> report of Germany, that none dared return
> thither but such as aspired to martydom....

> Jordan of Giano
> (in Ross, 1949)

Thomas Cummings taught languages of India to mission-
aries in the early part of this century, some seven hun-
dred years after the Franciscans' disagreeable experiences

310

with German. He published some of the fruits of his work in 1916, in a little book titled How to Learn a Foreign Language. One of his most characteristic emphases was that his students should know not only some answers, but also some questions to which each answer is appropriate, and not only some questions, but also a number of useful answers for each question. Cummings saw that each language has only a small number of question-words, and realized what power those few questions give to a student who wants to elicit new vocabulary. Furthermore, the same questions can be applied to one center of interest after another, in accordance with the student's changing needs. The answers to such a set of questions can readily be combined into meaningful and interesting texts, whether those texts be written exposition or genuine un-rehearsed conversation. Having more than one answer to each question insures that the student does not merely memorize a fixed sequence, but that he is always aware of the choices without which discourse cannot qualify as communication.

Half a century after Cummings, this writer was attempting to solve problems of materials development for Swahili and Hausa at the Foreign Service Institute, and for Chinyanja (now called Chichewa) in the Peace Corps. This work led to three observations:

1. The shorter a dialog, the less unexplained, confusing clutter it contains. The shortest possible dialog consists of two lines.

2. Differences in progress were less between trainees of low aptitude and trainees of high aptitude when material was true, important and, if possible, autobiographical, and greater when material was general, fictitious and of no immediate use.

3. Students seemed to retain material better when they have used it for communication of some kind.

Cummings' use of questions and answers made sense in all these respects. It thus became the historical source of what was called the 'microwave' format for writing language lessons. This unfortunate label was selected as part of an elaborate electronic metaphor; its meaning was that the length of one 'cycle' (defined as the length of time from first introduction of a new item until its use in communication) was extremely short.

The microwave format itself, in what we may a little wryly call its 'classical form,' contained a basic utterance (usually but not always a question) and from four to eight potential answers or other appropriate rejoinders. If the basic utterance and the rejoinders are well chosen, they can lead to almost immediate real or realistic (Chapter 2, p. 28-29) conversation in class, and are also likely to find use in real life outside of class. At the same time, new structures and new vocabulary can be kept to a minimum.

A microwave 'cycle' was divided into an M-phase and a C-phase. M stood for mimicry, manipulation, mechanics and memorization, and C for communication, conversation, and continuity. Within the M-phase, the first section usually introduced the answers or rejoinders, often in the form of a substitution drill with a separate column for cue words. The second section contained the question(s) or other basic utterance(s). The C-phase combined the elements of the M-phase with each other and, ideally, with material from earlier lessons, to form a short sample conversation.[1]

At least in the early stages, all sentences were kept fairly short (very few with as many as 12 syllables). They also were simple in their structure, and in most cycles all of the rejoinders exemplified a single surface structure. Cycles were therefore relatively light and transparent, in the sense of Chapter 3 (p. 47f). In the C-phase, parentheses (   ) were placed around those nouns, verbs, or adjectives that were subject to replacement, and users were urged to 'relexicalize' the cycle by adding their own vocabulary at those points.

From this brief description, it should be obvious that microwave cycles have potentially high ratings for usability (Chapter 2, Assumption I), responsiveness (Assumption III), and responsibility (Assumption IV). Just how much of this potential is realized for any one textbook or any one program depends on three factors:

1. The internal structure of individual cycles.

2. The relationship of the cycles to one another.

3. The degree to which the content is pertinent to the needs of the students--'strength' in the sense of Chapter 3.

The same three factors of course affect the success of non-microwave lessons. But while an inappropriate microwave lesson is no more unmotivating than an inappropriate course

---

[1]The terms 'M-phrase' and 'C-phrase' were applied by Garner and Schutz (1969) in much the same sense but on a quite different scale.

of any other kind, it was felt that an appropriate microwave lesson could go far beyond most other formats, at least for young American adults who were about to go abroad.

These ideas took shape in 1964, and were first discussed publicly at a conference in Bloomington, Indiana, in the spring of the following year (Stevick, 1966). This was a period in which the Peace Corps need for new materials in new languages was at its peak, and so it happened that the microwave format was adopted for use in dozens of courses, written under extreme pressure for time, by materials developers with highly miscellaneous backgrounds for the job. Results were sometimes surprisingly good, and in many cases were probably better than what the same writers would have produced in other formats, but the experience of the next five years also proved instructive in some negative ways:

1. 'Microwave' is not a theory, nor a method, but only a format.

2. There are certain pitfalls in writing individual cycles.

3. A course that consists of nothing but cycles violates Assumption V ('Pluralism,' p. 36), and is also unsatisfactory in other ways.

The remainder of this chapter will deal with the implications of these three statements.

MICROWAVES AND CUMMINGS DEVICES

First, on microwave as a format. A distressingly large number of people have talked and even occasionally written about microwave as a theory or as a method. This may be due

to the ease with which the term enters as the first member
into noun-noun constructions: 'the microwave method,' and so
forth. The only such construct that is justifiable is
'microwave cycle.' If that phrase is replaced by 'Cummings
device,' then the originator will receive credit for his idea,
and at the same time unwarranted collocations will be blocked
by the very mechanics of the English language: people will
not easily slip into talking about 'Cummings device theory,'
or 'the Cummings device method.' On the contrary, the term
'device' is intended to suggest a small part of a total
method, which may or may not be consonant with one or another
theory.

WRITING CUMMINGS DEVICES

Problems in writing Cummings devices arise in connection
with both the manipulative and the communicative phases.

<u>Example 1</u> (French)

Bonjour Monsieur.	Good morning. (said to a man)
Bonjour Mademoiselle.	Good morning. (said to an unmarried woman)
Bonjour Madame.	Good morning. (said to a married woman)
Comment allez-vous?	How are you?
Bien, merci. Et vous?	Well, thanks. And you?
Très bien, merci. Et vous?	Very well, thanks. And you?
Pas mal, merci. Et vous?	Not bad, thanks. And you?
Ça va bien, merci. Et vous?	Fine, thanks. And you?
Je vais bien, merci. Et vous?	I'm fine, thanks. And you?

Au revoir.	Good bye.
Au revoir, à bientôt.	Good bye, until later.

Summary: A. Bonjour (Monsieur).

B. Bonjour (Mademoiselle). Comment allez-vous?

A. (Très bien), merci. Et vous?

B. (Ça va bien), merci.

A. Au revoir.

B. Au revoir, à bientôt.

Comments on Example 1

The sentences are of suitable length. The subject matter is appropriate for most groups, and the sentences are all idiomatic. As shown in the summary, (   ) can be filled in various ways so as to make several different conversations.

Example 1 however departs from the format of a classical Cummings device in three ways: (1) It is actually a composite of three such devices, whose basic utterances are respectively (a) Bonjour, (monsieur) (b) Comment allez-vous?, and (c) Au revoir. (2) All of the rejoinders to Comment allez-vous? are practically synonymous with one another, (3) There is only one rejoinder to the last basic utterance. Meaningful choice, and hence communication, are thus impossible in two-thirds of this particular device.

Example 2 (English)

Basic utterance:	What is your name?
Potential rejoinders:	My name is Bill Williams.
	My name is Clyde Bonney.
	My name is Ethel Redd.
	My name is Carol Singer.
	My name is Fletcher Arrowsmith.

316

Summary: What is your name?

                            My name is (Bill Williams).

Comments on Example 2

The subject matter--getting people's names--is well-chosen if the cycle is used by trainees who are still getting acquainted with each other. It is also appropriate, but less so, for groups that have passed that stage, since any trainee can look forward to having to get people's names at some time in the future.

The length of the sentences (4-7 syllables) is ideal. The names that are selected for use in presenting the lesson may be chosen either for their phonetic problems or for their lack thereof. After initial presentation of the Cummings device, names of real people should be used at the point indicated by (   ).

This Cummings device has a serious flaw, and it is the kind of flaw that writers of language lessons most easily overlook. The short, uncomplicated sentences and the usefulness of the subject matter should not blind us to the fact that the question simply is not idiomatic. 'What is your name?' is used only to children and to inferiors. If I want to know the name of another adult, I must find it out in some other way. For example, I may volunteer the information that 'My name is _____' and expect him to reciprocate.

Example 3 (Swahili)

Basic utterance:

Unatoka mji gani?	What city are you from?
Unatoka jimbo gani?	What state are you from?
Unatoka nchi gani?	What country are you from?

Potential rejoinders:

Ninatoka mji wa Topeka.	I'm from (the city of) Topeka.
Ninatoka jimbo la Kansas.	I'm from (the state of) Kansas.
Ninatoka nchi ya Amerika.	I'm from (the country of) America.

Summary:

Unatoka (mji) gani?

Ninatoka (mji) (w)a (Topeka).

Comments on Example 3

Suitability of subject matter is as for Example 2. Length and complexity of sentences are still within the ability of beginners. This Cummings device provides a fairly realistic way of learning to choose among wa, la, ya in agreement with mji, jimbo, nchi.

Example 4 (French)

Basic utterances:

Qu'est-ce que vous faites à 6 heures du matin?	What do you do at 6 a.m.?
Et après,qu'est-ce que vous faites?	And then what do you do?

Potential rejoinders:

Je me réveille.	I wake up.
Après je me lève.	Then I get up.
Après je me lave.	Then I wash.
Après je m'habille.	Then I get dressed.
Après je vais au réfectoire.	Then I go to the dining hall.

| Après je prends un casse-croûte. | Then I have a bit to eat. |
| Après j'etudie le français. | Then I study French. |

Comments on Example 4

Experienced language teachers will recognize their ancient and trusty friend the action chain, disguised here as a Cummings device. The subject matter is appropriate for almost any group, although the questions themselves are seldom asked outside of a language classroom. The questions would have been a bit long for absolute beginners, but this was No. 68 in a series of Cummings devices.

Example 5 (Bini)

See pages 320-321.

Comments on Example 5

This is an excellent example of a Cummings device set out in standard microwave format. The list of key words in the left-hand column of M-1 makes that section of the lesson into a simple substitution drill. C-1 and C-2 could have been combined, by putting the noun into parentheses. As a good C-phase should, C-3 takes the user beyond mere mechanical combination of what was in the M-phase.

CYCLE 26

M-1

èpɛnì	èpɛnì nàkhin	pen	This is a pen.
èpɛnsò	èpɛnsò nàkhin	pencil	This is a pencil.
èbe	èbe nàkhin	book	This is a book.
ugbɛ̀kùn	ùgbɛ̀kùn nàkhin	belt	This is a belt.
aga	aga nàkhin	chair	This is a chair.
èteburù	èteburù nàkhin	table	This is a table.
ibâtà	ibâtà nàkhin	shoes	These are shoes.
ɛwû	ɛwû nàkhin	dress/shirt	This is a shirt.
èsìga	èsìga nàkhin	citarette.	This is a cigarette.

M-2

bh' ɔnà a-khin?   What is this?

C-1

A: Bh' ɔnà a-khin?   A: What is this?

B: èsìga nàkhin.   B: This is a cigarette.

C-2

A: Bh' ɔnà a-khin?   A: What is this?

B: ɛwù nàkhin.   B: This is a shirt.

C-3

Continue this cycle using actual objects in the room. Additional vocabulary should be given for objects present for which the Bini equivalent is unknown. Have the students try both asking and responding.

To The Student:

The prefix /a-/ attached to the verb occurs when the question word /bhɛ/ introduces a question. There are times when /a-/ becomes fused with a preceding vowel, or is elited since retention of the preceding vowel is required.

CYCLE 19

M-1

èmwan	èmwan ɔ ghi dì'à	here	He lives here now.
ghi	ὲbhò nâ ɔ ghi ye	now	He lives in this city now.
èbha	èbha ɔ ghi dì'à	there	He lives there now.
diya	òwa nâ ɔ ghi dì'à	live in	He lives in this house now.
ye	ìdùmwun nâ ɔ ghi ye	to be	He now lives (is) on this street.

M-2

k'èkè	d'èkè n' èjonì ghi dì'ǎ?	What place	Where does John now live?
kere	d'ὲbhò n' ɔ kerě?	come from	Where does he come from?

C-1

A: d'ὲbhò n˙ ejɔnì kerě?   A: Where is John from?

B: èshìkagò ɔ kerè.   B: He is from Chicago.

A: èbha ɔ ghi dì'a?   A: Does he live there now?

B: ὲò, ὲῒˑ ebha ɔ ghi dì'à.   B: No, he does not live there now.

   èmwan ɔ ghi ye.   He is here now.

Comments on Example 6

Again, the C-phase is relatively strong. Notice that it brings in yes-no questions, which had been covered in a previous lesson, and also that it recombines elements from the M-phase more boldly than C-1, C-2 of Example 5.

The sentences of the M-phase of Example 6 all exemplify very much the same surface structure, but the cue words in the left-hand column are chosen from three different parts of their sentences: verb, place expression, and time expression. The reason for this is not apparent, since it will probably make M-1 more difficult to use as a drill. In any case, the relationship between cue words and expected responses is one of the problems that writers of Cummings devices must recognize and deal with.

Example 7   (Swahili)

See pp. 323-324.

This lesson seemed to have much to recommend it. It was about air transportation, which all of the trainees expected to be using shortly after the end of their language study; it was illustrated with a reproduction of an authentic airline schedule; and it was obvious how the content of this lesson could be replaced by up-to-date information on actual flights that the trainees expected to take.

Nevertheless, this lesson was heavily criticized by nearly everyone who tried to use it, and eventually had to be dropped. It may therefore stand as a warning to other developers of language materials. Its chief flaws seem to have been the following:

(1)   The individual sentences are rather heavy, in the sense of Chapter 3 (p. 47). The heaviness results not only from their length, but also from the fact that in translating time into Swahili, one must add or subtract six hours: 7 o'clock is literally 'one o'clock' and 1 o'clock is literally 'seven o'clock.'

CYCLE 43

[Refer to the timetable which appears below.]

M-1

New York	Ndege namba 35 huo- ndoka New York saa 5 na dakika 30 asubuhi.	New York	Flight 35 leaves New York at 11:30 a.m.
Chicago	Ndege namba 35 huo- ndoka Chicago saa 7 na dakika 25 mchana.	Chicago	Flight 35 leaves Chicago at 1:25 p.m.
Kansas City	Ndege namba 35 huo- ndoka Kansas City saa 9 na dakika 20 mchana.	Kansas City	Flight 35 leaves Kansas City at 3:20 p.m.

M-2

Chicago	Ndege namba 35 hufika Chicago saa 6 na dakika 48 mchana.	Chicago	Flight 35 arrives in Chicago at 12:48 p.m.
Kansas City	Ndege namba 35 hufika Kansas City saa 8 na dakika 42 mchana.	Kansas City	Flight 35 arrives in Kansas City at 2:42 p.m.
Albuquerque	Ndege namba 35 hufika Albuquerque saa 10 na dakika 10 mchana.	Albuquerque	Flight 35 arrives in Albuquerque at 4:10 p.m.

C-1

Ndege namba 23 _____   What time does Flight 23 _____
       (fika/ondoka)   (arrive/leave)
_____ saa ngapi.   _____?
(jina la mji)   (name of city)

Hu _____ saa _____ .   It _____ at _____ .
(fika/ondoka)   (wakati)   (arrives/leaves)   (time)

C-2

[Ask and answer the same questions about Flights 27, 107, 137, etc.
The students should of course have the timetable before them for
this cycle.]

(2)   The upcoming air trip to East Africa, though
      a dramatic event, was one that would not be part
      of daily life.

(3)   Arrangements for any air travel that they might
      undertake within East Africa could best be made
      in English anyway.

<u>Example</u> 8   (Lao)

See pp. 326-327.

This example consists of the M-1 segments of Cycles 38
and 73 in <u>Lao Basic Course</u>. In their format, they are identical. The problem of interest here is again choice of
content. Each contains a miscellaneous list of predicate
expressions. In the C-phase of Cycle 38, it is easy to see
how the content of the lesson could be brought to bear on one
member of the class after another, so that they would get
better acquainted with one another at the same time that they
were practicing their Lao. No comparable focus is obvious
for the material of Cycle 73. Cycle 38 talks about what one
individual or another can do, while Cycle 73 is a list of
unconnected bits of information illustrating a grammatical
pattern.

One more question that arises in the writing of Cummings
devices is the extent to which they should depend on the use
of translation. The same problem of course comes up in connection with lesson material of other kinds, such as dialogs
and drills. Obviously, if the intent is to do with little
or no translation, then there is a correspondingly greater
premium on the quality of transparency (Chapter 3, p. 48).

CYCLE 38

M-1

<u>tiicák</u>   to type

    láaw tiicák dàɉ bɔɔ?   Can she type?

<u>sǎk hùup</u>   to take pictures

    láaw sǎk hùup dàɉ bɔɔ?   Can she take pictures?

<u>sỳy khɔ̌ɔŋ</u>   to shop

    láaw sỳy khɔ̌ɔn dàɉ bɔɔ?   Can he shop?

<u>tát phǒm</u>   to cut hair

    láaw tát phǒm dàɉ bɔɔ?   Can she cut hair?

<u>púk hýan</u>   to build a house

    láaw púk hýan dàɉ bɔɔ?   Can she build a house?

<u>khúakin</u>   to cook

    láaw khúakin dàɉ bɔɔ?   Can she cook?

M-2

<u>khúakin</u>

    bɔɔ dàɉ, phɔ̄waā láaw khúakin   No, because she doesn't
    bɔɔ pen   know how to cook.

<u>púk hýan</u>   build a house

    bɔɔ dàɉ, phɔ̄waá láaw púk   No, because he doesn't know
    hýan bɔɔ pen   how to build a house.

326

CYCLE 73

M-1

daŋ-fáɟ   to make a fire

    càw si sàɟ njǎŋ daŋ-fáɟ?   What will you use for making
                                           a fire?

hɔ́ɔŋ, nǎŋ   to underlay, place beneath; sit

    càw si sàɟ njǎŋ hɔ́ɔŋ nǎŋ?   What will you use to sit on?

lǎbaaɟ, nàm   to control the flow, water

    càw si sàɟ njǎŋ lǎbaaɟ nàm?   What will you use to control
                                           the water flow?

sǎmlûat, bə̄ŋ   survey, inspect, look at, see

    càw si sàɟ njǎŋ sǎmlûat   What will you use for
    bə̄ŋ?   inspecting?

lỳak, mâak màɟ   select, choose; fruit

    càw si sàɟ phǎɟ lỳak   Who will you use to select
    mâak màɟ?   fruit?

kinkhâw   to have one's meal

    càw si sàɟ njǎŋ kinkhâw?   What will you use to eat with?

phán, mýy   to wrap around, hand

    càw si sàɟ njǎŋ phǎn mýy?   What will you use to wrap
                                           around your hand?

RELATIONSHIPS BETWEEN CUMMINGS DEVICES AND OTHER COMPONENTS

We have already said (p. 314) that a number of sets of materials have appeared which consisted but nothing but series of Cummings devices. The advantages in writing textbooks in this way are that each individual device provides a sharp focus for one class hour, and that the absence of any further printed helps leaves no doubt in the teacher's mind that he must be creative, but in general this kind of textbook is inadvisable. Cummings devices have, however, entered into a number of other courses either as the central elements of the lessons, or in peripheral and supporting roles. Some of the possibilities that can be documented are the following:

1. Cummings device central in each lesson, supported by usual types of drill, glossary, grammar notes, and a few suggestions for use. (Stevick, Indakwa, et al., An Active Introduction to Swahili)

2. Cummings device followed by suggestions for a related 'cross-cultural experience' and 'routine language experience,' and information of interest to learners who also expect to teach English in their host country. (Kim, Lee, Crowley, Lessons in the Korean Language and Culture)

3. Cummings device paired with experience in singing folk songs and enjoying poetry. Often only a distant connection between the Cummings device and the poem. (Bailey, Jamaican Creole Language Course)

4. Cummings device followed by explanatory notes, followed by a series of self-testing frames related to something in the first two parts of the same lesson (Yates and Sayasithsena, Lao Basic Course).

5. Heavily modified Cummings device format as the
   'principal stage,' preceded by self-instructional
   frames which present other matters, and followed by
   detailed suggestions for other activities both in
   and outside of class. (Blair et al., Cakichiquel
   Basic Course)

6. Lessons that are built around Cummings devices are
   interspersed among other types of lesson. (Kamoga
   and Stevick, Luganda Basic Course)

7. Cummings devices as one of several components which
   lead to performance of well-defined objectives for
   use in and outside of class (Rehg and Sohl, Kitail
   Lokaiahn Pohnpei, see Appendix R, p. 346.
   See also Appendices E (Mauritian Creole) and G
   (Thai), which show the use of Cummings devices as
   subordinate parts of new materials, and all the
   appendices to Chapter 3, in which Cummings devices
   appear as one means for adapting existing lessons.)

SUMMARY

This chapter has described an ancient device, and to
some extent has chronicled a recent flurry of attention to it.
But to look only at the format itself would be a mistake.
Mueller (1968) has said that 'as soon as [a] pattern has been
mastered, the student must progress   further to the creative
stage, where he learns to use what he has mastered.'
[emphasis added] Even though it may be the case that in this
book we mean more by 'use' than Mueller did, still his words
may serve as a statement of what we can call 'the Cummings
principle.' Experiences of the past six or seven years

suggest that the Cummings <u>principle</u> deserves general
recommendation and wider application. The Cummings <u>device</u>,
with its shortness, clearly defined scope, and goal of
immediate use, is certainly an excellent way of realizing
the principle. Nevertheless, the device itself should play
a supporting, or at most a co-starring role in the design of
published lessons.

APPENDIX p TO CHAPTER 6

THE CUMMINGS PRINCIPLE

IN ANOTHER FORMAT: ENGLISH

The Cummings Principle may be embodied in formats that show no trace of the M-1, M-2, C-1, C-2 of the format described in Chapter 6. In 1969, the Foreign Service Institute was asked to begin conducting four-week courses in four languages for Marines who were to serve as security guards in embassies overseas. The content of these courses was to be much more sharply defined than is usually practicable for the training of other kinds of students. Other than the usual greetings and general phrases, the material was related to only three settings: 'At the Door,' 'On the Telephone,' and 'Dealing with the Clean-up Crew.' Within each of these settings, four problems were selected; in the first setting the problems were 'Checking Identification', 'Giving Information about Embassy Hours', 'Receiving or Refusing a Package', and 'Persons Seeking Asylum'. For each of these problems, two lists of sentences were established: a 'Production Inventory' which the trainees would be expected to memorize, and a 'Comprehension Inventory' which they would be expected to understand but not necessarily memorize. On the basis of these two inventories, a series of 15-20 short (4-6 line) dialogs were next written. Each sentence appeared in from 3-11 different dialogs. A few of the dialogs for each problem would later be used for intensive drill in class, but most would serve as comprehension practice in the tape lab.

331

A diagram may clarify the relations among the raw
materials of this course.

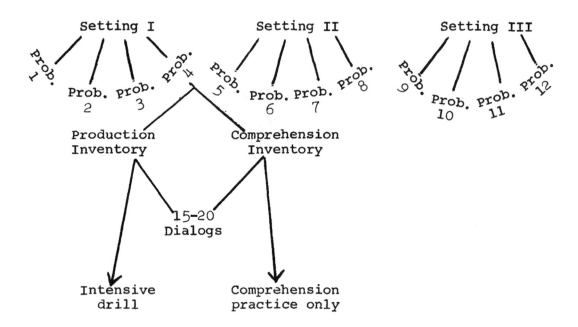

Each problem is developed as shown in the diagram for Problem
4. The inventories and a few sample dialogs for Problem 1
are reproduced on pp. 333-334 . The question, of course, is
how to use this mass of material. The Cummings principle was
applied to the initial presentation of the production inventory. The first half of the treatment of Problem 1 is
reproduced on pp. 335-336. It is apparent that the activities
labelled 'pronunciation' and 'meaning' in this lesson plan
correspond more or less to the M-phase of a Cummings device,
and that 'use' and 'cumulation' are in some sense a C-phase.
It is also easy to see how Cummings devices could be derived
from the materials as they stand. This superficial correspondence is however not the point. What is important is that the
student meets a very small amount of new material, manipulates
it, and then uses it.

SETTING: At the door.

PROBLEM: Checking identification.

PRODUCTION INVENTORY:

    May I see your (pass, identification)? (18)
    This pass is (not) valid. (7)
    This pass has expired. (8)
    You may (not) enter (without (pass, identification, I.D. card)). (25)
    I'm sorry. (10)
    Thank you (sir, madame). (5)
    Everything is in order. (4)
    Do you have (other) (pass, identification, I.D. card)? (2)

COMPREHENSION INVENTORY:

    Here is my (pass, identification, I.D. card). (15)
    Is this (pass, identification, I.D. card) valid? (3)
    I (don't) have (other) (pass, identification, I.D. card). (9)
    Would you like to see (other) (pass, identification, I.D. card)? (3)
    This is the only (pass, identification, I.D. card) I have. (5)
    Do I need (pass, identification, I.D. card) at this hour? (2)
    Is this (sufficient, all right)? (3)
    May I enter? (4)
    May I go in for just a minute? (6)

1. M. May I see your pass, sir?

    L. Here it is. Is it valid?

    M. Yes, this pass is valid.

        You may enter.

    L. Thank you.

2. M. May I see your pass, sir?

    L. I don't have a pass.

    M. You may not enter without a pass.

    L. I have some other identification here.

    M. I'm sorry. You may not enter without a pass.

3. L. Would you like to see my pass?

    M. Thank you, sir.

        You may enter.

    L. (It's a nice evening.)

    M. Yes, sir.

4. L. Would you like to see my pass?

    M. Thank you, sir.

        I'm sorry.

        This pass is not valid.

    L. But it is the only pass I have.

        *Can't you let me in just this time?

    M. I'm sorry. You may not enter without a pass.

5. M. May I see your pass?

    L. I'm sorry. I don't have a pass.

    M. May I see your identification?

    L. Will this do?

    M. Thank you, sir. You may enter.

6. L. This is the only pass I have. Is it valid?

    M. I'm sorry. This pass is not valid.

        May I see your identification?

    L. Here it is.

    M. Thank you, sir.

    L. I have some other identification also.

    M. Thank you, sir. You may enter.

Lesson 1, Section 1

PROPS: Two different passes, two different I.D. cards, two other
          forms of identification, a "booby prize".

PRONUNCIATION: May I see your pass?
                May I see your identification?
                May I see your I.D. card?

MEANING: Continue mimicry. After each sentence is mimicked, teacher
          holds up what was asked for.

USE: Individual students ask for one of the objects. If they
          are easily intelligible, teacher holds up the one asked for.
          If not, holds up booby prize (an autographed picture of
          Alfred E. Neumann?).

          Individual students continue to ask for the objects.
          Other students respond.

Lesson 1, Section 2

PROPS: As above.

PRONUNCIATION: This pass is valid.
                This pass is not valid.

MEANING: One of the passes is defined as valid, the other as not
          valid. Continue mimicry. After each sentence is mimicked,
          teacher holds up the appropriate pass. Do same with I.D.
          cards and other identification.

USE: Individual students rule on the validity of the passes held
          up by the teacher.

          Individual students rule on the validity of passes offered
          by other students.

CUMULATION: Student asks to see pass, then comments on its validity.

          Student asks to see I.D. card, then comments on its
          validity.

          Student asks to see other identification, then comments
          on its validity.

CHAPTER 6   CUMMINGS PRINCIPLE IN ANOTHER FORMAT (ENGLISH)

Lesson 1, Section 3

PROPS: Passes with various expiration dates.

PRONUNCIATION: This pass has expired.
                This pass is valid.

MEANING: Passes in two stacks: expired and valid. After each
          sentence is mimicked, teacher holds up an appropriate pass.

USE: Students are shown a pass. They reply either 'This pass
          has expired' or 'This pass is valid.'

CUMULATION: Three kinds of passes. One that was never valid, one
          that was formerly valid but now expired, and one that is
          valid. Student asks to see pass, then comments 'This pass
          is not valid,' 'This pass has expired,' or 'This pass is
          valid.'

Lesson 1, Section 4

PROPS: As above, plus pictures of men and women."

PRONUNCIATION: Thank you, sir.
                Thank you, madame.
                You may enter.

MEANING: Students take turns holding up a valid pass. Repeat after
          instructor: 'You may enter'.

          Same, except students repeat after instructor 'Thank you
          (sir, madame). You may enter.'

USE: Instructor places valid pass next to picture of woman or
          man. Students take turns saying 'Thank you (sir, madame).
          You may enter.'

CUMULATION: Student asks to see pass. When it is shown, he comments
          on its validity. If it is valid, he thanks the person and
          tells him he may enter.

336

APPENDIX Q TO CHAPTER 6

CUMMINGS DEVICES IN A DO-IT-YOURSELF KIT

(KIKUYU)

(with Carolyn Jackson and John Thiuri)

The worksheets which make up this appendix were designed for people who find themselves in a situation where they must learn a new language on their own, and who have, or can make for themselves, pictures of life being lived in the language.

The worksheets are of three kinds. The simplest deals with formulas and isolated useful phrases: greetings, 'thank you,' 'that is to say,' etc. The second kind of worksheet, which in effect produces Cummings devices, centers on questions based on pictures. The third type uses an action chain. In each type, the sequence of activities is (1) exploring, (2) establishing, (3) sorting, except that 'sorting' is not applied to the formulas.

The shorthand symbols in the 'establishing' sections of the worksheets are:

    A - answer

    C - correction

    E - English

    F - foreign language, complete utterance

    f -   "   "   , fraction of complete utterance

    G - gesture

    n - number of utterances chosen for learning

Q - question

S - student

T - teacher

x - some one utterance in category indicated
    by preceding capital letter

y - some other utterance

The questions to be asked on the second and third types
of worksheet might be drawn from some general list such as
the ones given for Thai in Appendix G (pp. 161-164). Both
the Cummings device (Worksheet Type 3) and the action chain
(Worksheet Type 2), because they tend to consist of sentences
with some one surface structure, allow for both lexical and
structural exploration. Neither in itself provides a convincing 'sample of language use' (Chapter 3, p. 57), but
such samples can readily be constructed by a native speaker
who is familiar with the content of one or more completed
worksheets. Payoff will be greater if the filling in of the
worksheets and the taking of the pictures can proceed hand-
in-hand, under the joint initiative of student and instructor.

EXPLORING: Formulas

1. Ask for 4-8 highly useful formulas. Examples are
    greetings, courtesy phrases, 'please say it again,'
    'I don't understand,' ways of expressing agreement
    or disagreement. Find out the approximate meaning
    of each and <u>when</u> and <u>with</u> <u>whom</u> you can use it. Write
    this down in E. DO NOT write in the FL yet!

ESTABLISHING

2. SE/G, TF, SF, TC (Fx max. 3)
3. SE/G, TF, SF, Tf, SF, TC
4. TE/G, SF
5. Write down F_{1-n}
6. S read F_{1-n}

	FL	English
F_1	ũrí mwega (?).	Hello-anyone, anytime
F_2	wenda .	please
F_3	nĩ wega .	thank you
F_4	cokera .	say it again
F_5	ndira menya .	I don't understand.
F_6	nĩ-guo .	I agree - (or yes) or both --
F_7	ti-guo .	I don't agree (or no) or both
F_8	tigwo na wega / thiĩ na wega .	a. Remain in peace } Goodbye b. Go in peace

Do not try to do 'sorting' for the words in Formulas.

CHAPTER 6   A DO-IT-YOURSELF KIT (KIKUYU)

CHAPTER 6   A DO-IT-YOURSELF KIT (KIKUYU)

EXPLORING: An action chain

General subject: <u>What one does in the morning</u>

Q$_1$ _____   What does one do first?

Q$_2$ _____   What does one do next?

1. Learn to ask these Q.

2. Get 8-12 short A. Discard the 4-8 most difficult, so
    that you are left with 4-8 answers. Write down the
    approximate meanings in E. DO NOT write in the FL yet!

ESTABLISHING

3-11. (As for questions based on pictures. Be sure to keep
       all A in the right order.)

A$_1$ <u>Njũkĩraga kĩroko.</u>   <u>I get up in the morning.</u>

A$_2$ _____ .   <u>I wash (my) face.</u>

A$_3$ _____ .   <u>I comb (my) hair</u>

A$_4$ _____ .   <u>I put on (my) clothes.</u>

A$_5$ <u>Ndĩaga irio</u>   .   <u>I eat breakfast.</u>

A$_6$ <u>Haicaga ngari</u>   .   <u>I catch the bus.</u>

A$_7$ <u>Thiaga wĩra-inĩ</u>   .   <u>I go to work..</u>
(Ngathiĩ - before the last member
          of a sequence
A$_8$ Thutha-inĩ - then, after   .   _____

342

EXPLORING: Question based on pictures

Q <u>Mũndũ ũyũ arĩ kũ</u> ? <u>Where is this person ?</u>

1. Learn to ask this Q.

2. Get 8-12 short A, based on the pictures. Discard the 4-8 most difficult, so that you are left with 4-8 answers. Write down the approximate meanings in E. DO NOT write in the FL yet!

ESTABLISHING

3. SQ, TA, SA, TC, (Ax max. 3)
4. SQ, TA, SA, Ta, SA, TC (Ax max. 3)
5. TAx?, SyesAx
6. TAx?, SyesAx/noAy
7. TAx?, SnoAy
8. TQ, SA, TC
9. SA_{1-n}
10. Write down A_{1-n}
11. S read A_{1-n}, $A_{1-n}TC$

	FL	English
A_1	(Mũndũ ũyũ) arĩ cukuru.	She is in school.
A_2	" " arĩ kiugũ.	He is in a cowshed.
A_3	" " arĩ gĩthũi-inĩ.	He is at the thresher.
A_4	" " arĩ wabici .	He is in an office.
A_5	.	
A_6	.	
A_7	.	
A_8	.	

12. Get 2-4 A that are demonstrable or known to be true outside the pictures. Treat as above.

SORTING

1. Which words in this set of sentences have occurred only once so far?

2. Which have occurred twice or more?

3. Of the words that have occurred more than once, which ones seem to have exactly the same form in all of their occurrences?

4. Which words have different prefixes, suffixes, tones, etc. from what they had in earlier occurrences?
    What exactly are the differences?

5. Which of these differences have already been found between other pairs of forms?

6. Which of these differences have not yet been found between other pairs of forms?

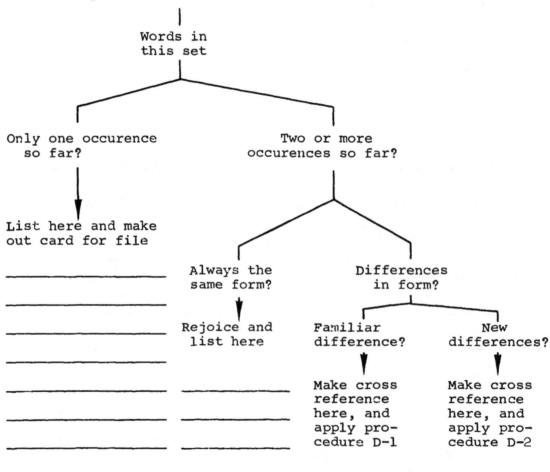

EXPLORING: Question based on pictures

Q _Areka atĩa_____?   <u>What is this person doing?</u>

1. Learn to ask this Q.

2. Get 8-12 short A, based on the pictures. Discard the 4-8 most difficult, so that you are left with 4-8 answers. Write down the approximate meanings in E. DO NOT write in the FL yet!

ESTABLISHING

3. SQ, TA, SA, TC (Ax max. 3)
4. SQ, TA, SA, Ta, SA, TC (Ax max. 3)
5. TAx?, SyesAx
6. TAx?, SyesAx/noAy
7. TAx?, SnoAy
8. TQ, SA, TC
9. SA$_{1-n}$
10. Write down A$_{1-n}$
11. S read A$_{1-n}$, TC

FL	English
A$_1$ <u>Arahe mwana irio</u> .	<u>She is feeding her child.</u>
A$_2$ <u>Arathekia mwana</u> .	<u>He̶She̶ is making the child laugh.</u>
A$_3$ _____ .	<u>He is mounting a horse.</u>
A$_4$ <u>Arathomithia Gĩthũngũ</u> .	<u>She is teaching English.</u>
A$_5$ <u>Arathĩa ngano</u> .	<u>He is grinding wheat.</u>
A$_6$ <u>Arararora ng'ombe</u> .	<u>He is looking at the cows.</u>
A$_7$ <u>Arathomithia Kĩbaranja.</u>	<u>She is teaching French.</u>
A$_8$ _____ .	_____

12. Get 2-4 A that are demonstrable or known to be true outside the pictures. Treat as above.

CHAPTER 6   A TASK-CENTERED COURSE (PONAPEAN)

APPENDIX R TO CHAPTER 6

CUMMINGS DEVICES IN A TASK-CENTERED COURSE

(PONAPEAN)

The textbook from which this lesson has been taken was
written in Ponape, for trainees who were living with Ponapean
families. The authors were therefore able to write lessons
which led very directly to real use of the language, with
equal emphasis on linguistic practice and entry into the
culture of the island.

Unlike most courses that have given prominence to
Cummings devices, this one does not make each 'cycle' the
center of its own lesson. Instead, there are several
'cycles' in each 'unit,' together with notes and dialogs.
All these components are aimed at enabling the student to
use Ponapean for clearly-stated purposes at the end of the
unit. Nor is the textbook as a whole just a series of units.
As the table of contents shows, there is a 'prelude,' which
consists of preliminary lesson material with detailed
instructions, followed by four 'books,' each of which contains four 'units' interrupted by 'interludes.' This format
is one of the most thoughtful, imaginative, and appropriate
in the recent spate of 'microwave' courses.

In addition to the table of contents and Unit I of Book
I, we have reproduced here the pages labelled Using these
Materials from the remaining units of Book I.

Table of Contents

Acknowledgements   i

Preface   ii

Instructor's Notes   iii

Prelude   1

Map of Ponape Island   26

Book I

    Unit I   27

    Unit II   39

    Map of the Trust Territory   40

    Interlude   51

    Unit III   63

    Unit IV   76

Book II

    Unit I   89

    Unit II   102

    Interlude   116

    Unit III   131

    Unit IV   142

    Pronoun Chart   154

Book III

    Unit I   155

CHAPTER 6   A TASK-CENTERED COURSE (PONAPEAN)

Unit II   169

Interlude   183

Unit III   193

Unit IV   203

Ponapean Counting System   218

. Book IV

Unit I   219

Unit II   237

Interlude   250

Unit III   261

Unit IV   272

Ponapean Verb Paradigm   290

Possessive Pronoun Chart   291

348

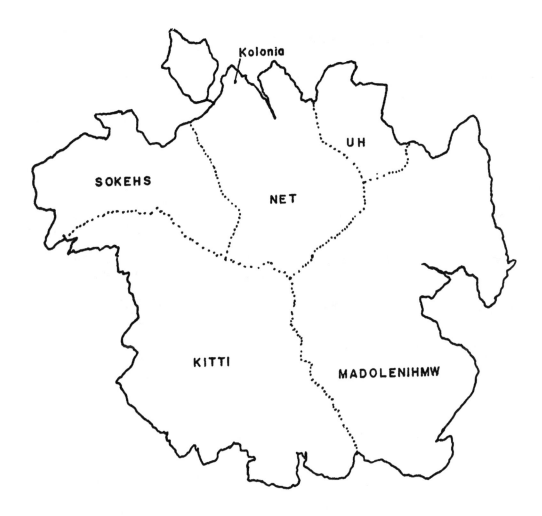

Kolonia

SOKEHS

UH

NET

KITTI

MADOLENIHMW

PONAPE ISLAND

BOOK I

"People and Places - Comings and Goings"

Proceed as you did for the Introductory Cycles.

Cycle 1

M-1

wehi(et)	Ia eden wehiet?	(this) municipality	What's the name of this municipality?
kousapw(et)	Ia eden kousapwet?	(this) section of land	What's the name of this section of land?
sahpw(et)	Ia eden sahpwet?	(this) piece of land	What's the name of this piece of land?
wasa(ht)	Ia eden wasaht?	(this) place	What's the name of this place?

M-2

Madolenihmw	Eden wehiet Madolenihmw.	The name of this municipality is Madolenihmw.
Uh	Eden wehiet Uh.	The name of this municipality is Uh.
Kiti	Eden wehiet Kiti.	The name of this municipality is Kiti.
Net	Eden wehiet Net.	The name of this municipality is Net.
Sokehs	Eden wehiet Sokehs.	The name of this municipality is Sokehs.

M-3

| Areu | Eden kousapwet Areu. | The name of this section of land is Areu. |
| Awak Powe | Eden kousapwet Awak Powe | The name of this section of land is Awak Powe. |

Pohrasapw	Eden kousapwet Pohra-sapw.	The name of this section of land is Pohrasapw.
Dolokei	Eden kousapwet Dolo-kei.	The name of this section of land is Dolokei.
Palikir	Eden kousapwet Pali-kir.	The name of this section of land is Palikir.

M-4

Nanengk	Eden sahpwet Nanengk.	The name of this piece of land is Nanengk.
wasa	Eden wasaht Nanengk.	The name of this place is Nanengk.
Peinais	Eden wasaht Peinais.	The name of this place is Peinais.
sahpw	Eden sahpwet Peinais.	The name of this piece of land is Peinais.
Pahn Pei Pwel	Eden sahpwot Pahn Pei Pwel.	The name of this piece of land is Pahn Pei Pwel.
wasa	Eden wasaht Pahn Pei Pwel.	The name of this place is Pahn Pei Pwel.
Luhke	Eden wasaht Luhke.	The name of this place is Luhke.
sahpw	Eden sahpwet Luhke.	The name of this piece of land is Luhke.
Iohl	Eden sahpwet Iohl.	The name of this piece of land is Iohl.
wasa	Eden wasaht Iohl.	The name of this place is Iohl.

Give accurate responses in C-1 according to the location of your class-room.

C-1

A: Ia eden (kousapwet)?

A: What is the name of (this section of land)?

B: Eden (kousapwet) (Pohrasapw).

B: The name of (this section of land) is (Pohrasapw).

TO THE STUDENT:

The noun suffix /-(e)t/ indicates a location in the immediate proximity of the speaker. Thus, /kousapw/ meaning 'section of land' may take the suffix /-(e)t/ to result in /kousapwet/ or 'this section of land.' (In the case of 'this place', the final vowel of /wasa/ is lengthened and /-t/ is suffixed to produce /wasaht/.)

When asking about the name of a piece of land, /wasa/ is commonly employed as an alternate to /sahpw/.

In M-2, the names of the municipalities of Ponape are listed as they are usually ranked. In M-3 and M-4, kousapws and sahpws of each of the five municipalities are listed in the order of M-2. Therefore, you may determine that Pahn Pei Pwel is the name of a sahpw which is located in the kousapw of Pohrasapw in the municipality of Kiti.

TO THE INSTRUCTOR:

Kataman ken sukuhlihkin irail eden sahpw, kousapw, oh wehi me kouson en sukuhl mihie.

Cycle 2

+--+
| Carefully imitate your instructor's pronunciation and gestures. |
+--+

M-1

Pohrasapw	E mi Pohrasapw.	It's in Pohrasapw.
Areu	E mi Areu.	It's in Areu.
Luhke	E mi Luhke.	It's in Luhke.
Palikir	E mi Palikir.	It's in Palikir.

M-2

peilong(o)	E mi peilongo.	inland	It's inland.
pali(o)	E mi palio.	over there	It's over there.
pah(o)	E mi paho.	down there	It's down there.
powe(o)	E mi poweo.	up there	It's up there.

352

M-3

pah	E mi paho.	It's down there.
Areu	E mi Areu.	It's in Areu.
powe	E mi poweo.	It's up there.
peilong	E mi peilongo.	It's inland.
Pohrasapw	E mi Pohrasapw.	It's in Pohrasapw.
Luhke	E mi Luhke.	It's in Luhke.
pali	E mi palio.	It's over there.

M-4

sidowa	Ia sidowahn?	store	Where is the store?
ohpis	Ia ohpisen?	office	Where is the office?
ohpisen Peace Corps	Ia ohpisen Peace Corpsen?	Peace Corps office	Where is the Peace Corps office?
ohpisen wehi	Ia ohpisen wehien?	municipal office	Where is the municipal office?

M-5

imwen wini	Ia imwen winien?	dispensary	Where is the dispensary?
ihmw sarawi	Ia ihmw sarawien?	church	Where is the church?
imwen sukuhl	Ia imwen sukuhlen?	school	Where is the school?

M-6

sidowa	Ia sidowahn?	Where is the store?
imwen wini	Ia imwen winien?	Where is the dispensary?
ohpis	Ia ohpisen?	Where is the office?
ohpisen wehi	Ia ohpisen wehien?	Where is the municipal office?
imwen sukuhl	Ia imwen sukuhlen?	Where is the school?

ohpisen Peace Corps	Ia ohpisen Peace Corpsen?	Where is the Peace Corps office?
ihmw sarawi	Ia ihmw sarawien?	Where is the church?

Ask meaningful questions and give accurate responses in C-1 and C-2 relative to the location of your training site and classroom.

C-1

A: Ia imwen winien?   A: Where is the (dispensary)?

B: E mi (Pohrasapw).   B: It's in (Pohrasapw).

C-2

A: Ia (ohpisen wehien)?   A: Where is the (municipal office)?

B: (Paho).   B: (Down there).

TO THE STUDENT:

/e/ is a third person singular subject pronoun and means 'he, she, or it.'

/ia/ in this cycle means 'where.'

/mi/ means 'exist or live' in the sense of being or dwelling in a particular location. (The short answer omitting /e mi/ as in C-2, B is perhaps the more common response to a question about location.)

/palio/ in sentence final position is idiomatically translated in this text as 'over there.' Literally, though, /pali/ means 'side'; /palio/ thus means 'side-that' or 'the further side.' 'Over there', then, must be interpreted as 'over (meaning beyond or on the other side of) there.' Cycle 6 will further explore the use of /palio/.

/imwen wini/ literally means 'house-of medicine.' It may be translated either 'dispensary' or 'hospital.'

In this cycle, as in Cycle E, the noun suffix /-o/ is employed. Note, however, that this suffix is not used with proper nouns; therefore, it does not suffix to proper names of places.

The noun suffix /-(e)n/ as in /ia ohpis-en/ functions to indicate that the speaker does not know, nor has ever known, the location of the object that he is inquiring about. (If a rhetorical question is being posed, or if the speaker once knew the location of the object but has forgotten, the /-o/ suffix is employed; therefore, /ia sidowao/.) This suffix will subsequently be referred to in this text as /-(e)n/² so as to distinguish it from the hypotactical suffix /-(e)n/¹ you encountered in Cycles E and 1.

Note that in M-5, the question word /ia/ sounds somewhat different than it does in M-4. This is due to the elision of the final vowel of /ia/ with the initial vowel of /i(h)mw/.

Inquiries about the location of people or places are commonly responded to only by a general indication of direction.

TO THE INSTRUCTOR:

Kihong irail pasapeng me uhdan pahn kasalehieng irail wasah me ihmw pwukat me ie.

Cycle 3

M-1

me(t)	E mi me(t).	here	It's here.
men	E mi men.	there by you	It's there by you.
mwo	E mi mwo.	there (away from both of us).	It's there (away from both of us).

M-2

palio	E mi palio.	It's over there.
me(t)	E mi me(t).	It's here.
paho	E mi paho.	It's down there.
mwo	E mi mwo.	It's there.
men	E mi men.	It's there by you.
peilongo	E mi peilongo.	It's inland.
poweo	E mi poweo.	It's up there.

M-3

| imwen kainen | Ia imwen kainenen? | outhouse | Where is the outhouse? |
| wasahn duhdu | Ia wasahn duhduen? | bathing place | Where is the bathing place? |

wasahn kuhk	Ia wasahn kuhken?	cooking place	Where is the cooking place?
rahs	Ia rahsen?	place of the stone oven	Where is the place of the stone oven?
wasahn kihd	Ia wasahn kihden?	garbage place	Where is the garbage place?

M-4

Iawasa?   Where?

The C phase of the cycle should be exercised in a real or simulated Ponapean compound, or with appropriate visual aids.

C-1

A: Ia (wasahn kuhken)?   A: Where is the (cooking place)?

B: E mi (rwo).   B: It's (there).

A: Iawasa?   A: Where?

B: (Mwo).   B: (There).

TO THE STUDENT:

The final consonant of /met/ is often omitted in informal speech.

Common alternates to /met/, /men/, and /mwo/ are, respectively, /iet/, /ien/, and /io/.

In this cycle, the noun suffix /-(e)n/[2] as in /men/ indicates a location in the direction and near proximity of the person being spoken to. Thus, it may be translated 'that (your way).'

You have now encountered the entire set of noun suffixes of location. In summary, they are /-(e)t/ 'this (my way),' /-(e)n/[2] 'that (your way),' and /-o-/ 'that (away from both of us).' As you will learn later in this book, an analogous set of directional suffixes exists for verbs.

The independent form of the question word 'where' is /iawasa/ - literally, 'what place.'

TO THE INSTRUCTOR:

C phase en Cycle wet uhdan pahn wiawi ni imwen mehn Pohnpei kan.

Cycle 4

M-1

Damian	Ia Damian?	Damian	Where is Damian?
Fred	Ia Fred?	Fred	Where is Fred?
Larry	Ia Larry?	Larry	Where is Larry?
Pernardo	Ia Pernardo?	Pernardo	Where is Pernardo?

M-2

pali(o)	E mihmi palio.	over there	He's over there.
Pahn Pei Pwel	E mihmi Pahn Pei Pwel.	Pahn Pei Pwel	He's at Pahn Pei Pwel.
mwo	E mihmi mwo.	there	He's there.
peiei(o)	E mihmi peicio.	toward the sea	He's toward the sea.
pah(o)	E mihmi paho.	down there	He's down there.
peilong(o)	E mihmi peilongo.	inland	He's inland.
Kiti	E mihmi Kiti.	Kiti	He's in Kiti.
powe(o)	E mihmi poweo.	up there	He's up there.

M-3

ohpis	E mihmi ni ohpiso.	He's at the office.
imwen sukuhl	E mihmi ni imwen sukuhlo.	He's at the school.
imwen wini	E mihmi ni imwen winio.	He's at the dispensary.
sidowa	E mihmi ni sidowaho.	He's at the store.
ihmw sarawi	E mihmi ni ihmw sarawio.	He's at the church.

M-4

met	E mihmi met.	He's here.
pah	E mihmi paho.	He's down there.
men	E mihmi men.	He's there (by you).
wasahn kuhk.	E mihmi ni wasahn kuhko.	He's at the cooking place.
sidowa	E mihmi ni sidowaho.	He's at the store.
ihmw sarawi	E mihmi ni ihmw sarawio.	He's at the church.
Uh	E mihmi Uh.	He's in Uh.
powe	E mihmi powco.	He's up there.
peiei	E mihmi peieio.	He's towards the sea.
imwen wini	E mihmi ni imwen winio.	He's at the dispensary.
wasahn duhdu	E mihmi ni wasahn duhduo.	He's at the bathing place.
mwo	E mihmi mwo.	He's there.
imwen kainen	E mihmi ni imwen kaineno.	He's at the outhouse.
peilong	E mihmi peilongo.	He's inland.

M-5

Pwurehng wia M-2, M-3, oh M-4, ahpw kieng /mwein/ ni tapi. Karasepe:	Practice M-2, M-3, and M-4 again, but precede each base sentence with /mwein/. For example:
pali(o) Mwein e mihmi palio.	over there He's probably over there.

C-1

> Ask or answer questions about the location of members of your class.

A: Ia (Fred)?	A: Where is (Fred)?
B: E mihmi (men).	B: He's (there - by you).

C-2

> Now ask or answer questions about people likely to be found in the
> directions or locations drilled in the M-phases of this cycle.

A:	Ia (Damian)?	A:	Where is (Damian)?
B:	E mihmi (ni ohpiso).	B:	He's (at the office).
A:	Ia (ohpisen)?	A:	Where is (the office)?
B:	E mi (paho).	B:	It's (down there).

TO THE STUDENT:

/-(e)n/² is not employed with proper names of people or places. Therefore,
the question in M-1 is /Ia Damian/ - not /Ia Damianen/. (Note that 'Peace
Corps office' is not considered a proper name; it is simply the office
that belongs to the Peace Corps).

With animate objects, the reduplicated form of /mi/, /mihmi/, is commonly
(though by no means always) employed. In Ponapean, reduplication conveys
the concept of a less definite, scattered, non-completive action or state
of facts.

/ni/ means 'at.' Do not expect to use /ni/, however, where you would use
'at' in English. In Ponapean, /ni/ is employed only with common nouns
like those in M-3.

/ia ih Damian/ is heard as a common alternate to /ia Damian/. This is
simply a dialect variation.

TO THE INSTRUCTOR:

Nan peidek oh pasapengen mwuhr kat, padahkiong irail ren idek aramas me
kalap mi wasah me re sukuhlkier de wasah me ke idek rehrail.

359

Dialogues for Practice

1) A: Oaron. Ia edcn sahpwet?   A: Oaron. What's the name of this
                                         piece of land?

   B: Eden sahpwet Pahn Pei Pwel.   B: The name of this piece of land
                                         is Pahn Pei Pwel.

   A: A ia eden kousapwet?   A: And what's the name of this
                                         section of land?

   B: Pohrasapw.   B: Pohrasapw.

/a/ is a conjunctive which is employed to link clauses with different subjects. Therefore, though it best translates as 'and,'
its meaning is closer to 'however.'

---

2) A: Largo. Ia wasahn kihden?   A: Largo. Where's the garbage
                                         place?

   B: Paho.   B: Down there.

   A: Iawasa?   A: Where?

   B: Kilang! E mi mwo.   B: Look! It's there.

/kilang/, like 'look' in English, is used either to direct someone's
eye or mental attention to something.

---

3) A: Maing. Ia eden soahng(o)?   A: Sir. What's the name of that
                                         thing?

   B: (Mwo)?   B: There?

   A: Ei, (mwo).   A: Yes, there.

   B: Rahs.   B: The place of the stone oven.

Using these Materials

Task 1

Find out the name of the /sahpw/ and the /kousapw/ where you are living. Record this information below.

Do the names that you listed above have any special meaning, or are they just names? What does /Pohnpei/ mean?

Task 2

At your home, establish the location of the /wasahn kihd/ and the /rahs/. Below, draw a sketch of the Ponapean home site (the main dwelling and the adjacent buildings) where you are staying, and label ... the principal landmarks. If you do not know the names of some of the places, use the question /Ia eden soahng-(et, en, o)?/.

Using these Materials

Task 1

With someone from the family you are staying with, or with your language instructor, visit your neighbors. Using the materials that you have learned thus far, converse about the following matters:

a) What are the names of the people at the household?

b) What are their titles?

c) What is the name of their /sahpw/ and /kousapw/?

d) Where is their cooking place, garbage place, bathing place, stone oven, and outhouse?

e) What are the names of other important places at their household? (For example, they may have a copra-drying shed; find out what it is called in Ponapean.)

When you approach the house, remember to use the greeting, /kaselehlie tehnpasen/.

Record any significant information that you may wish to remember below.

Task 2

Review all the lexical items or new structures that you have learned while carrying out the 'tasks' of this text.

Using these Materials

Two important sources of assistance while studying Ponapean are (1) children, because you need not be embarrassed about trying to speak Ponapean to them, and (2) sakau parties, because there everyone will be relaxed and most willing to help you in your language learning efforts. Therefore, carry out the following tasks:

Task 1

Talk to one of the children you know and find out what he plans to do for the remainder of the day and on the following day. If he has no opinions on the subject, which he may not, find out what someone in his family plans to do.

Task 2

Specifically find out when one of the men in your family, or some adult male that you know, plans next to pound sakau. Upon asking this question, you are likely to be asked to participate. If at all possible, accept the invitation.

Task 3

Find out the meaning of the following expressions connected with sakau drinking.

sakaula -

ohn sakau -

wungumung -

kelou -

Using these Materials

In addition to children and sakau parties, your training staff will be of great assistance in helping you to learn Ponapean. To tap this resource, carry out the following tasks:

Task 1

Find out when at least three of the American staff members of your training program came to Ponape, and when they plan to return to America. (Of course, do this in Ponapean.) Be prepared to report this information back to your class members.

Task 2

Find out the meaning of the following expressions:

kaunen kaiahnen Peace Corps -

kaun kariauen kaiahnen Peace Corps -

kaunen sukuhlen lokaiahn Pohnpei -

sounpadahken lokaiahn Pohnpei -

CHAPTER 7

MICROTEXTS

WHAT 'MICROTEXTS' ARE

A nineteenth-century German, Gabelentz, observed that
for elementary instruction the best language teacher is a
'talkative person with a limited range of ideas'. (in Jespersen
1904, p. 74) If a student meets too many words and too many
new grammar structures too soon, he is overwhelmed. Yet
students are motivated best by genuine use of the new language,
and genuine use, by definition, can place no restrictions on
vocabulary or on grammar. Gabelentz handled this dilemma by
the way he chose teachers. How can this formula be applied to
the development of textbooks and other teaching materials?

One answer to this question is found in a device which
we may call the 'microtext'. Although the term is new and
slightly modish, microtexts probably go back at least to the
time of Gabelentz himself. This writer first encountered
them as a student in second-year German in the United States
in 1942 and began to use them in 1956, as one expedient in the
teaching of Shona in Zimbabwe. He has also used them in courses
in Swahili, Luganda, Yoruba, French, Mauritian Creole, and
English as a Foreign Language, and in his own learning of Portuguese, and has demonstrated their use in other people's
courses in Hindi, Sotho, Chinyanja and other languages.
Language teachers and students from other parts of the world
have independently reported similar devices, always with
enthusiasm. Earlier drafts of this chapter have been

discussed with language teachers in Micronesia, Korea, Western Europe and Chile, as well as the United States.

'Microtexts' are actually a family of devices, all of which begin by presenting to the student a very small amount of monolog material on a subject in which he is already interested; they then go on to guide him in immediate use of the material in a series of different ways, progressing from tighter to looser control by the teacher and leading to genuinely communicative use of the language, all within an hour or less. The most important points of this chapter, however, lie outside of the listing of procedures. They are: (1) that microtexts may be developed on very short notice, even by a teacher with only modest qualifications in the language, and (2) that microtexts are therefore valuable in making a language course more responsive to the needs and interests of each class (Chapter 2, Assumption 3), and in thus sharing with the students much more initiative and responsibility than teachers can usually manage to delegate (Assumption 4). They are also highly useful to the individual student who is learning a foreign language from a non-professional teacher.

JUDGING INDIVIDUAL MICROTEXTS

The teacher may either select texts from the work of other people, or he may originate his own. In either case, he should keep in mind four criteria, some of which are easier to apply than others. The first and second criteria have to do with 'lightness' (Chapter 3, p. 47):

1. Is the text of suitable length? Students should be able to comprehend it, and practice it according to whatever format is being used, within 15-45 minutes.

In the less advanced classes, this may mean that a printed text will be 50 words or less in length, or that an oral text will not be longer than 20-30 seconds.

2.   Are the sentences short and uncomplicated?

The limitation on length of text is of course the source of the 'micro' in 'microtexts'. Its effect, however, seems to be qualitative as well as quantitative: there are differences between what students can do with a passage that they can take in as a whole almost immediately, and a passage which their minds must break up into subsections. Experience in collecting prospective microtexts in a dozen languages indicates strongly that a 30-second limit is empirically a good one to place on oral texts.

The third criterion measures 'strength' (Chapter 3, p. 46):

3.   Will the text be either real or realistic for the class with which it is to be used? 'Real' in this sense means that the students need and want the information at the time. An example would be today's menu in the cafeteria, or news about a forthcoming field trip. Humor is also a 'real' goal in this sense, and amusing anecdotes often make good microtexts.

A 'realistic' passage is one that contains information for which the students anticipate a future need. Here the range of topics is broad: descriptions of places and things, games, processes like changing a tire or cooking beans, brief biographical statements about prominent persons, these and many

others. The degree to which a given text is realistic
of course depends on the students with whom it is to
be used. Recipes will be more realistic for
(unliberated!) girls than for (unliberated!) boys;
texts on animal husbandry will be very realistic for
a few groups of students, but unrealistic for most.
Folk stories are comparatively unrealistic for everyone, except insofar as listening to and telling such
stories constitutes an essential social grace or an
intrinsic pleasure.

The fourth criterion relates to 'transparency' (p. 48):

4. How many new words does the text contain? How easy
will it be to explain the meanings of new words,
either by gesture, or by paraphrasing in words that
the students already know? Will unfamiliar grammatical
constructions cause trouble?

SOURCES OF MICROTEXTS

Microtexts may be taken from outside sources: newspapers,
cookbooks, radio broadcasts, etc. A simple example, useful
with students who expect to discuss food and nutrition in
Shona, is the following (Muswe et al., 1956):

Apo mukaka unoregerwa uchirara, mangwana unofuma une
mafuta awo ese ari pamusoro. Kuti mukabvisa mafuta
aya, unosara wacho, ndiwo mukaka unonzi skim milk.
Kune mashini inobvisa mafuta mumukaka nenzira
yekugaya. Mukaka unosara, tinoudayidza kuti mukaka
wakagayiwa, kana usina mafuta.

[When milk is left to stand, the next morning all

368

its fat is on top. If you then remove this fat,
what remains is milk which is called <u>skim</u> <u>milk</u>.
There is a machine which removes fat from the milk
by means of separation. The milk that is left
behind, we call 'separated,' or 'fat-free' milk.]

One advantage in texts taken from such sources is that
students know that they are working with something which was
intended as communication among speakers of the language, and
which therefore carries an unquestionable authenticity.
Another advantage is that these sources can be used even by a
teacher whose personal command of the target language is
limited. Such teachers are less common in the seldom-taught
languages, where most teaching is done by native speakers.
They are much more common in the frequently taught languages:
French in the United States, English in Korea, etc. But any
teacher who is able to make questions, simple paraphrases, and
other routine manipulations of a text can work as effectively
with this sort of microtext as he can with a reading selection
in the printed textbook. Such a teacher of German can find in
the following entry in a one-volume encyclopedia (<u>Der Volks-</u>
<u>Brockhaus</u>, 1938) the basis for discussing chess problems with
a class:

Schachspiel [ist ein] aus Indien stammendes altes
Brettspiel zwischen zwei Spielern , gespielt auf dem
Damebrett, mit 16 weissen, 16 schwarzen Figuren:
je 1 König, 1 Dame, 2 Türme, 2 Läufer, 2 Springer,
8 Bauern. Das Ziel ist, den König des Gegners matt
zu setzen.

[Chess is an old board game, which originated in
India, between two players, played on a chessboard

with 16 white and 16 black pieces: each player has one king, one queen, two castles, two bishops, two knights, and eight pawns. The goal of the game is to checkmate the opponent's king.]

If the students have had some hand in selecting the topic, and possibly the text itself, then even a prosaic text that is totally unsuited for inclusion in a published language textbook may be exciting and effective.

It is important to exploit the facts in a text, as well as its purely linguistic content. For   students who have at lease a potential interest in international affairs, or in the place of Quebec in the world, the following story from a random issue of the Montreal _Gazette_ can lead into a genuine discussion:

> Paul Emile Victor, a French explorer who has journeyed to the North Pole, will undertake explorations of Northern Quebec next spring as part of a Franco-Quebec agreement. At a press conference yesterday he called Quebec's north a gigantic reservoir of natural riches. The month-long mining exploration will be followed by another in 1971.

The same issue contains numerous articles that cast light on some aspects of life in Montreal:

> The Montreal Soldiers' Wives League is holding a gaslight era party and fun auction on Friday evening, November 21, at eight o'clock, in the Officers' Mess of the Canadian Grenadier Guards by kind permission of the Commanding Officer, Lt. Col. R.I. W_____, C.D., A.D.C. Music and refreshments will be provided. Parking space has been arranged for that evening. Mrs. J_____W_____ and Mrs. A_____D_____ are conveners.

Students can point out differences between this story and the customs that they are familiar with; they may also compare their inferences about this event and the people who will participate in it.

There are numerous ways to originate a microtext. The most dramatic is to allow the class to suggest a topic at the beginning of the same hour in which the text is to be used. The instructor is asked to speak on this topic, completely impromptu, for about 30 seconds. He is told that someone will signal him at the end of that time. He then begins to speak. There may be a fair number of hesitations and false starts, but most people seem to be able to do it. He then goes on and tells the story two or three more times, working out a stable form of it and at the same time giving the students genuine practice in oral comprehension.

Originating microtexts on the spot is dramatic, but it is not always practicable. Some instructors find that having to improvise aloud in front of a class is too much of a strain on them. Dwight Strawn (personal communication) reports that one of his own language tutors simply didn't like to try to say 'the same thing' so many times. But even when these objections do not exist, a group of two or more instructors teaching in the same program cannot make frequent use of impromptu microtexts, since the vocabulary given to one class would soon be quite different from that given to another class. Under these circumstances, a committee of instructors can originate a text in written form. The following day, this text is given to all the instructors, who use it in class the day after that. The purpose of the written text is to keep the instructors more or less together. It should not be distributed to the students. Each instructor should supply his own impromptu oral paraphrase of it in class.

371

In a school system, or in a group of neighboring school systems, where most of the teachers of a given language are non-natives, the telephone could enable a single native speaker to provide on 24 hours notice microtexts on topics requested by several different classes.

No matter how a microtext is originated, it should be natural and in an appropriate style. Within this general restriction, sentences should be kept rather short. The speaker should attempt to communicate with his hearers, rather than to amaze or baffle them.

Judith Beinstein, in a paper prepared for the United States Peace Corps and directed at Volunteers learning languages in a host country without professional supervision, outlined methods for eliciting simple microtexts. Informants can produce suitable texts on the basis of a picture, or their own associations with key words, or requests for information about processes, places, people, etc.

Microtexts can help to make the course livelier, and more responsive to the needs of the class. To the extent that a class participates in selecting topics, they also raise the level of responsibility, and allow the students to .feel that they, too, have an ego-investment in what is going on. They can thus make language study 'stronger' (p. 46) and also healthier as a total experience. Even from the point of view of language pedagogy in a narrower sense, Rivers (1968, p. 200) advises that 'for sheer practice in selection, the student should be given the opportunity to chatter on subjects of his own choice, where the production of ideas is effortless and most of his attention is on the process of selection.'

PREPARING A WRITTEN TEXT FOR USE

Once a written text has been selected, it may be edited in a number of different ways. From the least to the most drastic, they are:

1. Correction of typographical errors. Even this much editing is not always desirable: students must become accustomed sometime to making their own adjustments as they read.

2. Partial rewriting of one or two sentences which, though quite correct and idiomatic, nevertheless contain more than their share of difficult constructions.

3. Rewriting the entire original, using shorter, simpler sentences but retaining the same vocabulary.

Here is an example of complete rewriting. The original text is a single sentence:

'In 1919, under the post-World War I Treaty of Saint Germain the Italian frontier was established along the "natural" and strategic boundary, the Alpine watershed.'

Rivers (1968, p. 210) has said that the student 'must try...to express...meaning...with correct use of uncomplicated structural patterns and a basic general-purpose vocabulary.' The above sentence is neither extremely long nor extremely complicated, but it is still too long and complicated to be manageable for any but advanced students. If it is to serve as a basis for drills, it may be broken up into very short, very simple sentences that use the same vocabulary to say the same thing:

The nations signed the treaty of Saint Germain.

> The treaty was signed in 1919.
> The treaty was signed after World War I.
> The treaty established the frontier of Italy.
> The frontier followed a strategic boundary.
> Some people said the boundary was natural.
> The boundary was the Alpine watershed.

If, on the other hand, the text is to be used only for comprehension and as a general model for writing, these very short sentences may be recombined[1] into a more graceful version which is still much easier than the original:

> The Treaty of St. Germain, which was signed in 1919 after World War I, established the frontier of Italy. The boundary that the frontier followed was the Alpine watershed. This was a strategic boundary, and some people said that it was also a natural one.

With each text, the student's goal is to assimilate it, so that its contents -- its words, and the structures that they exemplify -- will be available to him for future use. Before he can assimilate it, he must digest it, and before food can be digested it must be chewed. Just how long digestion will take and just how much chewing is necessary of course depend on each student's ability and on his prior knowledge of the target language. Nevertheless, with beginning students the materials developer will want to supply a certain amount of 'apparatus', the purpose of which is to chop the text up so that the process of mastication can begin.

----

[1]For guided practice in preparing parallel versions of a single text, see Stevick (1963, pp. 59 - 68).

WAYS OF USING MICROTEXTS IN CLASS

Recent issues of <u>Neuere Sprachen</u> have included a series
of exchanges which began with K. Hepfer's 'Zur Frage der
Eignung der Nacherzählung als Form der sprachlichen Übung in
Englischunterricht' ['On the question of the suitability of
retelling as a form of linguistic exercise in the teaching
of English'] (1968). Hepfer's examples indicate that for
him 'retelling' applies to texts somewhat longer and more
complex than what we are here calling microtexts, but the
article and the ensuing discussion by Hohmann (1968) and
Herfurth (1968) are still relevant to the present topic.
Hepfer had concluded that in retelling, the original text is
badly diluted and distorted by students. Hohmann conceded
that this is the case, but argued that it was not sufficient
ground for rejecting this type of lesson entirely. Herfurth
distinguished between correctness of content and correctness
of language, and also between retelling as 'Klassenarbeit'
(writing in class) and 'Übungsform' (kind of practice). The
former depends on the latter. In Herfurth's opinion the
'Übungsform' is usually slighted in teaching, and impossible
results are then demanded of the 'Klassenarbeit.' In this
section of this chapter, we shall outline some of the classroom procedures which have proved useful in turning microtexts
into effective 'Übung.'

One basic procedure which has had considerable use over
the years is the following:

   1. Students listen to the text three to four times. For
       them, this is an opportunity to practice comprehension,
       and the quicker ones may notice certain variations in
       successive retellings. For the teacher, if he is
       originating the text on the spot, this is a way of
       settling in a fairly stable version that he will be
       using in later steps.

2. Students ask questions in the target language, in order to clarify the meaning of new words. It is important at this stage that they not try to go further with their questions into interesting matters that may be related to the text but which are not included in it.

3. The instructor warns the class that after repeating the text once more, he will ask the questions. It is essential at this stage that he try to choose his questions in such a way that students will give the right answer on the first try.
The first questions may suggest alternative answers, so that the student can reply by simply repeating part of what he has just heard: Q. <u>Did he go home, or to the market?</u> A. <u>(He went) to the market.</u> As the student answers the questions, he is reproducing parts of the original text.

4. Students take turns in telling things that they remember from the text. They are still reproducing parts of the text, but now the parts may be longer, and there is no question from the teacher to suggest form or content.

5. Students try to retell the entire original in their own words, until one of them can do it with no mistakes. Then they try to tell it in the length of time that the instructor used, still without mistakes. With a small class, (six to eight students) the first five steps of this procedure are normally completed in about 20 minutes. Because virtually all of the time is spent either in repeating the text or in asking questions about it, the time needed for these

steps is directly proportional to the length of the
text itself. This is an additional reason for being
fairly strict about the 30-second limit.

6. After this basic procedure has been completed, the
    class may move in one or more of several directions.
    For example:

    a. Students write the text down, either by dictation
        or from memory, and read it back. Now they have
        a permanent record of the text, for later review.

    b. Students ask two or three additional questions,
        to expand the scope of the text, or to get new
        details. (This is precisely the kind of ques-
        tioning that should be discouraged at Step 2,
        above.) They then retell the amplified version.

    c. Students and teacher discuss the content of the
        text. With the first story quoted above from
        the Montreal Gazette, for example, this is the
        time to talk about the implications of an agree-
        ment between a nation and one province of another
        nation.

    d. Students may be asked to relate comparable
        experiences from their own lives.

    e. The content of the text may be used for role-
        playing. The second story from the Gazette,
        for example, provides a starting point for two
        students, as Mrs. J___W_____ and her husband, to
        plan ·for a social event like the one described
        in the text.

7. A microtext may serve as the basis for ordinary
    drills. Thus, the construction 'month-long

exploration,' found in the first Gazette story
(above, p. 370) might lead to a transformation drill
which would produce sentences containing 'day-long
tour,' 'week-long conference,' etc.

GROUPS OF MICROTEXTS

What has been said up to this point applies to single
texts. But there are often advantages in presenting texts in
groups. From a linguistic point of view, a set of texts on
the same or closely related subjects will share much of their
vocabulary, so that the average number of new items per 100
running words of text is reduced. This of course means that
many words characteristic of the topic will be reintroduced in
a number of different texts. A small-scale example, in a
commonly taught language and from a readily available source,
consists of the entries for the inert gases in Nouveau Petit
Larousse (1968):

argon Corps simple gazeux, incolore, qui constitue
environ le centième de l'atmosphère terrestre.

[A colorless gaseous element, which constitutes
about 1% of the earth's atmosphere.]

hélium Corps simple gazeux, de numéro atomique 2
... découvert dans l'atmosphère solaire, et qui
existe en trés petite quantité dans l'air.

[A gaseous element, atomic number 2, discovered in
the sun's atmosphere, and which exists in minute
quantities in the air.]

krypton   Un des gaz rares qui existent dans
l'atmosphère.   (Numéro atomique 36.)

[One of the rare gases found in the atmosphere.
Atomic number 36.]

neon   Gaz rare de l'atmosphère, de numéro atomique
10, employé dans l'eclairage par tubes luminescents
à lumière rouge.

[Rare atmospheric gas, atomic number 10, used in
illumination by red luminescent tubes.]

radon   Elément gazeux radio-actif, de numéro
atomique 86.

[Radioactive gaseous element, atomic number 86.]

From the point of view of content, families of microtexts
allow for presentation of larger amounts of real information,
comparison among a number of partially similar incidents, or
the making of generalizations.

From the pedagogical point of view, one text of a group
may be treated in one way, and other texts in other ways.
These principles are illustrated in Appendix S.

In an experiment with groups of microtexts, the instructor selected from Swahili newspapers a large number of very
short news items, each of which told about some local activity
in the general area of 'nation-building' (kujenga taifa).
These include construction of schools and roads, making of
bricks, clearing of land, etc. The class was divided into
two groups, three students in Group I, and the rest in Group
II. Each member of Group I had his own news item to prepare.

379

The classroom procedure was as follows:

1. One member of Group I answers questions from Group II concerning his story. The other members of Group I listen. The teacher listens and makes necessary corrections.

2. The members of Group II ask the <u>same</u> questions of the <u>other</u> members of Group I.

3. The teacher asks the same questions of members of Group II.

Division into two unequal groups allows the stronger students, as members of Group I, to do more challenging work while using the same material as their classmates.

SUMMARY

Chapter 3 called for four 'basic components' in a language lesson: (1) reward(s) outside of language acquisition itself, (2) a sample of language in use, (3) structural and (4) lexical exploration moving from the sample and toward the extralinguistic goals. Chapter 6 dealt primarily with lexical exploration; Chapter 5 dealt with one way of presenting structure, and Chapter 8 will describe another. Chapter 7 has concerned itself with how to obtain or create, and use, a stable 'sample' relevant to the unstable but all the more potent readinesses of a 'them' in a here and a now.

APPENDIX S TO CHAPTER 7

MICROTEXTS AS PARTS OF A SHORT BASIC COURSE

The Foreign Service Institute's <u>Luganda Basic Course</u>
consists of 94 'lessons.' Lesson 38 and every fifth lesson
thereafter are based on microtexts. These texts cover three
topics: principal cities of Uganda, eating customs, and
interurban travel. The originator of the texts recorded them
impromptu, concentrating on giving useful general information,
rather than on composing language lessons. Each of nine
cities was a subtopic and formed the basis of one lesson. For
each subtopic, three versions ('takes') were recorded on tape.
Any one lesson uses each of the three versions in a different
way. In Lesson 38, which contains the first microtext, the
content of the first version has been converted into very
short, uncomplicated sentences. Following those sentences
are two or three questions based on each. The student is to
get the answers by listening to the first version. The second
version is to be written down off the tape, and checked by
reference to the book. Later, the student tries to fill the
blanks (orally) in a printed copy of the third version, and
then checks himself by listening to the tape.

One of the aims of the series of microtexts that runs
through this course was to give to the tape lab an independent
status of its own, rather than making it the slave of the
teacher-directed sessions.

LESSON 38

This lesson is based on a short monolog about Kampala.
Three slightly different versions of the monolog are on
the tape:

1. Listen to these monologs straight through, just to see
   how much you can understand.

2. Next, learn the following short sentences. Practice
   them until you can give them easily and correctly in
   response to the English translations.

a.	Kampala / kibuga.	Kampala is a city.
b.	Kye kibuga + ekikulu + mu Uganda.	It is the capital city of ('in') Uganda.
c.	Kampala / kiri mu Buganda.	Kampala is in Buganda.
d.	Kiri mu makkati ga Uganda.	It is in the centre of Uganda.
e.	Kirimu + abantu / bangi + ab'enjawulo.	Therein are many different people.
f.	Bava' mu mawanga / mangi.	They come from many tribes.
g.	Buganda / ggwanga.	Buganda is a tribe.
h.	Bunyoro ne Ankole / mawanga.	Bunyoro and Ankole are tribes.
i.	Abantu / bangi / babeera mu Kampala.	Many people live in Kampala.
j.	Bakola + emirimu / mingi + egy'enjawulo.	They do many different [kinds of] work.
k.	Babajja.	They do carpentery.
l.	Bazimba.	They do building.
m.	Bakola + emirimu + egy'omu ofiisi.	They do office jobs.
n.	Mulimu + ofiisi / nnyingi.	There are many offices.
o.	Mulimu + ebitongole / bingi.	There are many departments.

3.   Listen again to the first version of the monolog and
     answer the following questions asked by the instructor.
     Students' books should remain closed.

     1.   a.   Kampala kibuga?

          b.   Kampala nsi?

          c.   Kampala kye ki?

     2.   a.   Kampala kye kibuga ekikulu mu Uganda?

          b.   Kampala kye kibuga ekikulu mu nsi ki?

     3.   a.   Kampala kiri mu kitundu kya Buganda?

          b.   Kampala kiri mu kitundu ki mu Uganda?

          c.   Kampala kye ki?

     4.   a.   Kampala kiri mu makkati ga Uganda?

          b.   Kampala kiri ludda wa?

          c.   Kampala kye ki?

     5.   a.   Kampala kirimu abantu bangi ab'enjawulo?

          b.   Kampala kirimu abantu ba ngeri ki?

          c.   Kampala kye ki?

     6.   a.   Abantu b'omu Kampala bava mu mawanga mangi?

          b.   Abantu b'omu Kampala bava wa?

          c.   Kampala kye ki?

     7.   a.   Buganda ggwanga?

          b.   Buganda kibuga?

          c.   Buganda kye ki?

     8.   a.   Bunyoro ne Ankole mawanga?

          b.   Bunyoro ne Ankole bibuga?

          c.   Bunyoro ne Ankole kye ki?

     9.   a.   Abantu bangi babeera mu Kampala?

          b.   Abantu bameka ababeera mu Kampala?

10. a. Bo bakola emirimu mingi egy'enjawulo?

     b. Bo bakola mirimu ki?

11. a. Babajja?

     b. Bakola ki?

12. a. Bazimba?

     b. Bakola ki?

13. a. Bakola emirimu egy'omu ofiisi?

     b. Bakola ki?

14. a. Mulimu ofiisi nnyingi?

     b. Mulimu ofiisi mmeka?

15. a. Mulimu ebitongole bingi?

     b. Mulimu ebitongole bimeka?

4. <u>Dictation</u>: Before looking at the following text, listen
                  to the second version of the monolog and try
                  to write it down. Then check yourself by
                  looking at the printed version.

Kámpálá / kyè kìbúgà + èkìkúlù + mù Ùgáńdà. Kírí mú
Ùgáńdà, mù nsí + Bùgáńdà + mù mákkátí gá Ùgáńdà.
Kírí-mú + àbàntù / báńgì / àb'à-máwáńgà / máńgì,
ng'̣ + Àbàgáńda , Àbányóró, Àbànyáńkólè, n'Àbéérù,
ng'̣ + Àbazúńgù / n'Á-bayíńdì / n'á-bàlálá. Àbàntú +
báámú / bàkòlà + èmìrìmù / gya njàwùlo, ng'̣ + òkùbàjjá,
òkúzímbá, èrá / mùlí-mú / nè ófììsì / nyíńgì /
èz'è-bítóńgòlè + èbírálá.

5. DRILL: Concordial agreement.

emirimu   emirimu / mingi + egy'enjawulo
abantu   abantu / bangi + ab'enjawulo
amawanga   amawanga / mangi + ag'enjawulo
ebitongole   ebitongole / bingi + eby'enjawulo
Abeeru   Abeeru / bangi + ab'enjawulo

6. DRILL: Tone changes with [nga] 'such as'.

Abaganda   abantu / bangi + ng'+Abaganda, n'a-balala
Abanyoro   abantu bangi ng'Abanyoro n'abalala
Abanyankole   abantu bangi ng'Abanyankole n'abalala
Abeeru   abantu bangi ng'Abeeru n'abalala
Abazungu   abantu bangi ng'Abazungu n'abalala

7. Try to anticipate the whole word that belongs in each blank.
    Check yourself by listening to the third version of the monolog.

        Kiri mu _____, mu _____ ga Uganda. Kirimu _____
        bangi _____, ng'Abaganda, _____, Abanyankole,
        _____ ng'Abazungu _____. Abantu _____ bakola
        _____ mingi, ng'okuzimba, okubajja _____.

8. Tell in your own words as much as you can remember about
    Kampala.

385

Glossary:

e.n.jawulo (N) (stem [.awulo])	difference
_'_njawulo	different
e.g.gwanga (LI-MA) (stem [.wanga])	tribe
.bajja (.bazze)	do carpentry, cabinet work
.zimba (.zimbye˙)	build
o.mu.limu (MU-MI)	work, job
e.ki.tongole (KI-BI)	department (of gov't)
.lala	other
e.n.geri (N)	kind

APPENDIX T

TO

CHAPTER 7

MICROTEXTS AS CENTERS FOR A SERIES OF
PRINTED LESSONS (SWAHILI)

The following is one of 25 brief lessons, each of which was based on a short, complete news item about meetings in East Africa. The stories were chosen both for their linguistic simplicity and for the light which they shed on the holding of meetings in Kenya and Tanzania.

Each story is surrounded by a large amount of pedagogical apparatus, part of which was designed to enable students to use them as supplementary material almost from the beginning of their training. This apparatus progresses from very tightly controlled to relatively uncontrolled activities of the student. The lessons thus provide occasions for use, as well as a sample of the language and structural exploration. They do not, however, contain any explicit provision for lexical exploration beyond what is in the original sample.

LESSON 11

<u>Vocabulary</u> Listen to the Swahili sentences, repeat them aloud, and practice until you can give them easily and correctly in response to the English sentences.

Rais aliwahutubia Mawaziri kwenye mkutano.	The President addressed the Ministers at a meeting.
Watakutana mwisho wa mwaka huu.	They will meet [at] the end of this year.
Bw. Fulani ni mjumbe wa wilaya hii.	Mr. So-and-so is the representative of this district.
Mwenyekiti alisimamia uchaguzi.	The chairman supervised the election.
Mwenyekiti wa Mkoa huu ni nani?	Who is the chairman of this province?
Wanachama walimsaidia mwenyekiti.	The members helped the chairman.
Wanachama wote wanasaidiana.	All the members help one another.

<u>Text</u> Listen to the text, read it aloud, and then check with the English translation.

   Kwenye mkutano mkuu wa mwaka wa chama cha U. W. T. katika Wilaya ya Karagwe Bi Paulina Mkonge alichaguliwa kuwa Mwenye Kiti wa Wilaya na Bibi Cortrida Laurenti alichaguliwa Makamu wa Mwenye Kiti.

   Uchaguzi huo ulisimamiwa na mwenye kiti wa U. W. T. wa Mkoa Bi Amisa akisaidiana na mjumbe wa Mkoa Bi Mariani Farahani.

        Kiongozi, 15 Agosti 1966

  At the annual meeting ('principal meeting of the year') of the U. W. T. organization in the district of Karagwe, Miss Paulina Mkonge was elected to be chairman of the district and Mrs. Cortrida Laurenti was elected deputy (of the) chairman.

  The (aforementioned) election was supervised by the regional chairman of U. W. T., Miss Amisa in cooperation with ('cooperating with') the regional representative, Miss Mariani Farahani.

Supply concords   All blanks are to be filled orally. Writing in the book
                       would spoil it for future practice.

U.W.T. ni __ama __enye   U.W.T. ni chama chenye   U.W.T. is an organization
  _anachama __engi.   wanachama wengi.   with many members.

Morogoro ni mkoa _enye   Morogoro ni mkoa wenye   Morogoro is a Province (?)
  __jiji __ngi.   vijiji vingi.   with many villages.

Read the first sentence in each pair, and try to anticipate the second:

Wanachama waliwakuta Viongozi.   The members found the leaders
Viongozi walikutana.   The leaders met one another.

Wanachama waliwasaidia viongozi.   The members helped the leaders.
Viongozi walisaidiana.   The leaders helped one another/
                                          cooperated.

Rais aliwajulisha mawaziri.   The president introduced the
                                          ministers.

Mawaziri walijulishana.   The ministers introduced one
                                          another.

Viongozi walihutubia mkutano.   The leaders addressed the
                                          meetings.

Viongozi walihutubiana.   The leaders made speeches to
                                          one another.

Questions

1. Uchaguzi huo ulisimamiwa na mwenyekiti wa mkoa?
2. Bi Paulina Mkonge alichaguliwa kuwa mwenyekiti wa mkoa?
3. Bibi Laurenti alichaguliwa makamu wa mwenye kiti?

4. Uchaguzi huo ulisimamiwa na nani?
5. Bi. Mariani Farahani ni mjumbe wa mkoa gani?
6. Mkutano huo ulikuwa wa aina gani?
7. Sasa mwenyekiti wa Wilaya ni nani?

Glossary

-enye	who or which has; where there is
kwenye (17)	at
mwaka (3,4)	year
U.W.T.	(Umoja wa Wanawake wa Tanzania)
umoja (14)	union, unity
mwanamke (1)	woman
wanawake (2)	

wilaya (9, 10)	district
makamu (1)	deputy, vice-
-simamia	to oversee (lit: 'to stand by or over')
mkoa (3,4)	region, province
-saidia	to help
-saidiana	to help one another; to cooperate

Use each of these words in a short sentence based on the text. Then, if you have studied Swahili elsewhere, go on and use each word in a short sentence that is not based on the text. Ordinarily, these sentences should be factually true as well as grammatically correct.

CHAPTER 8

ROUTINE MANIPULATIONS

It is only by constant reiteration
that one can impress an alien concept
upon a recalcitrant mind.

Anon.

Negative advertising has been with us at least
since the days of 'No Stoop, No Squat, No Squint,'
and purveyors of $10.98 language courses have made
a fortune from offering 'No Tiresome Drills!' and
'No Confusing Grammar Rules!' Whether drills are
necessarily tiresome remains to be seen, but there
can be little doubt that they are necessary. Even
many cognitivists, although they do not emphasize
drill to the same extent that the behaviorists do,
are still willing to recognize a place for this kind
of activity. Thus Kuno (1969): 'Whatever may be
shown [through research] about pattern drill vs. true
communication..., the student must still be induced
to engage in such activities for any learning to take
place.' Kniesner (1969) concurs. Rivers (1968) sees
drills as being particularly suited for internalization
of the 'closed systems' of a language. Bolinger (1968)
quips that 'to imagine that drills are to be replaced
by rule-giving is to imagine that digestion can be
replaced by swallowing.'

The reason why drills are so hard to get away from is that a language does not consist of sounds and words alone. It also has its stock of constructions and processes and rules. Just as a speaker must choose the right words for his purpose, and the right sounds to make them intelligible, so he must develop facility in putting them into appropriate grammatical settings. Consider the following English examples, which could be matched from any other language. The principal words are <u>tank</u> and <u>leak</u>.

<u>Barely intelligible</u>.	<u>Clear and idiomatic</u>.
Tank leak.	The tank leaks. A tank is leaking. The tank is leaking.
Tank leak, no?	Is the tank leaking? The tank is leaking, isn't it? Does the tank leak? The tank leaks, doesn't it?
Tank no leak.	The tank doesn't leak. The tank isn't leaking. The tank hasn't leaked yet. The tank won't leak.

As these examples show, grammatical inadequacy not only sounds funny; it often carries with it a certain amount of ambiguity.

But to say that drills are concerned with the teaching of constructions would not be an adequate statement of their function. A grammatical construction cannot be mastered by itself. A student may repeat one or more examples of the construction after the teacher, and he may see other examples of it in

connected texts, and he still may not comprehend it
completely. The study of grammar is the study of
relationships, such as the contrast between <u>This tank
leaked</u> and <u>This tank has leaked</u>. Any relationship has
at least two terms, and the student will not internalize
a relationship by practicing only of its terms. This is
why Cummings devices (pp. 312-327), dialogs, and other
kinds of basically textual material are by themselves
inadequate. This is why we need systematic practice
material, both drills and exercises.[1] The essential
nature of a drill, therefore, is threefold:

(1)   The point on which it focusses, and the
      item which it repeats, is not a word or
      a construction, but a relationship between
      constructs. This relationship may be such
      that it can only be summarized by a trans-
      formational rule, or it may lend itself
      to summary in the shape of a simple sub-
      stitution table, but it is still a rela-
      tionship between constructs.

---

[1] A 'drill,' as the term is used here, is an activity
which allows for only one correct response to a given
stimulus: If the student is told to substitute the
word <u>pencil</u> for <u>pen</u> in the sentence <u>I forgot my pen</u>,
then the only possible correct reply is <u>I forgot my
pencil</u>. An 'exercise' allows the student some
latitude. If the student is instructed to 'substitute some other noun for <u>pen</u>' in the above sentence,
or if he is asked to make his own reply to the
question 'What did you forget?' then he is doing
an 'exercise.' (The need for texts <u>and</u> drills <u>and</u>
exercises is one example of the principle of pluralism
(Assumption V).)

(2)   These relationships are of a nature which
      keeps them from becoming the object of
      attention during normal language use.

(3)   No one of these relationships ordinarily
      gets repeated several times in a row in
      normal conversation, while the consecutive
      reiteration of such a relationship is
      essential to the successful completion
      of a drill.

For these reasons, it might be well to replace 'stimulus'
(or 'cue') and 'response' as terms for the two halves of
a line in a drill, calling them instead 'the first and
second terms of the relationship' that the drill is about.

   How and why drills work is a much-discussed question,
which we considered in Chapter 1 (p. 19). Some authorities
seem to believe that constant reiteration of samples of the
desired effect of a neurological potential will
produce that potential in the minds of their students.
It is quite possible that students' minds do work this
way, if only in self-defense. It may also be the case,
however, that drills are valuable first for exploring
and elucidating the relationships that they exemplify,
and second in establishing a short-term memory of the
relationship, which is then lengthened (Carroll in
Valdman 1966, p.99) by repeated real or realistic
application (Chapter 2, pp. 29-31).

   The two principal kinds of manipulative drill are
substitution, which deals primarily with 'enate' relationships (Chapter 1, p. 12), and transformation, which
deals with 'agnate' relationships. The purpose of a

substitution drill is to let the student see and
practice a large number of highly similar examples
of a single construction:

Pattern sentence: I brought my camera.

New cue: Expected response:

    flashlight   I brought my flashlight.
    raincoat   I brought my raincoat.
    gloves   I brought my gloves.
    homework   I brought my homework.
    golf clubs   I brought my golf clubs.

Even in such a simple drill as this, considerations of
realism (Assumption I) will encourage us to go beyond
such old standby nouns as book, pen, pencil; the same
considerations require us to use golf clubs or homework
only with students who are likely to have golf clubs
or homework that they sometimes carry around with them.

There are many other varieties of substitution
drill. This is not the place to catalog them. One
is 'substitution-correlation,' in which a change of
a major word at one place in the sentence entails a
grammatical change somewhere else.

Pattern sentence: I brought my camera.

New cue: Expected response:

    (John)   John brought his camera.
    (Mary)   Mary brought her camera.
    everyone   Everyone brought his camera.
    some people   Some people brought their
                                    cameras.

Obviously, John and Mary stand respectively for the names of men and women known to the students.

Substitution-correlation drills lend themselves to practice of gender-number concords, as in the above example, to matching tenses of verbs with appropriate time expressions, to matching prepositions with the nouns, verbs or adjectives in a sentence, and so forth. Some important relationships, however, cannot be drilled in this way. For these relationships, transformation drills are needed.

Sample pair of sentences:

Do you go swimming every day?	No, but I went swimming yesterday.

Additional pairs of sentences:

Do you buy cigarettes every day?	No, but I bought cigarettes yesterday.
Do you eat breakfast every day?	No, but I ate breakfast yesterday.
Do you get mail every day?	No, but I got mail yesterday.

The purpose of this drill is of course to practice the single relationship which unites go with went, buy with bought, eat with ate and get with got.

A different kind of transformation drill combines two short sentences into a longer one:

Sample set of sentences:

Cue: **Expected response:**

    Some trainees got mail.   The trainees who got
    Some trainees were happy.   mail were happy.

Additional sets:

    Some people ate custard.   The people who ate
    Some people got sick.   custard got sick.

    Some people took the bus.   The people who took
    Some people were late.   the bus were late.
    etc.

Again, one should try to keep from falling back on such
clichés as:

    Some students studied   The students who studied
      hard.   hard got good grades.
    Some students got good
      grades.

The design of drills is one thing; actually writing
them for a permanent set of materials is quite another.
What for one user are exactly enough drills on a given
point are for a second user too many, and for a third
user too few. The materials developer is certain only
that he cannot please everybody. To some extent this
problem can be eased by transferring to the user the
responsibility for deciding how many drills there will
be (Assumption IV). To do this, one must first make
a very useful but seldom noted distinction between
'routine manipulations' and other manipulative drills.
This distinction is based simply on the frequency,

importance and difficulty of a distinction. These
factors vary from language to language. In French,
for example, the tag question <u>n'est ce pas</u>? is added
to sentences about as often as the corresponding tag
questions are used in English. Yet <u>n'est ce pas</u>?
requires much less practice than is needed to master
English <u>isn't it</u>?, <u>won't it</u>?, <u>won't they</u>?, <u>can't I</u>?,
<u>haven't you</u>?, <u>mustn't she</u>? and so forth. On the
other hand, changing from present to past tenses in
the best-known European languages including English
is troublesome: <u>get</u>, <u>got</u>, but <u>set</u>, <u>set</u>; <u>sink</u>, <u>sank</u>,
but <u>think</u>, <u>thought</u>. In Swahili this difference is
always made by replacing the prefix <u>na</u> by the prefix
<u>li</u>. And in some languages, the verb doesn't change
to show tense at all. A French speaker, whose definite
and indefinite articles work something like <u>the</u> and <u>a</u>
in English, will need less drill on these words than
will a speaker of Russian, whose language lacks
articles altogether.

A difficult manipulation which is however infrequent
and relatively unimportant is the relationship between:

<u>We waited</u> four hours.	<u>Seldom have we waited</u> so long.
<u>I ate</u> fourteen pancakes.	<u>Seldom have I eaten</u> so many.

Points like this will not be made the subject of
'<u>routine</u> manipulation.' They are best handled by
writing manipulative drills ahead of time, as is
usually done in the preparation of language textbooks.

Here is a three-step outline for conducting routine manipulations:

1. Decide what grammatical points are to be made the subjects of routine manipulation. In English, for speakers of most other languages, one might list the following:

> a. Tense changes: <u>he goes</u>, <u>he went</u>, <u>he has gone</u>, etc.
>
> b. Relative constructions: <u>the speaker that we listened to most carefully</u>, etc.
>
> c. Negation: <u>he can't sleep</u>, <u>he doesn't sleep</u>, etc.
>
> d. Tag questions: <u>doesn't he</u>? <u>do they</u>? <u>won't I</u>?, etc.
>
> e. Prepositions: <u>in (a city)</u>, <u>on (a street)</u>, <u>at (an address)</u>, etc.
>
> f. Direct and indirect questions: <u>When does he have to leave</u>?, <u>Ask him when he has to leave</u>, etc.
>
> g. Articles, mass/count nouns: <u>I saw a key</u>. <u>I saw some charcoal</u>. <u>I saw Jacqueline</u>.

2. Prepare a sample drill for each point in the above list. Some will require more than one drill, but the total number should not be more than 20. Three samples for English are:

399

TENSE DRILL

In stimulus sentence: 'Simple' form of a verb

In response sentence: 'Past participle' of the same verb

When will they go?	Haven't they gone yet?
When will they leave here?	Haven't they left here yet?
When will they catch the bus?	Haven't they caught the bus yet?
When will they get back?	Haven't they gotten back yet?

TENSE DRILL

In stimulus sentence: 'Past' form of a verb

In response sentence: 'Simple' form of the same verb

They went yesterday.	When did they go?
They left here yesterday.	When did they leave here?
They caught the bus yesterday.	When did they catch the bus?
They got back.	When did they get back?

PREPOSITION DRILL

As stimulus: An adjective

In the response: The same adjective with an appropriate preposition

interested	Are you interested in it?
dependent	Are you dependent on it?
independent	Are you independent of it?
worried	Are you worried about it?

3.   Write a brief reminder of each of the sample
drills. This is usually a single line from the drill:

When will they go?	Haven't they <u>gone</u> yet?
They went yesterday.	When did they <u>go</u>?
dependent	Are you <u>dependent on</u> it?

Assemble a complete set of these reminders, for
all the routine manipulations. Affix a copy of this
list to the wall of the classroom, or to the front of
the instructor's notebook. (See Swahili example, p. 426.)

With a moderate amount of training, the instructor
will be able to make up his own drills on these points,
drawing his material from dialogs, stories, and other
meaningful use of the language. Suppose for example,
that the students have just finished working with an
impromptu 'microtext' like the following:

The grocery store we buy groceries from
is located about two blocks from our house.
It has a well-stocked dairy counter and a
well-stocked delicatessen counter. The food
is well displayed, it's a nice, bright, light
store; it has a very large parking lot;
there's no trouble finding parking; it's
located near other shops so that it makes--ah
--general shopping easier. It's located in
Bailey's Crossroads near the E. J. Korvette
store there.

The instructor might improvise drills like these:

TENSE DRILL: 'simple verb' <u>vs</u>. 'past participle'.

When will they buy groceries?	Haven't they bought groceries yet?
When will they stock the counter?	Haven't they stocked it yet?
When will they display the food?	Haven't they displayed it yet?
When will they find parking?	Haven't they found it yet?

PREPOSITION DRILL:

E. J. Korvette Store	It's near the E. J. Korvette Store.
Bailey's Crossroads	It's in Bailey's Crossroads.
our house	It's two blocks from our house.
far	It's far from here.
our house and Bailey's Crossroads	It's between our house and Bailey's Crossroads.

Drills constructed on this basis are no longer an obstacle course which the student must climb through before he can get to meaningful discourse. Instead, they are offshoots from and buttresses for his experience with real use of the language.

APPENDIX U TO CHAPTER 8

ROUTINE MANIPULATIONS BASED ON A
SERIES OF SIMPLE NEWS ITEMS
(SWAHILI)

The set of unpublished materials from which the
following examples are taken have two different purposes:

1. For students, they introduce simple examples
    of one type of routine news story (travel of
    officials), and provide drills based on the
    content of the stories.

2. For instructors, they show syllable-by-syllable
    a large number of drills based on the first two
    stories. From that point on, the same drills
    are repeated with each succeeding story, but
    in progressively more abbreviated forms, until
    finally the instructor is conducting the drills
    from a minimal list of reminders (p. 430).

Both students and instructor are led to break texts down
into two inventories: nouns and short sentences. The
former are important in Swahili because of the role played
by concordial agreement between nouns and many other words;
the latter serve largely as the basis for drills involving
changes of tense, and changes from affirmative to negative.

Included here are most of the drills to accompany
the first news item; a few, for comparison purposes,
derived from the second item; one more item with its
'inventories;' and the final list of key phrases which

serve as reminders of the full range of 'routine manipulations' for use with news items (or other text material)
that may be selected in the future.

Certain other types of pedagogical apparatus which
appear in the original have been omitted from these
examples. The 'thinking man's glossary,' however, has
been retained. English translations in [ ] have been
added for the benefit of readers who are not students
of Swahili. Note that in the sense of Chapter 3, these
are not fully developed lessons: they contain 'samples
of language use,' and opportunities for 'structural
exploration,' but they do not provide for 'lexical
exploration' or (more important) for using the materials
in ways that conform to the student's own non-linguistic
purposes.

ORIGINAL STORY 1:

BANDA SAFARINI   [BANDA ON A TRIP

Dr. Kamuzu Banda, Rais wa   Dr. K. B., President of
Malawi, atafanya ziara ya   M., will make a one-week
wiki moja katika Taiwan.   tour in Taiwan. He will
Atawasili mjini Taipei   arrive in the city of
Agosti 4.   Taipei August 4.]

'THINKING MAN'S GLOSSARY':

        safari: government? journey?
        rais: president? country?
        -fanya: pay for?   make?

404

```
ziara:     official tour?   official complaint?
moja:      every?  one?
-wasili:   inspect?  arrive?
```

INVENTORY OF NOUNS:

safari	(N class)	[trip]
rais	(MA-personal class)	[president]
ziara	(N class)	[official tour]
mji	(M-MI class)	[city]
wiki	(N class)	[week]

DRILLS BASED ON INVENTORY OF NOUNS:

1. Demonstratives (cf. Learner's Synopsis, par. 18).

      CUES (by teacher)   RESPONSES (by students)

KEY EXAMPLE:

    kitu hiki, vitu hivi   kitu hiki, vitu hivi
    [this thing, these things]

INVENTORY:

safari	safari hii, safari hizi
rais	rais huyu, (ma)rais[1] hawa
ziara	ziara hii, ziara hizi
mji	mji huu, miji hii
wiki	wiki hii, wiki hizi

---

[1] The prefix ma- in the plural of this word may be used
or not, according to the preference of the instructor.

KEY EXAMPLE:

kitu hicho, vitu hivyo   kitu hicho, vitu hivyo
[that thing, those things
(sufficiently specified)]

INVENTORY:

safari	safari hiyo, safari hizo
rais	rais huyo, (ma)rais hao
ziara	ziara hiyo, ziara hizo
mji	mji huo, miji hiyo
wiki	wiki hiyo, wiki hizo

KEY EXAMPLE:

kitu kile, vitu vile   kitu kile, vitu vile
[that thing, those things
(insufficiently specified)]

INVENTORY:

safari	safari ile, safari zile
rais	rais yule, marais wale
ziara	ziara ile, ziara zile
mji	mji ule, miji ile
wiki	wiki ile, wiki zile

(If students have trouble doing singular and plural together, go through these drills first with singular only, then with plural only, then with singular and plural together.)

2. Possessive pronouns (cf. Learner's Synopsis, par. 19).

          CUES   RESPONSES

KEY EXAMPLE:

    kitu chetu, vitu vyetu   kitu chetu, vitu vyetu
    [our thing, our things]

INVENTORY:

    safari   safari yetu, safari zetu
    rais   rais wetu, (ma)rais wetu
    ziara   ziara yetu, ziara zetu
    mji   mji wetu, miji yetu

    (The noun wiki has been omitted from this drill because
it does not easily make sense with possessive pronouns:
*wiki yetu 'our week'.)

KEY EXAMPLE:

    kitu changu, vitu vyangu   kitu changu, vitu vyangu
    [my thing, my things]

INVENTORY:

    safari   safari yangu, safari zangu
    ziara   ziara yangu, ziara zangu
    rais[2]   rais wangu, marais wangu
    mji[2]   mji wangu, miji yangu

_____

[2]These words may be used in this drill or not, according
  to whether the instructor feels that they make sense
  with singular possessive pronouns.

407

CHAPTER 8 MANIPULATIONS BASED ON NEWS ITEMS (SWAHILI)

CUES	RESPONSES

KEY EXAMPLES:

kitu chake, vitu vyake   kitu chake, vitu vyake
[his thing, his things]

INVENTORY:

safari	safari yake, safari zake
rais	rais wake[1], marais wake
ziara	ziara yake, ziara zake
mji	mji wake, miji yake

---

[1]This corresponds to 'its president', and not to 'his/her president'.

KEY EXAMPLE:

kitu chako, vitu vyako   kitu chako, vitu vyako
[your thing, your things]

CUES	RESPONSES

INVENTORY:

safari	safari yako, safari zako
rais	rais wako, marais wako
ziara	ziara yako, ziara zako
mji	mji wako, miji yako

KEY EXAMPLE:

kitu chenu, vitu vyenu   kitu chenu, vitu vyenu
[your thing, your things]

INVENTORY:

safari	safari yenu, safari zenu
rais	rais wenu, marais wenu
ziara	ziara yenu, ziara zenu
mji	mji wenu, miji yenu

KEY EXAMPLE:

kitu chao, vitu vyao   kitu chao, vitu vyao
[their thing, their things]

CUES	RESPONSES

INVENTORY:

safari	safari yao, safari zao
rais	rais wao, marais wao
ziara	ziara yao, ziara zao
mji	mji wao, miji yao

3. Adjectives, Vowel Stem (cf. Learner's Synopsis, par. 21)

CUES	RESPONSES

KEY EXAMPLE:

kitu kingine, vitu vingine   kitu kingine, vitu vingine
[another thing, other things]

INVENTORY:

safari	safari nyingine, safari nyingine
rais	rais mwingine, marais wengine
ziara	ziara nyingine, ziara nyingine
mji	mji mwingine, miji mingine

CHAPTER 8 MANIPULATIONS BASED ON NEWS ITEMS (SWAHILI)

KEY EXAMPLE:

Vitu vingi.[1]   vitu vingi.
[Many things.]

INVENTORY:

safari	safari nyingi
rais	marais wengi
ziara	ziara nyingi
mji	miji mingi

CUES   RESPONSES

[1]Since the singulars of these nouns do not make sense
with -ingi, they are not used in this drill.

KEY EXAMPLE:

kitu cheusi, vitu vyeusi   kitu cheusi, vitu vyeusi
[a black thing, black things]

INVENTORY:

safari[2]	_____
rais	rais mweusi, marais weusi
ziara[2]	_____
mji	mji mweusi, miji myeusi

----

[2]Colors, as modifiers, do not make sense with these nouns.

More drills of this kind may be done, using the adjective
stems -embamba 'narrow', -eupe, 'white', etc., as long as
they make sense with the nouns.

4.   Adjectives, Consonant Stem (cf. Learner's Synopsis, par. 20)

        CUES   RESPONSES

KEY EXAMPLE:

   kitu kizuri, vitu vizuri   kitu kizuri, vitu vizuri
   [a good thing, good things]

INVENTORY:

   safari   safari nzuri, safari nzuri
   rais   rais mzuri, marais wazuri
   ziara   ziara nzuri, ziara nzuri
   mji   mji mzuri, miji mizuri

KEY EXAMPLE:

   kitu kirefu, vitu virefu   kitu kirefu, vitu virefu
   [a long thing, long things]

INVENTORY:

   safari   safari ndefu, safari ndefu
   rais   rais mrefu, marais warefu
   ziara   ziara ndefu, ziara ndefu
   mji   mji mrefu, miji mirefu

More drills of this kind may be done, using the adjective stems -kubwa 'big', -kali 'fierce', -bovu 'spoilt' etc., as long as they make sense with the nouns.

411

5. Numerals (cf. Learner's Synopsis, par. 20)

CUES	RESPONSES

KEY EXAMPLE:

| kitu kimoja, vitu viwili | kitu kimoja, vitu viwili |
| [one thing, two things] | |

INVENTORY:

safari	safari moja, safari mbili
rais	rais mmoja, marais wawili
ziara	ziara moja, ziara mbili
mji	mji mmoja, miji miwili

Other numbers may of course be substituted for 'one' and 'two'.

6. Subject Prefixes (cf. Learner's Synopsis, par. 23, 28)

CUES	RESPONSES

KEY EXAMPLE:

Kitu kilikuwa kizuri.	Kitu kilikuwa kizuri.
Vitu vilikuwa vizuri.	Vitu vilikuwa vizuri.
[The thing was good.]	
[(The) things were good.]	

INVENTORY:

safari	Safari ilikuwa nzuri.
	Safari zilikuwa nzuri.
rais	Rais alikuwa mzuri.
	Marais walikuwa wazuri.

ziara   Ziara ilikuwa nzuri.
                               Ziara zilikuwa nzuri.

mji   Mji ulikuwa mzuri.
                               Miji ilikuwa mizuri.

7. Relative Affixes (cf. Learner's Synopsis, par. 25, 28, 42)

        CUES   RESPONSES

KEY EXAMPLE:

    Ndicho kitu alichotaja.   Ndicho kitu alichotaja.
    Ndivyo vitu alivyotaja.   Ndivyo vitu alivyotaja.
    [It is the thing which he mentioned.]
    [They are the things which he mentioned.]

INVENTORY:

    safari   Ndiyo safari aliyotaja.
                                Ndizo safari alizotaja.

    rais   Ndiye rais aliyetaja.
                                Ndio marais aliotaja.

    ziara   Ndiyo ziara aliyotaja.
                                Ndizo ziara alizotaja.

    mji   Ndio mji aliotaja.
                                Ndiyo miji aliyotaja.

413

CHAPTER 8 MANIPULATIONS BASED ON NEWS ITEMS (SWAHILI)

INVENTORY OF SHORT SENTENCES:

Malawi ina rais.
[M. has a president.]

Dr. Banda ni Rais wa Malawi.
[Dr. B. is President of M.]

Dr. Banda atafanya ziara.
[Dr. B. will make an official tour.]

Ziara itachukua wiki moja.
[The tour will take one week.]

Atawasili Taipei Agosti 4.
[He will arrive in T. on August 4.]

Taipei ni mji.
[T. is a city.]

Mji uko Taiwan.
[The city is on Taiwan.]

DRILLS BASED ON INVENTORY OF SHORT SENTENCES:

8. Six major tenses (cf. Learner's Synopsis, par. 28, 29, 33, 36)

        CUES   RESPONSES

KEY EXAMPLE:

Kitu hiki ni kizuri.   Kitu hiki ni kizuri.
[This thing is good.]

TENSE MODIFIERS:

sasa [now]	Kitu hiki ni kizuri sasa.
jana [yesterday]	Kitu hiki kilikuwa kizuri jana.
kesho [tomorrow]	Kitu hiki kitakuwa kizuri kesho.
Wanataka nini? [What do they want?]	Wanataka kitu hiki kiwe kizuri. [They want this thing to be good.]
ingewezekana [if it were possible]	Ingewezekana, kitu hiki kingekuwa kizuri. [If it were possible, this thing would be good.]
Watafanya nini? [What will they do?]	Kitu hiki kikiwa kizuri watafanya nini? [If this thing is good, what will they do?]

SENTENCE FROM THE INVENTORY:

Dr. Banda ni Rais wa Malawi.   Dr. Banda ni Rais wa Malawi.

TENSE MODIFIERS:

sasa[1]	Dr. Banda ni Rais wa Malawi sasa.
jana[2]	Dr. Banda alikuwa Rais wa Malawi jana.
kesho[3]	Dr. Banda atakuwa Rais wa Malawi kesho.

---

[1]If sasa doesn't sound good, use leo, mwaka huu, or some other present tense time expression.

[2]If jana doesn't sound good, use mwaka jana, mwezi uliopita, or some other past tense time expression.

[3]If kesho doesn't sound good, use mwaka kesho, mwezi ujao, or some other future time expression.

Wanataka nini?	Wanataka Dr. Banda awe Rais wa Malawi.
ingewezekana	Ingewezekana, Dr. Banda angekuwa Rais wa Malawi.
Watafanya nini?	Dr. Banda akiwa Rais wa Malawi, watafanya nini?

9. 'Have' (cf. Learner's Synopsis, par. 63)

KEY EXAMPLE:

Watoto wana vitabu.   Watoto wana vitabu.
[The children have books.]

TENSE MODIFIERS:

sasa	Watoto wana vitabu sasa.
zamani [long ago]	Watoto walikuwa na vitabu zamani.
siku zijazo [in the future]	Watoto watakuwa na vitabu siku zijazo.
Anataka nini?	Anataka wawe na vitabu.
Atafanya nini?	Atafanya nini, watoto wakiwa na vitabu?
ingewezekana	Ingewezekana, watoto wangekuwa na vitabu.

SENTENCE FROM INVENTORY:

Malawi ina rais.   Malawi ina rais.
[Malawi has a president.]

TENSE MODIFIERS:

sasa	Malawi ina rais sasa.
zamani	Malawi ilikuwa na rais zamani.
siku zijazo	Malawi itakuwa na rais siku zijazo.
Anataka nini?	Anataka Malawi iwe na rais.
Atafanya nini?	Atafanya nini, Malawi ikiwa na rais?
ingewezekana	Ingewezekana, Malawi ingekuwa na rais.

10. 'Have not'

KEY EXAMPLE:

Watoto wana vitabu?	La, hawana.
[Do the children have books?]	[No, they haven't.]

TENSE MODIFIERS:

Watoto wana vitabu sasa?	La, hawana vitabu sasa.
Watoto walikuwa na vitabu zamani?	La, hawakuwa na vitabu zamani.
Watoto watakuwa na vitabu siku zijazo?	La, hawatakuwa na vitabu siku zijazo.
Anataka watoto wawe na vitabu?	La, anataka wasiwe na vitabu.
Watoto wangekuwa na vitabu?	La, wasingekuwa na vitabu.
Atafanya nini, watoto wakiwa na vitabu?	Atafanya nini, wasipokuwa na vitabu?

EXAMPLE FROM INVENTORY:

Malawi ina rais?   La, haina.

[Does Malawi have a president?]

TENSE MODIFIERS:

Malawi ina rais sasa?   La, haina rais sasa.

Malawi ilikuwa na rais   La, haikuwa na rais
  zamani?   zamani.

Malawi itakuwa na rais   La, haitakuwa na rais
  siku zijazo?   siku zijazo.

Anataka Malawi iwe na rais?   Anataka Malawi isiwe na
                                      rais.

Malawi ingekuwa na rais?   La, isingekuwa na rais.

Watafanya nini, Malawi   Watafanya nini, Malawi
  ikiwa na rais?   isipokuwa na rais?

11. '**Be located**' (cf. _Learner's Synopsis_, par. 62)

KEY EXAMPLE:

Kitu kiko huko.   Kitu kiko huko.

[The thing is there.]

TENSE MODIFIERS:

sasa   Kitu kiko huko sasa.

zamani   Kitu kilikuwa huko zamani.

siku zijazo   Kitu kitakuwa huko siku
                                      zijazo.

Wanataka nini?   Wanataka kitu kiwe huko.

418

ingewezekana   Ingewezekana, kitu
                                       kingekuwa huko.

Watafanya nini?   Watafanya nini, kitu
                                       kikiwa huko?

SENTENCE FROM INVENTORY:

    Mji uko huko.   Mji uko huko.
    [The city is there.]

TENSE MODIFIERS:

    sasa   Mji uko huko sasa.

    zamani   Mji ulikuwa huko zamani.

    siku zijazo   Mji utakuwa huko siku
                                       zijazo.

    Wanataka nini?   Wanataka mji uwe huko.

    ingewezekana   Ingewezekana, mji ungekuwa
                                       huko.

    Watafanya nini?   Watafanya nini, mji ukiwa
                                       huko?

FURTHER SENTENCE FROM INVENTORY:

    Dr. Banda yuko safarini.   Dr. Banda yuko safarini.
    [Dr. Banda is on a trip.]

TENSE MODIFIERS:

    sasa   Dr. Banda yuko safarini
                                       sasa.

    siku zijazo   Dr. Banda atakuwa safarini
                                       siku zijazo.

419

ingewezekana

Ingewezekana, Dr. Banda angekuwa safarini.

Watafanya nini?

Watafanya nini, Dr. Banda akiwa safarini?

Wanataka nini?

Wanataka Dr. Banda awe safarini.

jana

Dr. Banda alikuwa safarini jana.

FURTHER SENTENCE FROM INVENTORY:

Dr. Banda atafanya ziara.   Dr. Banda atafanya ziara.
[Dr. Banda will make an official tour.]

TENSE MODIFIERS:

kesho

Dr. Banda atafanya ziara kesho.

Wanataka nini?

Wanataka Dr. Banda afanye ziara.

sasa

Dr. Banda anafanya ziara sasa.

ingewezekana

Ingewezekana, Dr. Banda angefanya ziara.

Watafanya nini?

Watafanya nini, Dr. Banda akifanya ziara?

jana

Dr. Banda alifanya ziara jana.

12. Affirmative vs. negative.   (cf. Learner's Synopsis,
                                    par. 53-61)

KEY EXAMPLE:

Watoto watasoma?   La, hawatasoma.
[Will the children study?]   [No, they won't study.]

AFFIRMATIVE QUESTIONS:

Watoto wanasoma sasa?   La, hawasomi sasa.

Watoto walisoma jana?   La, hawakusoma jana.

Watoto watasoma kesho?   La, hawatasoma kesho.

Wanataka watoto wasome?   La, wanataka watoto wasisome.

Ingewezekana, watoto   La, hawangesoma.
  wangesoma?

Watoto wamesoma?   La, hawajasoma.

Watoto wakisoma, tutafanya   Au, wasiposoma, tutafanya
  nini?   nini?

SENTENCE FROM THE INVENTORY:

Rais atafanya ziara?   La, hatafanya ziara.
[Will the president make an official trip?]

AFFIRMATIVE QUESTIONS:

Rais anafanya ziara sasa?   La, hafanyi ziara sasa.

Rais alifanya ziara jana?   La, hakufanya ziara jana.

Rais atafanya ziara kesho?   La, hatafanya ziara kesho.

Anataka rais afanye ziara?   La, anataka asifanye ziara.

Ingewezekana, rais ange-   La, hangefanya ziara.
fanya ziara?

Rais akifanya ziara   Asipofanya ziara tutafanya
tutafanya nini?   nini?

Rais amefanya ziara?   La, hajafanya ziara.

13. Relative affixes. (cf. Learner's Synopsis, par. 42-47)

KEY EXAMPLE:

Watoto wanasoma.   Alitaja watoto wanaosoma.
[The children are reading.]   [He mentioned the children
                                who are reading.]

TENSES:

Watoto wanasoma sasa.   Alitaja watoto wanaosoma
                              sasa.

Watoto walisoma jana.   Alitaja watoto waliosoma
                              jana.

Watoto watasoma kesho.   Alitaja watoto watakaosoma
                              kesho.

Watoto wamesoma mara   Alitaja watoto waliosoma
nyingi.   mara nyingi.

SENTENCE FROM INVENTORY:

Ziara itakachukua wiki   Alitaja ziara itakayochukua
moja.   wiki moja.
[The tour will take one week.] [He mentioned a tour that
                                will take one week.]

TENSES:

Ziara inachukua wiki   Alitaja ziara inayochukua
moja sasa.   wiki moja sasa.

Ziara ilichukua wiki
  moja mwaka jana.

Ziara itachukua wiki moja
  mwaka ujao.

Ziara imechukua wiki moja
  mara nyingi.

Alitaja ziara iliyochukua
  wiki moja mwaka jana.

Alitaja ziara itakayochukua
  wiki moja mwaka ujao.

Alitaja ziara iliyochukua
  wiki moja (inayochukua).

ORIGINAL STORY 2:

Bw. KAWAWA KAREJEA

Makamu wa Pili wa Rais,
Bw. Rashidi Kawawa, amerejea
Dar es Salaam jana kutoka
ziara yake ya kirafiki ya
nchi ya Scandinavia. Bw.
Kawawa alikuwa safarini kwa
muda wa wiki mbili.

[Mr. KAWAWA RETURNS

The second vice-president
Mr. R. K., returned to
D. yesterday from his
friendly tour of Scand-
inavia. Mr. K. was on the
trip for a period of two
weeks.]

'THINKING MAN'S GLOSSARY':

-rejea: return?   amaze?
makamu: deputy?   bodyguard?
wa pili: chief?   second?
kutoka: leaving on?   from?
kirafiki: friendly?   expensive?
safari: home?   trip?
muda: period?   end?

CHAPTER 8 MANIPULATIONS BASED ON NEWS ITEMS (SWAHILI)

INVENTORY OF NOUNS:

bwana (MA-personal class)	[gentleman, Mr.]
makamu wa rais (personal class)	[vice-president]
ziara (N class)	[official tour]
rafiki (MA-personal class)	[friend]
nchi (N class)	[land]
safari (N class)	[journey]
muda (M-MI class)	[period of time]
wiki (N class)	[week]

MANIPULATIONS BASED ON THE INVENTORY OF NOUNS:

1. Demonstratives. (cf. Learner's Synopsis, par. 18)

CUES	RESPONSES

KEY EXAMPLE:

kitu hiki, vitu hivi [this thing, these things]	kitu hiki, vitu hivi

INVENTORY:

bwana	bwana huyu, mabwana hawa
makamu wa rais	makamu huyu wa rais, makamu hawa wa rais
ziara	ziara hii, ziara hizi
rafiki	rafiki huyu, (ma)rafiki hawa
nchi	nchi hii, nchi hizi
safari	safari hii, safari hizi
muda	muda huu
wiki	wiki hii, wiki hizi

KEY EXAMPLE:

    kitu hicho, vitu hivyo   kitu hicho, vitu hivyo

INVENTORY:

bwana	bwana huyo, mabwana hao
makamu wa rais	makamu wa rais huyo, makamu wa rais hao
ziara	żiara hiyo, ziara hizo
rafiki	rafiki huyo, marafiki hao
nchi	nchi hiyo, nchi hizo
safari	safari hiyo, safari hizo
muda	muda huo
wiki	wiki hiyo, wiki hizo

KEY EXAMPLE:

    kitu kile, vitu vile   kitu kile, vitu vile

INVENTORY:

bwana	bwana yule, mabwana wale
makamu wa rais	makamu wa rais yule, makamu wa rais wale
ziara	ziara ile, ziara zile
rafiki	rafiki yule, marafiki wale
nchi	nchi ile, nchi zile
safari	safari ile, safari zile
muda	muda ule
wiki	wiki ile, wiki zile

INVENTORY OF SHORT SENTENCES:

Bw. Kawawa ni Makamu wa Pili wa Rais.
   [Mr. Kawawa is Second Vice-President.]

Bw. Kawawa amerejea Dar es Salaam jana.
   [Mr. Kawawa returned to D. yesterday.]

Bw. Kawawa alitoka ziara yake.
   [Mr. Kawawa came from his official tour.]

Ziara ilikuwa ya kirafiki.
   [The tour was unofficial ('friendly').]

Scandinavia ni nchi.
   [Scandinavia is a land.]

Bw. Kawawa alikuwa safarini.
   [Mr. Kawawa was on a trip.]

Six major tenses. (cf. Learner's Synopsis, par. 28, 29, 33, 36)

KEY EXAMPLE:

Kitu hiki ni kizuri.   Kitu hiki ni kizuri.
[This thing is good.]

TENSE MODIFIERS:

sasa [now]   Kitu hiki ni kizuri sasa.

jana [yesterday]   Kitu hiki kilikuwa kizuri
                                   jana.

kesho [tomorrow]   Kitu hiki kitakuwa kizuri
                                   kesho.

426

Wanataka nini?
[What do they want?]

Wanataka kitu hiki kiwe
  kizuri. [They want this
  thing to be good.]

ingewezekana [If it
  were possible.]

Ingewezekana, kitu hiki
  kingekuwa kizuri. [If
  it were possible, this
  thing would be good.]

Watafanya nini? [What
  will they do?]

Kitu hiki kikiwa kizuri
  watafanya nini? [If
  this thing is good,
  what will they do?]

SENTENCE FROM THE INVENTORY:

Bw. Kawawa ni Makamu wa
  Pili wa Rais.

Bw. Kawawa ni Makamu wa
  Pili wa Rais.

[Mr. Kawawa is Second Vice-President.]

TENSE MODIFIERS:

sasa

Bw. Kawawa ni Makamu wa
  Pili wa Rais sasa.

jana

Bw. Kawawa alikuwa Makamu
  wa Pili wa Rais jana.

siku zijazo

Bw. Kawawa atakuwa Makamu
  wa Pili wa Rais siku
  zijazo.

Wanataka nini?

Wanataka Bw. Kawawa awe
  Makamu wa Pili wa Rais.

Watafanya nini?

Watafanya nini Bw. Kawawa
  akiwa Makamu wa Pili wa
  Rais?

Ingewezekana

Ingewezekana, Bw. Kawawa
  angekuwa Makamu wa
  Pili wa Rais.

427

FURTHER SENTENCE FROM THE INVENTORY:

Bw. Kawawa amerejea Dar es Salaam.
[Mr. Kawawa returned to Dar.]

TENSE MODIFIERS:

sasa	Bw. Kawawa anarejea D. sasa.
jana	Bw. Kawawa alirejea D. jana.
kesho	Bw. Kawawa atarejea D. kesho.
Watafanya nini?	Watafanya nini Bw. Kawawa akirejea D?
Wanataka nini?	Wanataka Bw. Kawawa arejee D.
ingewezekana	Ingewezekana, Bw. Kawawa angerejea D.

ORIGINAL STORY 3:

Rais wa Liberia, Bw. William Tubman aliwasili Ujerumani ya Magharibi jana kwa matembezi. Dr. Tubman aliandamana na wanawe, John na Eli. Watatembelea sehemu kadha.	[The President of Liberia, Mr. Wm. Tubman, arrived in West Germany yesterday for a visit. He was accompanied by his sons John and Eli. They will visit various parts of the country.]

INVENTORY NOUNS:

    rais (MA-personal class)   [president]
    matembezi (MA class)   [visit]
    mwana (MU-WA class)   [offspring]
    sehemu (N class)   [part]

INVENTORY OF SHORT SENTENCES:

    a.
        [.]

    b.
        [.]

    c. Rais (atafanya) matembezi.
        [The President (will make) a visit.]

    d. Rais _____ wanawe.
        [The President _____ his sons.]

    e. _____ (wanaitwa) John na Eli.
        [_____ (are called) John and Eli.]

    f.
        [.]

[The 'inventory of short sentences' has been left
 incomplete, to encourage users to begin making
 their own. Words in (   ) are common Swahili words
 which the student can be expected to know, but which
 do not occur in the story itself.]

429

NOUN CONCORDS

Demonstratives:
(kitu) [hiki, hicho, kile]

Personal possessives:
(kitu) [chetu, chake, chao etc.]

Adjectives, vowel-initial:
(kitu) [kingine, cheusi, etc.]

Adjectives, consonant-initial:
(kitu) [kikubwa, kibaya, etc.]

Numerals:
(kitu) [kimoja, viwili, etc.]

Subject prefixes:
(kitu) [kilikuwa kizuri.]

Object prefixes:
(kitu) Alikitaja).

DRILLS BASED ON SHORT SENTENCES:

Tenses:
(Watoto wanasoma.) [sasa, kesho, jana,
   ingewezekana, Watafanya nini?
   Wanataka nini?]

Affirmative & negative of above

Relative prefixes:
(Kitu kilitajwa.) → Kitu kilicho-
   tajwa ni kipi?

Compound tenses:
(Sasa wana soma) → Jana walikuwa
   wakisoma.

(Sasa wamechoka) → Kesho
   watakuwa wamechoka.

Emphatic capula:
Alitaja (kitu hicho) → Kitu hicho,
   ndicho· alichotaja.

CHAPTER 9

IN NATURE, UNIVERSE AND TIME

It seems to us only proper that words
Should be withheld from vegetables and birds.
....
We, too, make noises when we laugh or weep,
Words are for those with promises to keep.

Among the stars
There is no speech or language;
Their voice is not heard.

The rest is silence.

9 781438 2614